The 1992 Presidential
Election in the South

The 1992 Presidential Election in the South

CURRENT PATTERNS OF
SOUTHERN PARTY
AND ELECTORAL POLITICS

Edited by
Robert P. Steed,
Laurence W. Moreland, and
Tod A. Baker

PRAEGER

Westport, Connecticut
London

Library of Congress Cataloging-in-Publication Data

The 1992 presidential election in the South : current patterns of
  southern party and electoral politics / edited by Robert P. Steed,
  Laurence W. Moreland, and Tod A. Baker.
      p.   cm.
    Includes bibliographical references and index.
    ISBN 0–275–94534–0 (alk. paper)
      1. Presidents—United States—Election—1992.   2. Southern States—
  Politics and government—1951–   I. Steed, Robert P.   II. Moreland,
  Laurence W.   III. Baker, Tod A.
  JK526   1992e
  324.973'0928—dc20   93–11894

British Library Cataloguing in Publication Data is available.

Library of Congress Catalog Card Number: 93–11894
ISBN: 0–275–94534–0

First published in 1994

Praeger Publishers, 88 Post Road West, Westport, CT 06881
An imprint of Greenwood Publishing Group, Inc.

Printed in the United States of America

The paper used in this book complies with the
Permanent Paper Standard issued by the
National Information Standards Organization (Z39.48–1984).

10 9 8 7 6 5 4 3 2 1

Contents

Tables and Figures

FIGURES

Acknowledgments

This volume continues a series of analyses of presidential elections in the South. The previous two volumes, covering the 1984 and 1988 elections and also published by Praeger, provide a basic foundation for the current study, and we are therefore indebted to those who participated in those earlier projects.

As with any project of this nature, numerous people contributed to its successful completion. The Citadel Development Foundation provided essential financial support for the project through its funding of the 1992 Citadel Symposium on Southern Politics and through its ongoing program of support for research and faculty development at The Citadel. The foundation deserves much credit for its role in helping to create the academic and intellectual environment that makes such work possible. The contributors to this volume were all involved in a major study of local political party activists in the South, and we are indebted to Lewis Bowman and Charles Hadley, the directors of that project, for their consenting to the joint participation necessary for the development of this manuscript. Finally, we are grateful to our editors at Praeger, especially Jim Dunton, for their usual patience and guidance; the project could not have been completed without their help.

PART I

INTRODUCTION: THE SETTING AND THE NOMINATING PROCESS

Southern Electoral Politics as Prelude to the 1992 Elections

ROBERT P. STEED

Not long before the 1992 electoral season began in earnest, students of southern politics could reasonably question whether there would be anything remotely resembling a competitive presidential election contest in the South. Even outside the region, prospects for an effective Democratic challenge for the White House were dim in light of the party's dismal presidential election record since 1964 and George Bush's extraordinary popularity following Operation Desert Shield/ Desert Storm. But in the South, which has emerged in recent years as "the most pro-Republican region in the nation,"[1] the competitive outlook was particularly bleak. Strong personal support for Bush in the South dating back to 1988 and a clear trend of southern presidential Republicanism dating back at least to 1972 combined to present the region's Democrats with what initially seemed an impossible task in 1992.

In 1988, George Bush's strength in the South had been a major factor in his winning the Republican nomination. His strong showing in the Super Tuesday primaries, following closely on the heels of his primary victory in South Carolina the week before, essentially eliminated his opponents and virtually ensured his nomination.[2] He then proceeded to sweep the South in November, defeating Michael Dukakis by a ratio of almost three to two, the largest regional margin of victory in the nation.[3]

Bush's success in the South in 1988 continued a trend toward Republican support in presidential elections since Lyndon Johnson's administration. As Earl Black and Merle Black have demonstrated in the most thorough explication of this development written to date, "Over the past half-century . . . the South has shifted [in presidential politics] from an overwhelmingly Democratic area to a region characterized initially by balanced competition between the two parties (1952–1964) and, more recently, by a distinct Republican advantage."[4] This partisan shift has come at a time when population shifts have given the South control of 27 percent of the nation's electoral votes (and 54 percent of the number needed for victory), more than any other region. In consequence of their new-found southern strength and the South's normal regional unity, the Republicans enjoy a significant advantage over the Democrats in contemporary presidential politics.

Unfortunately for the Democrats, this regional picture changes relatively little when we examine individual states. In both 1984 and 1988, all southern states voted strongly Republican. One important dimension of this pattern is found in the post–Great Society white vote in the region. Since white voters constitute over 80 percent of the South's electorate, their voting tendencies are of crucial importance to both parties. In each state except Georgia, majorities of white voters supported the Republican ticket in each of the presidential elections held during the 1980s; moreover, in eight of the eleven southern states, majorities of whites cast their votes for the Republican ticket in all five of the elections held from 1972 through 1988.[5] Only Georgia (1976 and 1980 with Georgian Jimmy Carter at the head of the Democratic ticket), Tennessee (1976), and Arkansas (1976) deviated from this pattern. While whites in the Deep South have been somewhat more inclined to vote Republican than whites in the Rim South, over the entire period from 1968 to 1988 these intraregional differences were slight.

On the plus side for the Democrats, this movement toward presidential Republicanism in the region was not accompanied by an equal growth of Republican support for candidates at other electoral levels. Although there were Republican gains in down-ticket elections, especially during the period since 1980, there was certainly no evidence of a general Republican realignment. Even in the landslide election victories of Ronald Reagan in 1984 and Bush in 1988, Republican gains in state legislative elections and other state and local elections remained modest.[6]

The formidable southern problem facing the Democrats as the 1992 presidential election season approached, then, was how to compete with an incumbent president popular in the region who was strengthened by the recent, and virtually uninterrupted, trend toward increased presidential Republicanism in the South. For the Democratic Party nationally, solving this problem was crucial in light of the South's mathematical importance in the electoral college. Indeed, as Black and Black point out, "In every one of the nine presidential elections between 1932 and 1988 in which a single party captured all or nearly all of the South's electoral votes, the South has been on the winning side."[7]

The strategic possibilities for the Democrats were generally limited to three: (1) write off the South completely, (2) go all out in every southern state, or (3) campaign in selected southern states. Noting that conceding the South to the Republicans would be extremely risky inasmuch as it would require a virtual sweep of targeted states outside the region, and observing that the likelihood of carrying all, or even most, of the South (even with a southerner at the head of the ticket) was very remote, Black and Black concluded a full three years before the election that

Absent a total Republican collapse, the most reasonable strategy for the Democrats would be to concentrate on states outside the region, but to allocate some of their campaign resources to a small number of southern states—Arkansas and Tennessee, for example, plus any others that might be experiencing severe economic difficulties in the election year—where majority biracial coalitions might be constructed.[8]

Whether any other strategy would have worked for the Democrats in 1992 is impossible to say, but as events unfolded, the strategy defined by Black and Black came extremely close to realization. By 1992, George Bush had become progressively more vulnerable, largely because of a widespread perception of economic decline. And, ultimately, the Democrats nominated not only a southerner, but also a southerner from *Arkansas* who proceeded to name as his running mate another southerner from *Tennessee*. The Democrats then ran a campaign that refused to concede upfront any southern state to Bush/Quayle, even though the realistic hope was to carry only selected states in the region (particularly Arkansas, Tennessee, Georgia, Louisiana, and North Carolina).

The uncanny congruence of Democratic nomination outcomes and campaign strategy with the formula outlined by Black and Black almost tempts one to conclude that a handful of Democratic leaders not only read something by the two political scientists, but then also shuffled into the proverbial smoke-filled room and anointed Clinton and Gore as their party's standard bearers. The actuality, however, is undoubtedly quite different. While the possibility that some important Democratic leaders have read some political science literature is not too remote, the possibility that the nomination and campaign were then tailored accordingly by some small band of party influentials is far-fetched, indeed. The nomination process, especially in light of the reforms of the past twenty-five years, is simply not subject to this type of manipulation by organizational leaders.

The election of 1992, then, is not reducible to simple explanations. The seemingly impregnable strength of Bush evaporated as 1992 approached, and the seemingly safe South became a contested battleground, both during the nomination and during the general election. While the main nomination battles occurred in the Democratic Party, the challenge to Bush's renomination by Pat Buchanan and David Duke raised regional interest in the Republican contest as well. The general election contest was further enlivened by the entry, withdrawal, and reentry of H. Ross Perot as an independent candidate. In short, what had initially appeared to be a dull election with an easily predictable outcome developed into an exciting contest marked by a number of unexpected twists. Not only was there genuine electoral conflict, but also 1992 turned out to be one of the most interesting presidential elections in recent years.

The volume examines in detail the 1992 presidential election in the South. An initial chapter by Charles S. Bullock III discusses the nomination process in the region as a whole. This is followed by a series of chapters exploring the key events and developments in the election in each of the eleven states of the South. Additionally, some attention is given to other important electoral contests in the various states. The goal, as in the previous volumes on the 1984 and 1988 presidential elections in the South,[9] is not only to describe presidential election politics, but also to consider the implications for political patterns in the individual states and in the region generally. While the state chapters address this goal, a concluding chapter by Harold W. Stanley helps bring the key threads together. These chapters combine to show that in spite of early appearances, there is more dynamism in southern presidential politics than most observers had thought, and they also help underscore that the region is, indeed, an important part of the nation's presidential election system and is worthy of continued attention.

NOTES

1. Earl Black and Merle Black, "The 1988 Presidential Election and the Future of Southern Politics," in *The 1988 Presidential Election in the South: Continuity Amidst Change in Southern Party Politics*, ed. Laurence W. Moreland, Robert P. Steed, and Tod A. Baker (New York: Praeger, 1991), 272.

2. For an extended examination of the 1988 nomination, see Charles S. Bullock III, "The Nomination Process and Super Tuesday," in *The 1988 Presidential Election in the South: Continuity Amidst Change in Southern Party Politics*, ed. Laurence W. Moreland, Robert P. Steed, and Tod A. Baker (New York: Praeger, 1991), 3–19. See also Earl Black and Merle Black, *The Vital South: How Presidents Are Elected* (Cambridge, Mass.: Harvard University Press, 1992), 282–287.

3. For a full state-by-state discussion of the 1988 presidential election in the South, see Laurence W. Moreland, Robert P. Steed, and Tod A. Baker, eds., *The 1988 Presidential Election in the South: Continuity Amidst Change in Southern Party Politics* (New York: Praeger, 1991).

4. Black and Black, *The Vital South*, 5. Much of the following discussion draws from the materials presented in this book.

5. See the data and the related discussion in Black and Black, *The Vital South*, chapter 11, especially 295.

6. For fuller discussions of this point, see Robert P. Steed, Laurence W. Moreland, and Tod A. Baker, "Preface," in *The 1988 Presidential Election in the South: Continuity Amidst Change in Southern Party Politics*, ed. Laurence W. Moreland, Robert P. Steed, and Tod A. Baker (New York: Praeger, 1991), xi–xiii; Harold W. Stanley, "The Reagan Legacy and Party Politics in the South," in *The 1988 Presidential Election in the South: Continuity Amidst Change in Southern Party Politics*, ed. Laurence W. Moreland, Robert P. Steed, and Tod A. Baker (New York: Praeger, 1991), 21–33; and Charles S. Bullock III, "The South in Congress: Power and Policy," in *Contemporary Southern Politics*, ed. James F. Lea (Baton Rouge: Louisiana State University Press, 1988), 177–193.

7. Black and Black, *The Vital South*, 344.

8. Black and Black, "The 1988 Presidential Election and the Future of Southern

Politics,'' 276. They develop this same theme in even more detail in *The Vital South*, chapter 13, especially 360–362.

9. Moreland, Steed, and Baker, *The 1988 Presidential Election in the South*; Robert P. Steed, Laurence W. Moreland, and Tod A. Baker, eds., *The 1984 Presidential Election in the South: Patterns of Southern Party Politics* (New York: Praeger, 1986).

2

Nomination: The South's Role in 1992 Nomination Politics

CHARLES S. BULLOCK III

In 1988, all southern states except South Carolina held their presidential preference primaries on a single day. The rationale for this concerted action was that the South would be able to determine the Democratic nominee. The region failed miserably in this effort, as its votes were split among three candidates, each of whom won at least two states.[1] The ultimate Democratic nominee, Michael Dukakis, won only the two least southern states (Florida and Texas), while the winner of the most states and delegates, Jesse Jackson, was certainly not the intended beneficiary of the reform effort. Super Tuesday 1988 was as successful as Gettysburg had been for the South.

The modified southern strategy of 1992 achieved many of the goals held out for its predecessor. A southerner swept all of the region's Democratic primaries held in March and less than two weeks after Super Tuesday 1992 had driven all serious opponents from the field. By March 20, Arkansas Governor Bill Clinton had a virtually unobstructed path to the nomination.

CHANGES FROM 1988

Almost immediately after the 1988 Super Tuesday, some states that felt slighted by the candidates indicated that they would shift the date of their primary. Four states moved the date of their presidential primary to some point after March 10. Georgia, which had received substantial attention from candidates and the media in 1988, made a surprise, last-minute change. In late 1991, Governor Zell Miller, who was leading most of the state's prominent Democrats into the Clinton camp, unveiled a proposal to shift Georgia's primary forward to March 3. Miller wanted Georgia to become the New Hampshire of the South.

He reasoned that if Georgia voted before the bulk of the region, it would not have to share the attention of the candidates or the media.

A second advantage for Miller was that if Georgia provided strong support for Clinton, this might give a New Hampshire–like bump as the Arkansan went on to the Super Tuesday states. With extra attention focused on Georgia, a Clinton victory would receive extensive coverage, which should promote the Arkansan's name recognition and fund raising.

SETTING THE SCENE

As 1991 drew to a close, Bill Clinton and George Bush were the candidates to beat in the 1992 marathon. In what was widely seen as a weak field, the governor of Arkansas was leading in fund raising and support from party leaders. As a possible indicator of preliminary southern attitudes, two months before the nation's first primary Clinton was the choice of 54 percent of the delegates at the Florida Democratic state convention, while Paul Tsongas, a former Massachusetts senator, attracted a barely discernible 2 percent. Clinton was helped in early January when Governor L. Douglas Wilder of Virginia, the sole black in the field, withdrew.

The sitting president, who had broken his 1988 "no new taxes" pledge, had drawn two opponents, but neither seemed too serious. Pat Buchanan, a Nixon speech writer and frequent guest of Washington talk shows, appealed to those who felt that Bush had betrayed Ronald Reagan's legacy. Former Ku Klux Klan leader David Duke, who had taken 39 percent of the vote in the Louisiana gubernatorial runoff in November 1991, was seen as more of an embarrassment than a viable candidate.

Suddenly in the weeks before the campaign moved South, Bush and Clinton suffered unexpected setbacks, which heightened the significance of the seven states scheduled to make their choices between March 3 and 10. Clinton was rocked by two blows, which in previous years would have felled even a strong front-runner. First, a tabloid story accusing Clinton of an extended affair with Gennifer Flowers, a state employee who had previously been a Little Rock television reporter, was widely disseminated by the mainstream media. Clinton met this charge head on. He and wife Hillary appeared live on a special edition of "60 Minutes" immediately after the Super Bowl. The poise under fire displayed by the couple went a long way toward defusing the issue.

The second challenge involved what Clinton did or did not do to avoid the Vietnam draft. Clinton seemed to live up to the "Slick Willie" label he had been given in Arkansas, as he repeatedly modified his story when pressed by reporters on apparent inconsistencies.

In New Hampshire, Clinton proved that the charges of infidelity—which sank Gary Hart in 1988—could be survived. The Flowers allegations did have a cost, however, as Clinton struggled before rebounding to a second-place finish. Lightly regarded Paul Tsongas led the Democratic field in his neighboring state. As attention turned southward, pundits wondered whether the fabled New Hampshire bump would provide Tsongas with the momentum to derail Clinton. There was speculation that southerners might be less willing to forgive a man accused of cheating on his wife and dodging the draft than were New Hampshire voters.

On the GOP side, New Hampshire proved to be Buchanan's coming-out party. The conservative television personality campaigned nonstop in the snowy state, while George Bush remained in Washington wrapped in the cloak of the presidency. Buchanan's 37 percent of the vote was judged to be impressive. As they sifted the ashes, commentators wondered if Buchanan might be yet another political Samson. Did Buchanan's unexpected strength indicate Bush was so weakened that he, like Harry Truman in 1952 and Lyndon Johnson in 1968, would withdraw rather than continue limping toward a tarnished nomination? Could Buchanan actually win some primaries in the more conservative South?

NEW HAMPSHIRE OF THE SOUTH?

Democrats

The March 3 Georgia primary was expected to preview the region's preferences. Atlanta pollster Claibourne Darden spoke for many when he opined, "We think that the framework laid out in Georgia will be fundamentally duplicated in the southern states to follow on Super Tuesday."[2] Candidates hoped that a strong showing in the Peach State would inspire favorable media coverage, campaign workers, and financial contributors so that a Georgia success could be replicated elsewhere.

In the northern preliminaries, Clinton, the putative front-runner, had yet to be a winner. Tsongas earned boasting rights in New Hampshire. Senator Bob Kerrey (D–Neb.) won the South Dakota primary with 40 percent of the vote, with Clinton struggling to a weak third. Iowa Senator Tom Harkin had been challenged in his home state's caucus. While the pre-March winners might be denigrated as mere regional candidates, Clinton had to demonstrate that he, too, could win in his region and in so doing secure a base before the campaign moved into the nation's heartland.

As a native southerner, Clinton had an advantage as he and the other candidates introduced themselves to the region's voters. Clinton also had an edge with Democratic leaders, many of whom had met him during his twelve years as governor. Several leaders, including Governors Zell Miller (Georgia) and Ned McWherter (Tennessee), had already endorsed their fellow chief executive.

In the amorphous days before serious campaigning began in the South, polls showed Clinton to be the Democrat to beat. In a regional poll released by the *Atlanta Journal and Constitution* in mid-January, Clinton led former California Governor Jerry Brown 30 to 21 percent.[3] Shortly after the New Hampshire primary, Clinton led Tsongas by nineteen percentage points in Georgia.[4]

Other candidates lost interest in Georgia after Governor Miller, House Speaker

Tom Murphy, and many other leading Democrats endorsed Clinton. Although the state Democratic Party tried to maintain an appearance of neutrality, the Clinton campaign used the party's telephones while their campaign headquarters was being set up. Moreover, the Miller organization played Cupid by introducing Clinton to campaign gurus James Carville and Paul Begala, who had directed Miller's 1990 election.

The dean of Georgia political journalists, Bill Shipp, observed a few days after the New Hampshire primary that "Governor Bill Clinton of Arkansas will be playing political solitaire in Georgia."[5] But Clinton's failure to win New Hampshire prompted Tsongas and Kerrey to reconsider and campaign in Georgia, even though Miller was openly critical of Tsongas.[6] The delay in mounting Georgia campaigns, however, proved insurmountable for Clinton's opponents. Tsongas could not fully exploit the New Hampshire bump, since at the time of his New England victory his Georgia organization consisted of a single volunteer.

Despite being poorly positioned, opponents had some hope of stopping Clinton. The South's traditional pro-military stance might boost Congressional Medal of Honor winner Kerrey, who was endorsed by Georgia Secretary of State Max Cleland, a Vietnam triple amputee, and Agriculture Commissioner Tommy Irvin. Kerrey hoped to broaden his appeal by emphasizing proposals for restructuring health care.

Tsongas tried to assuage fears that he was another northern liberal by stressing that he was friendly to business, was fiscally conservative, and would not launch a new spate of social programs. While largely absent in the days leading up to the Georgia primary, Jerry Brown had made early forays into the state and been received enthusiastically on college campuses. The January poll mentioned earlier indicated that Brown, largely on the strength of his earlier presidential bids and his unconventional approach in 1992, might win votes from Democrats who found nothing particularly appealing in the lackluster field.

Clinton's opponents hoped that social conservatives and veterans would find their fellow southerner morally unacceptable. They also sought to convince Democratic leaders, eager to reclaim the White House, that Clinton was unelectable. Kerrey spoke for the anti-Clinton forces when he warned that in the general election "I think [Clinton's] going to get opened up like a boiled peanut."[7]

A key unknown involved the black vote. In 1988, Jesse Jackson won Georgia and other Deep South states. In mid-January of 1992, only 10 percent of the South's blacks preferred Clinton, who trailed Jerry Brown by 24 points in this critical component of the electorate.[8] When Clinton heard a rumor that Jackson was supporting Tom Harkin, the Arkansan erupted. "It's an outrage. It's a dirty, double-crossing, back-stabbing thing to do." Former state legislator Hosea Williams, an associate of Martin Luther King, was unhappy with the inattention accorded black needs and urged African Americans to support none of the Democratic aspirants.[9] Had Clinton put African Americans into an "anyone but Clinton" frame of mind?

Table 2.1

Candidate Strength in the 1992 Southern Presidential Primaries (in percent)

	DEMOCRATS					REPUBLICANS		
	Clinton	Tsongas	Brown	Kerrey	Harkin	Bush	Buchanan	Duke
March 3								
Georgia	57.1	24.0	8.1	4.9	2.2	64.3	35.7	N
March 7								
So. Carolina	63.0	18.5	6.0	W	6.2	66.9	25.7	7.1
March 10								
Florida	51.7	34.0	12.3	W	W	68.1	31.9	N
Louisiana	69.3	11.1	6.6	W	W	62.0	27.0	8.8
Mississippi	73.4	7.9	9.6	W	W	72.3	16.7	10.6
Tennessee	67.4	19.3	8.1	W	W	72.5	22.2	3.1
Texas	65.4	19.2	8.0	W	W	69.8	23.9	2.5
May 5								
No. Carolina	64.0	W	10.4	W	W	70.7	19.5	W
May 26								
Arkansas	68.1	W	11.1	W	W	83.1	11.9	W
June 2								
Alabama	68.2	W	6.8	W	W	74.3	7.6	W

Note: N = not on ballot; W = withdrawn. Votes for other candidates, uncommitted slates, and no preference are not shown.
Source: Table compiled by the author with data from Congressional Quarterly Weekly Reports, issues as appropriate.

Ultimately several prominent black leaders joined their white counterparts. Representative John Lewis, Atlanta Mayor Maynard Jackson, and former Congressman and Altanta Mayor Andrew Young climbed aboard the Clinton bandwagon. Among those charting other courses, Legislative Black Caucus Chair Michael Thurmond was Paul Tsongas's most visible supporter in the state, and spirited state representative Mabel Thomas introduced Kerrey to Spelman College students, saying that the nation needed a commander in chief, not a "commander in chicken."

Clinton did far better than anyone had predicted. Using the same strategy he followed in the general election when he targeted a limited number of states, Clinton concentrated on forty north Georgia counties. He won 57 percent of the vote, seventeen points more than a poll at the end of February had indicated and almost three times the strength shown in January.[10] Clinton swept 158 of Georgia's 159 counties.

Tsongas's New Hampshire showing enabled him to do substantially better than he would have otherwise done. Yet his 24 percent of the vote, as reported in Table 2.1, was a poor second. No other Democrats broke into double figures.

Exit polls revealed that Clinton was the choice among most subsets of Georgia Democrats. He took 52 percent of the white vote and outpaced Tsongas by a 5-to-1 margin among black voters.[11] Neither the voter's sex nor the voter's ideology was related to candidate preference. Clinton did best among the least-educated voters, with 80 percent support among high school dropouts, while support for Tsongas was positively related to level of education, allowing him to beat Clinton 44 to 34 percent among Georgians having more than a baccalaureate education. Clinton won a majority in every age group except the 30–44 category, but even the baby boomers gave the Arkansan a plurality.

Avoidance of the draft hurt Clinton, but did not cripple him in Georgia. Only 22 percent of the voters troubled by this issue supported Clinton, while 47 percent went for Tsongas. Unfortunately for the former Massachusetts senator, only one in five Georgia Democrats viewed Clinton less favorably because of this issue. It had no effect on two-thirds of the electorate, and Clinton got the bulk of the veterans' votes.

Republicans

Georgia was especially critical for Buchanan. With the entire GOP hierarchy convinced that Buchanan could not win the nomination, but might weaken Bush in November, the challenger had to do more that win the silver medal if he was to stay in the hunt. Therefore, even though Maryland and Colorado also voted on March 3, Buchanan concentrated on Georgia, assuming that he would make a stronger showing with the more conservative southern electorate.

In New Hampshire, Buchanan had concentrated his fire on Bush's economic policies. Since the Georgia economy was more robust than that of New England, Buchanan shifted his emphasis. In an effort to demonstrate that he was the real conservative, Buchanan launched an expensive television campaign, which used a backdrop of dancing gays to accuse the president of supporting "so-called art [that] has glorified homosexuality, exploited children and perverted the image of Jesus Christ." This ad sought to link Bush to National Endowment of the Arts' expenditures, which Senator Jesse Helms (R–N.C.) had sharply criticized. Criticism of Bush for signing an affirmative action bill—which Buchanan characterized as a quota bill—was another Helms issue adopted by Buchanan.

Buchanan attempted to demonstrate his "southernness" by pointing out that his ancestors had fought for the South in the Civil War. He also rattled the xenophobic saber, promising to restore U.S. dominance in trade.

The Buchanan campaign pioneered what became the symbol of the Clinton general election campaign. The Republican conservative toured Georgia in a bus that he dubbed Asphalt One, in contrast to the president's Air Force One.

Despite outspending President Bush on television advertising by more than $170,000, Buchanan failed to improve on his New Hampshire showing. His 36 percent of the vote was one point below his share in the frozen North. There were a few bright spots in the gloom for the challenger, who captured majorities among Republican voters who believed their economic conditions had deteriorated and among those who were late in deciding for whom they would vote.[12] The third of the GOP electorate troubled by Bush's reneging on the "no new taxes" pledge went for the challenger by a 3-to-1 margin. Buchanan fought the president on an almost even footing with male voters, taking between 44 and 47 percent of the vote. He lost badly to the president among women, attracting just over a quarter of the vote. Only 19 percent of Buchanan's voters thought him to be the best presidential candidate, while 86 percent said they voted as they did in order to send the president a message.

SUPER TUESDAY

Democrats

Between Georgia and Super Tuesday, the Democratic field narrowed as Kerrey and Harkin bowed out. Harkin, who had appeared at South Carolina rallies accompanied by native son Jesse Jackson, failed to inspire voters of either race and, after securing only a 6 percent share in South Carolina, where ballots were cast on March 6, withdrew.

As Claibourne Darden had predicted, the patterns established in Georgia persisted in the six southern states that voted in the next week, as Clinton rolled up majorities in every state.[13] Most Democratic leaders, black and white, who took stands rallied to the Arkansan. *Congressional Quarterly* reported that twenty-one U.S. House members in Super Tuesday states committed to the southern candidate, while only one backed a rival.[14] The front-runner duplicated his feat in Georgia by taking the bulk of the black vote.

Going into Super Tuesday there had been some thought that Tsongas might duplicate the showing of his fellow Bay Stater Michael Dukakis in 1988 by winning an atypical southern state. Dukakis had acknowledged his relative weakness in the South and therefore focused his efforts on Florida and Texas, which, due to in-migration, are the least southern states in the region. The Dukakis strategy paid off, for while he showed little appeal in most of the South, his plurality victories in those two states, combined with victories in New England and Washington State, allowed him to claim that he could win in all regions of the country.[15] Encouraging to Tsongas partisans were polls done in late February and early March, which showed their man and Clinton running even in Florida and a sizable undecided vote.[16]

The 1992 results bore only the faintest resemblance to those of four years earlier. Tsongas did his best in Florida, taking 34 percent of the vote. But in what was essentially a two-person contest, he lost to Clinton by a 3-to-2 margin, with Jerry Brown taking one vote in eight. As in Georgia, Clinton's superior organization left insufficient room for Tsongas to make inroads. In Texas, Tsongas was routed 65 to 19 percent, and Clinton attracted support from well over 60 percent of the Democrats in every southern state except Florida on Super Tuesday. Tsongas came nowhere near duplicating his 34 percent in Florida, and in Mississippi he failed to make double figures.

Clinton in a well-funded television campaign promoted doubts about the costs of a Tsongas victory. The former senator had boasted that he was not afraid to give voters bad news by alerting them to the costs of the nation's profligate policies. But voters in 1992 were no more receptive to bad news prophets than they had been eight years earlier when Walter Mondale never recovered from his acceptance-speech promise to raise taxes. Clinton pilloried Tsongas for proposing to curb the growth in social programs for the elderly and for suggesting that the affluent elderly might have to pay for some items they now receive free. Tsongas's proposal to raise federal gas taxes curried little favored with voters. Efforts by Tsongas to counterattack by ridiculing Clinton as "pander bear" fell on deaf ears.

Outside of the South, the former senator fared better, winning majorities in his home state and neighboring Rhode Island, and taking pluralities in the Arizona and Delaware caucuses. These wins allowed Tsongas to continue in the race for a few more days, but his universal defeat in Dixie deflated the balloon of hope launched in New Hampshire, making a win in Illinois or Michigan essential for him to stay in the hunt.

Republicans

Super Tuesday sealed Pat Buchanan's fate on the Republican side. Buchanan continued to attract support from those who wanted to send the president a message, but he was unable to equal the 36 percent of the vote he won in Georgia. The Washington insider came closest in Florida, where he took 32 percent, and, like Tsongas, slumped worst in Mississippi, garnering only 17 percent of the vote.

Buchanan's inability to win, or even to attract much more than a quarter of the vote, eliminated him as a serious candidate. The Super Tuesday results also removed the GOP *bête noire*, David Duke. After winning majorities of the white vote in 1990 when he challenged U.S. Senator Bennett Johnston (D) and in 1991 when he faced Edwin Edwards (D) in a runoff for governor, Duke had compiled a nationwide list of contributors and become the nation's best-known state legislator.

The former neo-Nazi with the blow-dried hair and face lift was kept off the ballot in Georgia, so that the first reading of his strength in the region, which voted for George Wallace in 1968, did not come until Super Tuesday week. In the Deep South, it appeared that Duke cut into the Buchanan vote by providing an alternative to those who had soured on George Bush, but found little solace in Buchanan's Yankee accent. But while the anti-Bush vote continued in the 25 to 35 percent range, Duke consistently got the smaller share. His best showing came in Mississippi, but even here he barely managed 10 percent.[17] In his home state of Louisiana where he had been a force in the two previous years when seeking state offices, he struggled up to a scant 9 percent. In the Rim South states of Tennessee and Texas, the Duke vote was a paltry 3 percent. Two months before Super Tuesday, Duke had only a 10 percent favorable rating and even that eroded.[18]

Georgia and Florida officials had ruled that Duke was not a bona fide Republican candidate and had denied him a spot on their ballots, a decision upheld by the federal courts.[19] In light of Duke's weak showing, the president, whose backers had urged the exclusion of the Louisiana legislator, might have profited from his presence in Georgia; had the anti-Bush vote been split, Buchanan might have been held below 30 percent. Recall that Buchanan broke 30 percent in the only two southern states (Georgia and Florida) where Duke was not an available option.

THE REST OF THE SOUTH

Alabama, Arkansas, North Carolina, and Virginia opted out of the early March primaries. By choosing delegates to the national party conventions later in the year, they made their primaries (or in the case of Virginia, a caucus) irrelevant to the nomination decision. They fretted in obscurity in 1988, but voting later in 1992 attracted no great interest in these states. As the Bush and Clinton campaigns went about wrapping up the delegates needed for first-round nominations, much like a baseball team that has a fifteen-game lead going into September, the front-runners swept the remaining contests.

Bush took 74 percent of the vote in Alabama and performed even better in Arkansas. In North Carolina, Buchanan's attempt to attract voters who had given Jesse Helms (R) four terms in the Senate failed. Playing the race card by criticizing affirmative action as quotas and castigating the Justice Department for forcing the state to draw two gerrymandered black-majority House districts were unavailing.

On the Democratic side, in the last three southern primaries Clinton's closest opponent was not a named candidate, but the uncommitted slate or the "no preference" option. Clinton won majorities in every southern state, typically finishing up with about two-thirds of the votes.

SUPER TUESDAY: WHY WAS IT BETTER THE SECOND TIME AROUND?

Hollywood sequels are notorious for not being as good as the originals. Sylvester Stallone should be envious of Super Tuesday. In 1992, Super Tuesday worked as its creators had hoped it would, but failed to do in 1988. A southern moderate succeeded in rallying united support in his home region. By sweeping the South, its favorite son developed such a head of steam that he succeeded in quickly driving all viable opponents from the field. Less than two weeks after Super Tuesday, the path to the nomination was clear. What accounts for the improved performance in 1992?

The most significant single factor was the absence of Jesse Jackson or some other candidate able to command the black vote. Without Jackson or a white candidate with the credentials of Walter Mondale, who attracted a share of the

African-American vote in 1984, Clinton could assemble the kind of coalition that has elected Democrats in the South for the last generation. Clinton's moderate message attracted solid black support and sufficient white backing to win.[20] The black vote was up for grabs in January when most of the region's African Americans were undecided and another third professed support for Jerry Brown.[21] But with the departure of black governor Doug Wilder, prominent African-American political leaders were free to make endorsements. Given the fluid situation and the consistency in the choice of the endorsers, these endorsements were influential.

Clinton was also helped by the weakness of the field. Big-name Democrats opted not to run when President Bush, riding the wave of unequaled support derived from the 100-hour war against Saddam Hussein, was anointed "George the Unbeatable." Of those who chose to run, only Jerry Brown had national name recognition, and much of his image was that of "Governor Moonbeam," a wilting flower child whose message found little favor save among environmentalists and some college students.

Two competitors fared so poorly in the early going that they had struck their colors before Super Tuesday, with Kerrey withdrawing on March 5 and Harkin following suit four days later. Embarrassing performances in Georgia and South Carolina helped convince the two midwesterners that 1992 was not their magic year. Harkin tried to mobilize organized labor, a hopeless task in the right-to-work South, while Kerrey seemed unable to articulate a message. These departures meant that where Gore had faced what appeared to be two or even three serious candidates in Super Tuesday 1988, Clinton could concentrate his fire on Tsongas.

Not only were the names of the Democratic choices largely unknown in the South, but also their weak followings nationwide kept them from raising the funds necessary for media blitzes that might have attracted a following. Clinton, the leading fund-raiser, developed a more extensive organization than any of his rivals. A Texan supporting Kerrey observed that "Clinton has spent so much time in Texas, it's like he's running for governor of the state."[22] Without the rudiments of an organization, Tsongas could not capitalize on his New Hampshire win, which enabled Clinton to become the first president in forty years to overcome a New Hampshire defeat. The bump factor was still there for Tsongas as his share of the Georgia vote (24 percent) was substantially above his minuscule support in mid-January. But the underfunded and understaffed Yankee could not become a force in the two weeks between New Hampshire and Georgia.

To some extent, then, Clinton's success was the product of an absence of a viable alternative—to some extent, but not exclusively. Clinton was a stronger candidate than the white southern hope of 1988, Tennessee Senator Al Gore. The Tennessean, while having the pedigree of a father who had served in both the House and the Senate, was a first-term senator himself. In contrast, Clinton had lived in the governor's mansion for twelve of the previous fourteen years— so long that he owned no home. Clinton also had the advantage of being a leader

in the moderate Democratic Leadership Council (DLC). Gore, although supporting DLC ideas, was not a leader, and some saw him as a less than wholly
acceptable replacement for DLC leaders Senator Sam Nunn of Georgia and
former Virginia Governor (now Senator) Charles Robb. Nunn and Robb declined
entreaties to become the southern standard bearer in 1988 and 1992.

White Democratic leaders in the South were more united in 1992 than four
years earlier. In 1988, many white members of Congress rallied to the cause of
their colleague Representative Richard Gephardt (D–Mo.), while state politicians
more often smiled on Gore. In 1992, both national and state Democratic leaders
joined the Clinton effort.

As the clear winner in the South, Clinton emerged with far more momentum
than had Gore in 1988. While Gore was the preferred candidate among white
southern Democratic voters that year, the outcome was muddled. Jesse Jackson
actually took the largest share of the popular vote and delegates and thus claimed
to have won. Even Dukakis, who finished behind Jackson and Gore, could argue
that he had bagged what he set his sights on—the region's two largest states—
and, therefore, in light of his nonsouthern heritage, he, too, was a winner.
Clinton did not have to share the awards ceremony with anyone.

Finally, as the creators of Super Tuesday and everyone else recognized, southern votes alone are insufficient to win the nomination. A candidate whose strength
was confined to the South, like Richard Russell of Georgia in 1952, would not
be nominated. It was essential that Clinton continue winning as the campaign
moved into other regions. His chief adversary, Paul Tsongas, did not cease
campaigning until he was soundly beaten in Illinois and Michigan a week after
Super Tuesday. Had Clinton been no more successful in the Midwest than Gore
was in 1988, Tsongas could have held on and in time might have overtaken the
southerner.

As in 1988, Bush put away his opponents in the South. In 1988, Bush swept
the region and by doing so ended the hopes of Bob Dole (Kan.), Jack Kemp,
and Pat Robertson.[23] In 1992, the field of opponents was weaker, and the consequences of big wins on Super Tuesday were the same. David Duke was shown
to be a noncandidate. Buchanan tried to play a Jesse Jackson role, staying in
the contest long after it became obvious that he would not be the nominee, hoping
to publicize an ideological agenda and build support for a future day.

TURNOUT

Voter turnout in the South provided further evidence of the continuing realignment. Southerners demonstrated a marked disinterest in the Democratic
contest, while participation on the Republican side reached new heights. South
Carolina, where most whites now identify with the Republican Party, became
the first southern state in which a GOP presidential primary actually drew more
voters than the Democratic contest. In Georgia the ability of the GOP to match
the Democrats vote for vote in the presidential primary foreshadowed the re-

markable gains registered by the minority party later in the year when it picked up a U.S. Senate seat, three U.S. House seats, and a nation-high number of new state house slots.[24]

Much of the turnout decline in the Democratic contests can be laid to black disinterest. Without the enthusiasm engendered by Jesse Jackson, or the presence of blacks running for lesser offices, the early March contests provided little incentive for African Americans to get ballots. Black turnout in states that voted on Super Tuesday in both 1988 and 1992 may have declined by as much as 25 percent.

In the six states that held early March primaries in 1988 and 1992 (South Carolina Democrats used a caucus in 1988), the Republican share of the votes cast increased by an average of 6.6 percentage points. The Republican share fell only in Texas, and that drop was but a single point. The GOP primary drew voters even though the prospects of Bush not being nominated were substantially less in 1992 than they had been when he sought to become Ronald Reagan's successor. Not only are whites increasingly identifying with the GOP, since nominees for other offices are not chosen at the time of the presidential primary, but also Republican identifiers are not dissuaded from taking GOP ballots as some are later in the year when nominees for state and local offices are chosen.

CONCLUSIONS

It is probably hyperbole to claim that Georgia has replaced New Hampshire as the oracle that identifies future presidents. There are, however, some lessons to learn from Super Tuesday. To be nominated, a candidate need not win all of the southern states, but to be closed out is fatal. Candidates who have swept the South (Bush in 1988 and 1992 and Clinton) have quickly passed from uncertainty in the North to the calm that surrounds a candidate who is building an insurmountable lead. When candidates have split the early southern states (Democrats in 1984 and 1988), the struggle has continued.

As Tsongas, Kerrey, and Harkin learned, only a foolish candidate does not early on develop at least a rudimentary organization in some, if not all, southern states. The long shot may opt to concentrate exclusively on the Iowa caucuses or the New Hampshire primary, believing that to be the only viable strategy. The flaw in a strategy that seeks one early victory in hopes of being launched, as Jimmy Carter was in 1976, is that the concentrated vote of the South can be too high a hurdle for the undernourished long shot. A plan to gradually expand outward from a single upset has been made obsolete by front loading (that is, the placement of many primaries and caucuses early in the primary season). Candidates no longer have the luxury of focusing on one state per week until they build momentum. A candidate who is closed out in the South has little room for failure in the states balloting immediately after the South.

Super Tuesday was adopted, in part, because southerners felt that candidates popular in their region were too often eliminated before southern states had a chance to vote. In 1992, the South returned the favor as the two midwesterners failed to survive Super Tuesday and Tsongas was mortally wounded.

The 1992 primaries show that the Super Tuesday approach can work for both Democrats and Republicans. When a candidate, either through his own strength (Bush) or his opponents' weaknesses (Clinton), succeeds in sweeping the South, he has gone on to the nomination. A southern sweep requires a strong and far-flung organization and widespread support among party leaders. On the Democratic side, another prerequisite is the ability to run well with both black and white voters. As both parties' electorates increasingly resemble those in the North, resounding success in the South presages victory in other regions. Clinton's election confirmed an observation made on the eve of Super Tuesday 1988: "You find me a candidate of the Democratic party . . . who can carry Ohio and Pennsylvania, and I'll show you a candidate that can carry North Carolina and Arkansas.[25]

NOTES

I greatly appreciate the careful reading of an earlier draft of this manuscript by Paul Gurian, one of the leading scholars of presidential nomination politics.

1. For a discussion of the expectations behind Super Tuesday 1988 and the outcomes, see Charles S. Bullock III, "The Nomination Process and Super Tuesday," in *The 1988 Presidential Election in the South: Continuity Amidst Change in Southern Party Politics*, ed. Laurence W. Moreland, Robert P. Steed, and Tod A. Baker (New York: Praeger, 1991), 3–19; and Harold W. Stanley and Charles Hadley, "An Analysis of Super Tuesday: Intentions, Results, and Implications" (Revision of a paper delivered at the 1988 Annual Meeting of the Midwest Political Science Association, Chicago, 14–16 April 1988).

2. Quoted in Don Melvin, "No More Mr. Nice Guy Now," *Athens Banner-Herald* (1 March 1992), 1A.

3. A. L. May, "Clinton Is Early Favorite," *Atlanta Journal and Constitution* (18 January 1992), A1.

4. Tom Baxter, "Tsongas Poised for Big Payoff," *Atlanta Journal and Constitution* (28 February 1992), B1.

5. Bill Shipp, "Clinton Is Sure Thing, But Is Bush?" *Athens Banner-Herald* (23 February 1992), 2D.

6. As Miller shook off any pretense of neutrality, it became clear that his argument that Georgia should advance its primary ahead of Super Tuesday in order to secure more publicity was a ruse. Clearly Miller was more interested in helping his friend Clinton than in promoting a wide-open primary, the kind of event that would attract extensive media coverage.

7. A. L. May and Mark Sherman, "Kerrey Rips into Clinton on Vietnam," *Atlanta Journal and Constitution* (27 February 1992), A1.

8. May, "Clinton Is Early Favorite," A1.

9. *Atlanta Journal and Constitution* (3 March 1992), A4.

10. A. L. May, "Clinton Hangs On to Georgia Lead," *Atlanta Journal and Constitution* (29 February 1992), A1.

11. This discussion draws on the *Atlanta Journal and Constitution* (4 March 1992), A8, and the *New York Times* (5 March 1992), A10.

12. This discussion draws on the *Atlanta Journal and Constitution* (4 March 1992), A8, and the *New York Times* (5 March 1992), A10.

13. Florida, Louisiana, Mississippi, Tennessee, and Texas voted on March 10; South Carolina voted three days earlier, but will be discussed as a Super Tuesday state.

14. *Congressional Quarterly Weekly Report* (14 March 1992), 638.

15. For a fuller discussion of the 1988 Dukakis strategy, see Bullock, "The Nomination Process and Super Tuesday."

16. David E. Rosenbaum, "Florida Becomes Main Battlefield for Democrats on Super Tuesday," *New York Times* (6 March 1992), A1, A10.

17. For an argument that Duke did poorly in the Republican presidential primaries because his natural constituency was in the Democratic Party, see Ronald F. King, Douglas D. Rose, and Matthew Crozat, "White Knight Fades to Black: David Duke and the 1992 Presidential Campaign" (unpublished).

18. A. L. May, "Bush in Political Hot Water with Voters Across South," *Atlanta Journal and Constitution* (17 January 1992), A7.

19. *Duke v. Cleland*, 1:92-cv–116-RCF (N.D. Ga., January 21, 1992).

20. On the success of moderate Democrats, see Earl Black and Merle Black, *Politics and Society in the South* (Cambridge, Mass.: Harvard University Press, 1987).

21. May, "Clinton Is Early Favorite," A1.

22. Gwen Ifill, "Clinton Moves on 2 Fronts to Widen Support in South," *New York Times* (22 January 1992), A12.

23. For discussions of the 1988 Super Tuesday consequences for the GOP, see Bullock, "The Nomination Process and Super Tuesday," and Earl Black and Merle Black, *The Vital South: How Presidents Are Elected* (Cambridge, Mass.: Harvard University Press, 1992), chapter 5.

24. For a discussion of Republican gains in Georgia in 1992, see Charles S. Bullock III, *The Georgia Political Almanac 1993–1994* (Decatur, Ga.: Cornerstone), 1193.

25. Comments made by Donald Fowler at the Super Tuesday Roundtable at The Citadel Symposium on Southern Politics, Charleston, S.C., 3–4 March 1988.

PART II

ELECTIONS IN THE DEEP SOUTH

3

Alabama: No Winners or Losers

PATRICK R. COTTER

More than most elections, 1992 was a year in which, at least in Alabama, there were no clear winners or losers. George Bush won the state's presidential election, but by a margin much reduced from that he had achieved four years previously. Bill Clinton lost Alabama's presidential contest, but ran a competitive race while expending little of his time or resources on Alabama. H. Ross Perot faired poorly in the state, and his candidacy did not affect the outcome of the presidential contest; yet his presence had a clear impact on the tone and visibility of the race. After some uncertainty, the state's Republican Party held onto an open congressional seat and gained another. Yet the Democratic Party swept both the U.S. Senate election and the contests for all the other statewide positions on the ballot.

Despite, or perhaps because of, the absence of any clear electoral winners or losers, 1992 was a particularly interesting political year in Alabama. It was also a year that provides some valuable information concerning the current status of partisan politics in the state.

THE CAMPAIGN

The outcome of the 1992 presidential election in Alabama was uncertain until the very end of the campaign. As a result, unlike previous years when the eventual outcome of the campaign was obvious early in the election year, the presidential candidates, and particularly the Bush/Quayle campaign, were forced to focus a fair amount of their attention on Alabama.

The candidates' courtship of Alabama occurred, however, toward the end, rather than at the beginning, of the campaign. Indeed, during the early months of 1992, presidential candidates from both parties paid very little attention to

Alabama. Despite the absence of much electoral activity in the state, however, Alabama's Democratic leaders made it clear early in the election cycle that they wanted the party to nominate a mainstream, moderate candidate for president. "Home, mother and heaven won't hurt a Democratic candidate," declared U.S. Senator Howell Heflin.[1] What was not needed, Democratic leaders made clear, was another candidate like Walter Mondale or Michael Dukakis. Referring to Dukakis, freshman U.S. Representative Bud Cramer said, "I had to wear that albatross around my political neck . . . I don't want to go through that again. Anything I can do to get a mainstream Democrat elected, I'll do."[2]

A wide range of the state's Democratic leaders also made it clear that Bill Clinton was the type of candidate they had in mind. Most echoed the views stated by Congressman Ben Erdreich: "The things he's done as governor in Arkansas and his position on the issues seem to be very close to a lot of Alabama views on a range of issues."[3]

On the Republican side, most party leaders backed President Bush, and only a few expressed support for challenger Pat Buchanan.[4] Most Republicans also expressed optimism about the upcoming election.[5]

As in other states, efforts began in the spring of 1992 to put Ross Perot on the ballot as a presidential candidate. Petitions began to circulate to obtain the necessary 5,000 signatures of registered voters.[6]

During the early months of 1992, George Bush, Dan Quayle, and both Bill and Hillary Clinton visited the state.[7] None of these trips was exceptionally newsworthy. Bush went fishing, Quayle talked about the space program in Huntsville, and the Clintons' visit was overshadowed by the outbreak of rioting in Los Angeles. Also during this period, Perot obtained substantially more than enough signatures to be placed on the state's presidential ballot.[8]

As expected, the nomination contests in both parties were essentially decided by the middle of the spring. As a result, the Alabama presidential primary generated little interest or attention. Indeed, the most news generated by the contest was the (distant) second-place finish in both parties of "uncommitted."[9]

Naturally, given their earlier statements, Alabama Democratic leaders were happy that Clinton had gained their party's nomination. They also expressed optimism that Clinton could carry the state in November.[10]

Survey data supported the Democrats' optimism. A May *Birmingham News/* Southern Opinion Research survey found George Bush (42 percent) had a relatively narrow lead over Bill Clinton (31 percent) and (the not-yet-announced candidate) Ross Perot (24 percent).[11] A June *Birmingham News/*Southern Opinion Research survey found Bush (34 percent) with an even smaller margin over Clinton (29 percent) and (the now-formally-announced) Perot (24 percent).[12]

The pre-convention selection of Al Gore from Tennessee as the party's vice-presidential candidate further increased the optimism and enthusiasm of the state's Democrats. The executive director of the Alabama Democratic Party, Al LaPierre, said, "This is a ticket that Democrats in local elected offices can be proud to get out and campaign for. This is something we haven't had in a long time.''[13]

Republican leaders downplayed the influence of having Gore on the ticket with Clinton. Elbert Peters, state Republican chair, revived images from previous campaigns when he said that ''Gore shouldn't be that attractive in Alabama. He's just another liberal Democrat.''[14]

The conduct of the Democratic National Convention did nothing to reduce the enthusiasm of the party's faithful in the state. And, as elsewhere, the mid-convention withdrawal from the presidential race by Ross Perot gave Democrats (and Republicans) even more reasons for hope and concern.[15]

As the Republican National Convention neared, Dan Quayle made two trips to the state, arguing that Bush, and not his opponent, shared the values of southerners. He also claimed that a Clinton presidency would lead to higher taxes, deep cuts in defense spending, and ''socialized medicine.''[16]

During this period, Alabama Republicans also expressed optimism about the presidential election. GOP leaders acknowledged, however, that 1992 was going to be a closer race than were the 1984 and 1988 contests.[17]

The fact that 1992 was a substantially more competitive contest was clearly signaled by the Bush campaign's decision to hold a rally in the Birmingham suburb of Hoover two days after the close of the Republican convention. In his talk at the rally, Bush repeated the themes included in his convention acceptance speech, involving family values, taxes, Clinton's character, and the problem of congressional gridlock. The election, the president claimed, ''is a choice about the character of the person you want to lead the nation and the direction you want us to go.''[18]

The use of these themes, which were repeated in a general way for the remainder of the campaign, made it clear that the Republican campaign strategy was similar to the one they had used in 1988. In particular, the GOP tried to focus attention on the character of the Democratic candidate and thus convince voters that Bill Clinton did not share their values and therefore could not be trusted. The Republicans' job, Bush/Quayle Chair Emory Folmar said, was to show voters that Clinton and Gore ''talk Southern but vote another way. They come out of the mold of Dukakis, Mondale, Carter and McGovern and we're going to make sure people in Alabama are acquainted with that.''[19]

In contrast, the Democrats tried to focus attention on the economy and related issues, such as health care and education. Their goal was to convince voters that George Bush had not done a good job and did not understand the needs and problems of the average citizens. Democrats also believed that they had a pres-idential candidate who, unlike Michael Dukakis, was immune to Republican attacks on his character. For example, in a July statement that anticipated the future course of the campaign, Democratic Secretary of State Billy Joe Camp argued that ''Here we've got the governor of Arkansas, elected six times, and people in the South know the people in Arkansas are not flaming liberals. It's going to be a lot more difficult for the Republicans to attempt to take away the decency of this ticket."[20]

Throughout the fall, the Bush campaign continued to devote time and resources to Alabama. On these trips, Republican spokesmen followed Bush's lead at the Hoover rally and said little about economic conditions; instead they tried to focus attention on other concerns, and particularly on Bill Clinton's character. Dan Quayle made a campaign trip to Huntsville and again raised questions about Clinton's support of the space program.[21] Marilyn Quayle visited the state in late September and attacked Clinton's advocacy of big government and the bias of the mass media.[22] Both Dan and Marilyn Quayle returned to the state in mid-October, the day after the vice-presidential debate. At a rally held at Auburn University, the vice-president repeated the claim that he made several times during the debate, that "Bill Clinton has trouble telling the truth."[23]

George Bush himself returned to Alabama in late October. At a campaign rally in Montgomery, Bush attacked Clinton's draft record, his "waffling" on the issues, and his tax proposals. "This guy," Bush said, "talks about change; that's all you're going to have left in your pocket if we listen to his program."[24]

During the last days of October, Mrs. Quayle returned to the state and again attacked Clinton's character.[25] She also said that a Clinton administration would be "Jimmy Carter No. 2."[26] Coinciding with Mrs. Quayle's visit were campaign stops made by Pat Buchanan, South Carolina Senator Strom Thurmond, and Jonathan Bush, brother of the president.[27]

The Democratic ticket devoted substantially fewer resources to Alabama. Al Gore made several short trips to the state.[28] His father, the former senator from Tennessee, made one trip to the state.[29] Hillary Clinton visited Birmingham in late October. During this visit, Mrs. Clinton focused, as the Gore father and son did earlier, on the economy. She stated that "This country cannot afford four more years of trickle-down economics."[30]

Published polls showed why the Bush campaign was devoting resources to Alabama. A September *Birmingham News*/Southern Opinion Research survey, conducted shortly before Ross Perot reentered the contest, found that Clinton led Bush by a 50 to 44 percent margin. When respondents were asked how they would vote in a three-person race, Clinton led with 46 percent, while Bush got 39 percent, and Perot received 11 percent.[31]

A mid-October *Birmingham Post-Herald* survey found Clinton (45 percent) with a 10 percent lead over Bush (35 percent). Perot trailed with 12 percent.[32] A late October Mason-Dixon survey, conducted the same weekend as Bush's campaign visit to Montgomery, found a closer race, with Clinton supported by 39 percent, Bush by 38 percent, and Perot by 14 percent.[33]

By the end of the campaign, reflecting both national trends and the resources the GOP had put into the state, Bush had regained the lead in the presidential race. The final *Birmingham News*/Southern Opinion Research survey found Bush leading Clinton by a 45 to 38 percent margin.[34] Perot was supported by 14 percent of likely voters. A University of South Alabama survey found Bush ahead by a 41 to 37 percent margin (with Perot at 12 percent).[35]

RESULTS AND ANALYSIS

The Presidential Election

On election day, George Bush defeated Bill Clinton in Alabama by a 48 to 41 percent margin. Ross Perot trailed with 11 percent, considerably less than he achieved nationwide. While winning the state, Bush's margin of victory and his level of support were considerably lower than those he had achieved in 1988, when he defeated Michael Dukakis by about a 60 to 40 percent margin.

The results of the final *Birmingham News*/Southern Opinion Research survey show that Bush did relatively well among white, older, and more-educated voters.[36] (See Table 3.1.) Bush received an equal amount of support from men and women. The results also show that Bush, not surprisingly, did well among Republican identifiers and independents. Finally, the results show that Bush received more support in the central and southern parts of Alabama than in the northern section of the state.

Bill Clinton received strong support from black and less-educated voters as well as those living in northern Alabama. Like Bush, Clinton did better among older than among younger voters. Women were more likely than men to support Clinton. Democratic identifiers were about as unified in their support of their party's candidate as were Republican identifiers.

Ross Perot's strongest support came from whites, males, and younger voters. He also did well among political independents.

Prior to election day, there were a number of reports, based on registration rates and requests for absentee ballots, that turnout would be high in the 1992 election.[37] These indicators proved to be correct, as turnout increased by about 5 percent over 1988.[38] Clinton ran well among the "new" voters. Among respondents who said that they did not vote in 1988, Clinton led Bush by a 48 to 36 percent margin. Perot was supported by about 16 percent of the new voters.

Why Did Bush Win? Examining voters' perceptions of the candidates helps explain why George Bush defeated Bill Clinton and Ross Perot in Alabama. The *Birmingham News*/Southern Opinion Research pre-election survey asked respondents which of the candidates would do the best job in a number of different issue areas. Bush had a clear advantage over his opponents when voters were asked about social or foreign policy issues. (See Table 3.2.) For example, about 48 percent of the state's registered voters said that of the presidential candidates, Bush would do the best job of upholding family values, compared to about 29 percent for Clinton and 9 percent for Perot. Similarly, more than 60 percent of voters said that Bush was the best candidate for maintaining the nation's defense.

Table 3.1

Presidential Preferences Among Alabama Voters by Background Characteristic (in percent)*

Characteristic	Clinton	Bush	Perot	(N)
Respondent's race				
White	27	56	17	(617)
Black	85	10	6	(165)
Respondent's age				
18-30	38	42	20	(174)
31-40	36	45	19	(167)
41-60	41	46	14	(289)
61+	43	51	6	(165)
Respondent's education				
High school or less	45	43	12	(326)
More than high school	36	48	16	(475)
Respondent's gender				
Male	34	46	19	(354)
Female	43	46	11	(448)
Respondent's party				
Strong/weak Republican	4	86	11	(227)
Independent Republican	6	71	23	(135)
Independent	32	45	23	(051)
Independent Democrat	60	13	26	(074)
Strong/weak Democrat	81	10	10	(273)
Region of state				
North	45	39	16	(179)
Central	39	48	14	(451)
South	35	50	16	(173)
Voted in 1988?				
Yes	38	48	14	(670)
No	48	36	16	(118)

* Question asked: "If a presidential election was held today and the candidates were Bill Clinton for the Democrats, George Bush for the Republicans and Independent candidate Ross Perot, for whom would you vote?" (If undecided, respondent was asked: "As of today, do you lean towards Clinton, Bush or Perot?") Note: total of each row equals 100 percent (may vary slightly because of rounding).
Source: Compiled by author from data generated for *Birmingham News*/Southern Opinion Research.

Bush did not do as well when voters were asked about domestic/economic issues. Even on these issues, however, Bush showed some strength. In particular, Bush and Clinton received about equal support when voters were asked which candidate would do the best job in the areas of improving education, bringing about the changes needed in the country, and promoting jobs and economic development. All three candidates received about equal support in the area of reducing the federal deficit. Only on the issues of health care, the environment, and race relations did Bush significantly trail Clinton.

Table 3.2
Expectations of Presidential Candidates Among Alabama Voters (in percent)*

	Clinton	Bush	Perot	Equal	None	DK/NA
Maintain the nation's defense	2 2	6 2	6	2	1	6
Keep peace in the world	2 4	5 8	6	3	3	6
Uphold family values	2 9	4 8	9	6	2	6
Hold down taxes	2 5	4 4	9	2	1 3	7
Fight crime	3 0	4 1	1 1	4	3	1 0
Protect the rights of citizens	3 2	4 1	1 0	6	3	7
Improve education	3 9	3 6	1 2	2	4	7
Bring about the changes needed in the country	3 4	3 5	1 8	2	4	6
Promote jobs and economic development	3 7	3 4	1 9	2	2	6
Protect the environment	4 3	3 4	8	2	2	1 0
Improve health care	4 4	3 2	1 0	2	4	8
Improve race relations	3 9	3 1	6	5	8	1 2
Reduce the federal deficit	2 4	2 9	2 9	1	1 1	7

* Question asked: "Which of the presidential candidates, George Bush, Bill Clinton or Ross Perot, is most likely to do each of the following?"
Note: total of each row equals approximately 100 percent (may vary slightly because of rounding).
Source: Compiled by author from data generated for *Birmingham News*/Southern Opinion Research.

Respondents in the *Birmingham News*/Southern Opinion Research survey were also asked to evaluate the candidates on characteristics or traits such as honesty and strength. (See Table 3.3.) In these evaluations, Bush held a clear advantage over his opponents on job-related characteristics, such as making good decisions in times of crisis, being a good leader, and having the skills necessary to be a good president. Bush also had an advantage over Clinton and Perot on character concerns, such as strength, honesty, trustworthiness, and standing up for one's beliefs. Only on the trait of understanding the needs of the voters did Clinton's rating exceed Bush's.

Given these issue and trait evaluations, it is not surprising to find that Bush ended the campaign with a somewhat favorable overall image among Alabama voters. Specifically, about 44 percent of the state's voters said that they felt positively about Bush, while slightly fewer (40 percent) said that they felt negatively about the president (the remaining respondents either failed to express an opinion or gave Bush a neutral rating). In contrast, both Bill Clinton and Ross Perot ended the campaign with more negative than positive images among Alabamians. About 31 percent gave Clinton a positive rating, while almost half the public (49 percent) gave the Arkansas governor a negative rating. Ross Perot was even more disliked by Alabamians. His negative ratings outnumbered his positive ratings by a 48 to 20 percent margin.[39]

Thus, in terms of issues, characteristics and traits, and overall evaluations, Alabama citizens generally preferred George Bush to either Bill Clinton or Ross

Table 3.3

Evaluations of Personal Characteristics of Presidential Candidates Among Alabama Voters (in percent)*

Characteristic	Clinton	Bush	Perot	Equal	None	DK/NA
Makes good decisions in times of crisis	20	62	7	1	2	8
A good leader	29	50	10	3	2	6
Has skills necessary to be a good president	31	48	9	5	2	4
Strong	29	47	16	3	2	3
Trustworthy	25	42	13	4	9	6
Honest	20	40	21	3	10	6
Stands up for what he believes	25	38	25	7	2	3
Understands the needs of people like you	35	32	21	2	7	3

* Question asked: "Which of the presidential candidates -- George Bush, Bill Clinton or Ross Perot -- is *best* described by each of the following phrases?"
Note: total of each row equals approximately 100 percent (may vary slightly because of rounding); N = 839.
Source: Compiled by author from data generated for *Birmingham News*/Southern Opinion Research.

Perot. Given that citizens liked him more than his opponents, it is not surprising that Bush won the popular vote in the state.

Why Did Bush's Margin Decrease? Several pieces of evidence help explain why George Bush's victory margin was considerably smaller in 1992 than it was in 1988. First, a number of the issue and trait items included in the 1992 pre-election survey were also included in an equivalent, or roughly equivalent, form in the final 1988 *Birmingham News*/Southern Opinion Research pre-election survey.[40] On all but two of the issues and traits that can be compared, Bush's rating declined from 1988. (See Table 3.4.) The two exceptions to this pattern, probably reflecting the president's success in the Persian Gulf War, involved the items asking about which candidate would make the best decisions during a crisis and which would do the best job of maintaining the nation's defense.

Bush's overall image also declined between 1988 and 1992. In 1988, 50 percent of Alabamians rated Bush positively, compared to 44 percent in 1992. Similarly, in 1988, only 26 percent of Alabama voters gave George Bush a negative evaluation, compared to 40 percent in 1992. Thus, while George Bush ended the 1992 campaign with a more favorable image than his opponents, the public's evaluation of him was not nearly as favorable as it had been in 1988.

Second, the president's victory margin declined because, despite Bush's best efforts, the election agenda was dominated by one issue, jobs, on which George Bush did poorly, as Table 3.2 shows. In the 1992 pre-election survey, 56 percent of Alabama voters said that jobs and the economy was the most important issue facing the nation. Among those saying that jobs was the most important issue,

Table 3.4
Evaluations of Presidential Candidates in 1988 and 1992 (in percent)

Issues/Traits and Characteristics	1992		1988		
	Clinton	Bush	Perot	Bush	Dukakis
Issues					
Maintain the nation's defense	2 2	6 2	6	6 0	2 4
Hold down taxes	2 5	4 4	9	5 2	2 6
Fight crime	3 0	4 1	1 1	5 2	2 7
Promote jobs and economic development	3 7	3 4	1 9	4 8	3 7
Protect the environment	4 3	3 4	8	4 8	3 3
Reduce the federal deficit	2 4	2 9	2 9	4 4	3 4
Traits and characteristics					
Makes good decisions in times of crisis	2 0	6 2	7	5 2	2 9
Honest	2 0	4 0	2 1	4 1	3 2
Stands up for what he believes	2 5	3 8	2 5	4 7	3 2
Understands the needs of people like you	3 5	3 2	2 1	4 4	3 7

Source: Compiled by author from data generated for *Birmingham News*/Southern Opinion Research.

Clinton (44 percent) rather than Bush (42 percent) was the leading vote getter. (Perot was supported by 14 percent of these citizens.)

Ross Perot is a final reason George Bush's support declined from 1988. In particular, as Table 3.1 shows, much of Perot's support came from younger, white, male, and independent voters who, based on the results of previous elections, under more normal circumstances would probably have voted for George Bush. This conclusion is further supported by the results of a question included in the pre-election survey that directly asked Perot supporters how they would vote in an election limited to Bill Clinton and George Bush. About 38 percent of Perot's supporters said they would back Bill Clinton. However, a larger number (54 percent) said they would vote for George Bush (7 percent were undecided or would not vote).

In sum, George Bush's victory margin declined from 1988 because of his relatively unfavorable image, a campaign agenda dominated by an unfriendly issue, and the presence of Ross Perot. Despite these obstacles, George Bush won in Alabama. Obviously, this was not a feat that he duplicated in many other states. Thus, another important topic to examine is why Alabama went for Bush while most other states, including some southern states, did not.

Why Did Bush Win Alabama, but Not Other States? Two related factors seem to account for Bush's winning Alabama, but not other states. First, in terms of relative effort, the Bush campaign devoted many more resources to winning Alabama than did the Clinton campaign. Bill Clinton made no post-convention campaign trips to the state. As we have seen, George Bush made two campaign stops in Alabama. Dan Quayle also was a frequent visitor to Alabama throughout the year, while Al Gore only made occasional visits. Similar differences are found when the activities of campaign surrogates are examined.

The second reason for Bush's winning Alabama, but not other states, helps explain the Clinton campaign's apparent decision to ignore the state. In particular, as we have seen, jobs and the economy was the major issue among Alabama voters. However, throughout 1992, the unemployment rate in Alabama was below or about equal to the national average. This meant, given Alabama's economic history, that times were not all that bad in the state.[41] Thus, while important, the economy may not have played as central a role in Alabama as it did elsewhere.

Thus, it appears that George Bush won Alabama, but not other states, because the Clinton campaign largely conceded the state to the Republicans. They did this because economic conditions in the state, and the resulting concerns of Alabama citizens, made it difficult, in comparison to other states, for Clinton to carry Alabama.[42] By conceding the state, even though election surveys through the fall indicated it was a close contest, the Clinton campaign freed up resources it could use elsewhere. In contrast, the Bush campaign was required to expend resources on a state that Republicans had easily won the previous two election years.

Congressional and State Campaigns

Like the presidential campaign, little occurred at the state level in the 1988 election. In that year, neither of the state's U.S. Senate seats was up for reelection, none of the state's congressional seats was seriously contested, and the other statewide contests on the ballot, mostly for judicial positions, generated little news.

The situation was quite different in 1992. There was a U.S. Senate election in the state. Several of the state's congressional contests featured tight campaigns. The competition for the statewide offices up for election in 1992 remained, however, largely invisible.

In the U.S. Senate election, Richard Shelby was seeking reelection to a second term. Shelby, who barely defeated incumbent Republican Jeremiah Denton in 1986, was considered vulnerable by a number of observers in the state. Yet Shelby drew little opposition in his reelection effort.

In the primary election, Shelby was opposed by Chris McNair, a well-respected black Jefferson County (Birmingham) commissioner and former state legislator. It was thought that despite Shelby's considerable financial resources, McNair had a chance to defeat the incumbent if he could receive a high proportion of the black vote in an otherwise low-turnout primary election. This possibility was dashed, however, when the state's two major black political organizations, the Alabama Democratic Conference and the New South Coalition, gave dual endorsements to Shelby and McNair.[43] It was later revealed that Shelby made a substantial financial contribution to both of these organizations shortly after the endorsements were announced.[44] In the end, Shelby won more than 60 percent of the vote in the primary election.

The Republican Party did not mount a serious challenge to Shelby, perhaps because the party had suffered a serious loss in seeking to defeat Senator Howell Heflin in 1990. As a result, Shelby drew a weak opponent, Montgomery small-business consultant Richard Sellers, in the general election. Sellers's campaign was poorly financed and largely ignored by Republican Party leaders. Shelby won the general election by more than a two-to-one margin.

As elsewhere, there was considerable controversy in the state concerning the post–1990 census redrawing of the state's congressional district lines. The redistricting plan ultimately used (developed by a panel of Republican federal judges) created a majority black district in the state. By doing so, the plan made two of the state's other districts more Republican than they were previously.

The majority black district, which stretched in a crescent shape from Birmingham through the western black belt and back to Montgomery, attracted a large field of candidates. However, attention soon focused on three of these candidates, each of whom was endorsed by one of the state's important black political organizations. Earl Hilliard, a state senator from Birmingham, was endorsed by Mayor Richard Arrington's Jefferson County Citizens Committee. Montgomery County Commissioner John Knight was endorsed by the Alabama Democratic Conference. State Senator Hank Sanders, from Selma, received the support of the New South Coalition.[45]

Knight finished third in the primary. With its candidate out of the race, the Alabama Democratic Conference threw its support in the runoff to Hilliard. This, plus the fact that almost half the district's population came from the Birmingham area, allowed Hilliard to narrowly defeat Sanders in the runoff.

In the Second Congressional District (which covers southeastern Alabama), Republican incumbent Bill Dickinson retired after holding the seat for almost thirty years. Since Dickinson had barely survived several recent Democratic challenges, the GOP's chances for retaining this seat were not high.

The surprise winner of the Republican primary to replace Dickinson was wealthy Enterprise businessman Terry Everett.[46] The winner of a runoff election on the Democratic side was State Treasurer George Wallace, Jr., the son of the former governor.

Given his family's long involvement in Alabama politics, Wallace was given a real chance to win the congressional seat. However, Everett narrowly won the general election. Among the explanations given for Wallace's defeat was the removal of more than 20,000 black voters from the district as a result of redistricting. This led to the ironic (given recent Alabama history) headline, which read, "White Vote to Blame for Wallace Loss, Democrats Say."[47]

The Sixth Congressional District was redrawn so that it now contained heavily Republican Shelby County, the suburbs of Birmingham, and parts of Tuscaloosa and Bibb County. The redistricting plan also forced Tuscaloosa Congressman

Claude Harris to either seek reelection in the new black-majority district or oppose fellow Democrat Ben Erdreich in the newly redrawn Sixth District. Harris resolved his dilemma by retiring from Congress.

Spencer Bacchus, a former state Republican chair, state legislator, and state school board member, won the Republican nomination for the Sixth District in a runoff election against Marty Connors. After a particularly negative campaign on the part of both candidates, Bacchus won the general election over Erdreich by about a 55 to 45 percent margin.

CONCLUSION

Two general conclusions about Alabama's partisan politics can be drawn from the 1992 election. First, the closeness of the presidential race and the mixed results of the other contests show again that Alabama has become a politically competitive state.[48] Second, a review of the 1992 contests shows that the general factors that influence elections in Alabama are the same as those that influence elections elsewhere. These factors include the composition of the campaign agenda, the power of incumbency (particularly access to campaign funds), group endorsements, and the racial and class compositions of districts.

Overall, these conclusions suggest that in its broad outlines the partisan politics of Alabama are now similar to those found in other states. At this level, Alabama is not isolated, alienated, or particularly distinctive from other states or the nation as a whole. Rather, like many of its counterparts throughout the region and the nation, Alabama is now a competitive state whose elections are determined by the same general factors that determine elections in other locations. Thus, in considering Alabama's partisan politics, it is not safe to assume that one of the parties has a monopoly or a lock on a particular office. Nor, in seeking to explain the state's partisan politics, is reference to uniquely Alabama factors necessary.

NOTES

1. *Birmingham News* (3 November 1991), 21A.
2. *Birmingham News* (3 November 1991), 21A.
3. *Birmingham News* (3 November 1991), 21A. See also *Birmingham News* (23 February 1992), 18A; (28 May 1992), 5B; *Birmingham Post-Herald* (10 March 1992), C1; (27 March 1992), D1.
4. *Birmingham Post-Herald* (10 March 1992), C1.
5. *Birmingham News* (8 March 1992), 18A.
6. *Tuscaloosa News* (6 April 1992), 7A.
7. *Anniston Star* (5 March 1992), 6A; (7 March 1992), 2A; *Birmingham News* (8 March 1992), 1A, 18A; *Tuscaloosa News* (1 May 1992), 1A; (15 May 1992), 1B.
8. *Tuscaloosa News* (19 May 1992), 7A.
9. *Birmingham News* (3 June 1992), 1A.
10. *Birmingham News* (27 May 1992), 3B.
11. *Birmingham News* (28 May 1992), 1A.

12. *Birmingham News* (25 June 1992), 1A.

13. *Tuscaloosa News* (10 July 1992), 1B.

14. *Tuscaloosa News* (10 July 1992), 1B.

15. *Birmingham News* (17 July 1992), 1A.

16. *Anniston Star* (26 July 1992), 1A; *Birmingham Post-Herald* (5 August 1992), C7.

17. *Birmingham News* (16 August 1992), 1A.

18. *Birmingham News* (23 August 1992), 1A.

19. *Tuscaloosa News* (23 August 1992), 8A.

20. *Birmingham News* (19 July 1992), 7A.

21. *Montgomery Advertiser* (24 October 1992), 4A.

22. *Birmingham News* (26 September 1992), 1A.

23. *Birmingham Post-Herald* (15 October 1992), D1.

24. *Montgomery Advertiser* (25 October 1992), 1A.

25. *Tuscaloosa News* (31 October 1992), 1A.

26. *Birmingham News* (31 October 1992), 1A.

27. *Tuscaloosa News* (31 October 1992), 1A; *Birmingham Post-Herald* (30 October 1992), E1.

28. *Montgomery Advertiser* (28 October 1992), 1A.

29. *Montgomery Advertiser* (23 September 1992), 8C.

30. *Birmingham Post-Herald* (26 October 1992), A6.

31. *Birmingham News* (27 September 1992), 1A.

32. *Birmingham Post-Herald* (19 October 1992), A1.

33. *Anniston Star* (27 October 1992), 1A.

34. *Birmingham News* (3 November 1992), 1A.

35. *Mobile Press Register* (3 November 1992), 1A.

36. The results presented here are based on telephone interviews with a random sample of Alabama registered voters. The interviews were conducted between October 25 and October 31, 1992.

37. See, for example, *Tuscaloosa News* (31 October 1992), 1A.

38. *New York Times* (5 November 1992), B4.

39. Gore received a positive rating from 39 percent of the respondents and a negative rating from 36 percent. Vice-President Quayle was rated positively by 33 percent and negatively by 44 percent of the respondents. Ross Perot's vice-presidential running mate, Admiral James Stockdale, received a positive rating from 10 percent of the respondents and a negative rating from 46 percent.

40. The 1988 survey is based on telephone interviews with a random sample of 692 Alabama registered voters. The interviews were conducted between November 2 and November 5, 1988.

41. *Birmingham Post-Herald* (29 December 1992), C1.

42. Another indication of the relative weakness of the economy as an issue is found in the results of a series of Southern Opinion Research surveys, which were conducted among adults in seven southeastern states (Alabama, Arkansas, Florida, Mississippi, North Carolina, South Carolina, and Virginia) during the summer and fall of 1992. In each of these surveys, respondents were asked what the most important issues facing their state were. In every state except Alabama the economy was the most frequently mentioned issue facing the state. A plurality of Alabamians said that education was the state's most important issue.

43. *Birmingham News* (26 April 1992), 17A.

44. *Birmingham News* (6 September 1992), 1A.

45. *New York Times* (23 May 1992), 8Y.

46. *Tuscaloosa News* (3 June 1992), 3B.

47. *Montgomery Advertiser* (5 November 1992), 1A.

48. Patrick R. Cotter, "Alabama: Further Steps toward a Competitive Party System," in *The 1988 Presidential Election in the South: Continuity Amidst Change in Southern Party Politics*, ed. Laurence W. Moreland, Robert P. Steed, and Tod A. Baker (New York: Praeger, 1991) 37–50; Patrick R. Cotter, "Alabama: The Unsettled Electorate," in *Party Realignment in the American States*, ed. Maureen Moakley (Columbus: Ohio State University Press, 1992), 91–105.

4

Georgia: A State in Transition

BRAD LOCKERBIE AND JOHN A. CLARK

In Georgia, 1992 represented a year of change for the political parties. At the presidential level, the Democratic Party gained its first victory, albeit narrowly, since Jimmy Carter won in 1980. Below the presidential level, however, the Republican Party improved its position considerably, picking up an increasingly larger share of both the congressional delegation and the state legislature.

With the nomination of Bill Clinton and Al Gore, the Democrats hoped to recapture the southern base that had eluded their party for the last twenty-five years save the election of 1976, with Jimmy Carter, a Georgian, on the ballot. It has not always been this difficult for the Democratic Party to do well in the South. At the presidential level, Georgia had been one of the most solidly Democratic states in the Solid South. As recently as the presidential election of 1960, Georgia was the second most Democratic state in the nation. In a complete turnabout, the state became one of the more Republican at the presidential level, being one of the few states to support Barry Goldwater in the presidential election of 1964. In 1968, the Republican percentage dropped, but the Democratic percentage also dropped. George Wallace's bid for the presidency as the candidate of the American Independent Party siphoned a great deal of support from the major parties, thereby allowing Wallace to gain victory in Georgia. In 1972, with George Wallace off the ballot and George McGovern on the ballot as the Democratic nominee, the Republican Party rocketed upward to 75 percent of the vote (see Table 4.1).

Not surprisingly, this percentage of the vote was not repeated in the subsequent election. First, Richard Nixon, the Republican presidential candidate in 1972, had won in a landslide across the nation. Second, and most important, the Democratic nominee in 1976 was Jimmy Carter, a native of Georgia and a former governor. The support for the Republican candidate, Gerald Ford, dropped back

Table 4.1
Proportion of the Vote for the Parties in Presidential Elections in Georgia, 1900–1992 (in percent)

Year	Republican	Democratic	Other
1992	42.9	43.5	13.3
1988	59.8	39.5	
1984	60.2	39.8	
1980	41.0	55.8	2.3
1976	33.0	66.7	
1972	75.0	24.6	
1968	30.4	26.7	42.8
1964	54.1	45.9	
1960	37.4	62.5	
1956	33.3	66.4	
1952	30.3	69.7	
1948	18.3	60.8	20.3
1944	18.3	81.7	
1940	14.9	84.8	
1936	12.6	87.1	
1932	7.8	91.6	
1928	44.0	56.0	
1924	18.2	74.0	7.6
1920	28.7	71.0	
1916	7.0	79.5	12.9
1912	4.3	76.6	18.1
1908	31.2	54.6	12.6
1904	18.3	63.7	17.3
1900	28.2	66.9	

Sources: Table compiled by authors from *America Votes* and *Congressional Quarterly's Guide to U. S. Elections,* issues as appropriate, and from data provided by the office of the Georgia Secretary of State.

down to the level of the Republican Party in the 1950s. Carter ran less well in 1980, but still carried the state by an impressive margin.

With Jimmy Carter off the ballot, the Republican party had improved its position once again. While not in the stratosphere as in 1972, the Republican candidates for president in 1984 and 1988 had impressive margins of victory. In fact, when one looks at the electoral history of the 1980s, one should not be terribly surprised by the poor performance of the national Democratic Party in Georgia. As Alan I. Abramowitz and Wendy Davis point out, the state Democratic Party leadership, including Governor Joe Frank Harris, shunned the Mondale/Ferraro ticket in 1984.[1] The situation in 1988 was somewhat different in that the leadership of the state Democratic Party did endorse the Dukakis/Bentsen ticket, but again the activities on behalf of the ticket were rather sparse. The Democratic campaign had scheduled a trip to Georgia for the middle of October, but by that point the ardor of the Democratic leadership had cooled considerably; most of the prominent state Democrats announced they had scheduling conflicts and would be unable to attend. The Dukakis campaign subsequently canceled the trip. Tom Murphy, the speaker of the Georgia General Assembly, withdrew his endorsement of the Dukakis/Bentsen ticket in early October.[2]

Was 1992 any different? In one important respect, the answer is an emphatic yes. State Democratic officials endorsed the Clinton/Gore ticket and maintained their support throughout the campaign.

THE CAMPAIGN

The Democratic Primary

One of the most significant events of the 1992 Democratic nomination race occurred before the Iowa caucuses or the New Hampshire primary. In September of 1991, Georgia Governor Zell Miller proposed holding the state's presidential primaries on March 3, one week prior to Super Tuesday. On Super Tuesday, Georgia would be overshadowed by larger states such as Florida and Texas. By moving the primary date up a week, Georgia could become the "Southern New Hampshire" in the nomination process.[3]

The change proved to be difficult, but not impossible. In addition to passage in the General Assembly, approval was required from the U.S. Department of Justice and the Democratic National Committee. The state legislature enacted the change in January, allowing just enough time for the new date to meet the guidelines of the 1965 Voting Rights Act and the Democratic Party regulations.

The impact of the Georgia primary did not become apparent until after Bill Clinton's large victory. Clinton's success in Georgia catapulted him into Super Tuesday with tremendous momentum and put him in the driver's seat for the Democratic nomination.

Governor Miller was an early supporter of the Clinton campaign. The two had known one another through their interactions as governors and as "New South" politicians. Also, Clinton advisors James Carville and Paul Begala had run Miller's 1990 gubernatorial campaign. As the primary approached, Miller was particularly critical of Paul Tsongas, who had emerged as Clinton's chief rival. The former Massachusetts senator would lead the Democratic Party "right back down that same well-worn path of defeat," the governor charged. While Tsongas was being treated kindly by the media, Clinton had been attacked "like the only fire hydrant at a dog show."[4] Miller was able to continue his sharp-tongued rhetoric as one of three keynote speakers at the Democratic National Convention. There he aimed his criticisms at George Bush.

Most of the state's political leaders endorsed Clinton, too. United States Senator Sam Nunn, Georgia House Speaker Tom Murphy, and black leaders such as Congressman John Lewis, Atlanta Mayor Maynard Jackson, and former Mayor and United Nations Ambassador Andrew Young campaigned on Clinton's behalf. Not everyone supported the Arkansas governor, however. Bob Kerrey was endorsed by Secretary of State Max Cleland, a wounded Vietnam veteran like Kerrey, and Mabel Thomas, a black state representative. Paul Tsongas received the support of state representative Michael Thurmond, who chaired the Legislative Black Caucus.

Of the Democratic candidates, only Clinton and Tsongas broadcast television advertisements in their Georgia campaigns. Both candidates spent heavily on the influential Atlanta media market. Tsongas focused most of his resources on the Maryland primary, held on the same day. Still, he narrowly outspent Clinton in Atlanta ($122,295 to $115,740), although Clinton made greater use of the rest of the state.[5] Jerry Brown purchased advertising time only on cable television, while Kerrey and Tom Harkin did not enter the advertising wars in Georgia.

When the ballots were counted, Clinton was the clear winner in Georgia. He captured 57 percent of the primary vote and carried every region of the state convincingly. Under the Democratic Party's proportional delegate allocation procedures, Tsongas also qualified for convention delegates with 24 percent of the vote. Tsongas ran best in the Atlanta area, where he received 31 percent of the vote, but Clinton still managed to pull a majority, with 52 percent. The other Democrats ran well behind, with Brown winning 8 percent statewide, Kerrey 5 percent, and Harkin 2 percent.[6]

The Republican Primary

The Republican battle between President George Bush and challenger Patrick Buchanan garnered the largest share of attention in the Peach State. Buchanan, who captured more than 40 percent of the Republican primary vote in New Hampshire, hoped to use Georgia as a breakthrough state for his campaign. Bush was hoping to force Buchanan out of the race in a state that he won convincingly in 1988.

Buchanan campaigned heavily in Georgia, touring the state in the same chartered bus used by Bush in 1988. He outspent Bush for television time ($387,723 to $216,053).[7] In contrast to the economic message he used in New Hampshire, Buchanan focused on social and racial issues in the South. In his most controversial advertisement, he accused the Bush administration of using taxpayers' money to support "pornographic and blasphemous art," while images of leather-clad gay men gyrated in the background. Buchanan also appealed to racial divisions in the state, telling voters of his ancestors who fought for the Confederacy in the Civil War and visiting Confederate cemeteries in Georgia and surrounding states.[8] His efforts earned him an endorsement from former Democratic Governor Lester Maddox, an avowed segregationist.

For all his effort, Buchanan captured only 36 percent of the Republican primary vote. Still, participation in the state's Republican primary represented on all-time high. More than half of the nearly 1 million voters selected a Republican ballot. Many observers attributed this phenomenon to Buchanan's appeal to conservative white Democrats to cross over to the Republican primary, combined with poor turnout among the state's black voters.[9] The closeness in turnout foreshadowed the tight general election outcome eight months later.

The General Election Campaign

Despite the success enjoyed by Republican presidential candidates in the past two elections, Georgia emerged as a battleground state in the 1992 election. Both campaigns focused resources here as the GOP hold on the South's electoral college votes seemed tenuous. In the end, the candidates fought to a virtual draw.

Both candidates frequently visited the state. Clinton, along with vice-presidential nominee Al Gore and former President Jimmy Carter, helped build a house for a low-income family in Atlanta during the Republican convention. The Democratic ticket also took a bus tour through south Georgia in late September. Bush countered with a train trip through the northern part of the state one month later. Both candidates were represented by a variety of surrogate campaigners. Barbara Bush, Dan and Marilyn Quayle, cabinet members Jack Kemp and Louis Sullivan, and actor Charlton Heston represented George Bush; vice-presidential nominee Al Gore, Democratic National Committee Chair Ronald Brown, Jesse Jackson, actress Kim Basinger, and singer Michael Stipe campaigned for the Clinton ticket. The Republicans called out the heavy artillery with a campaign visit by former President Ronald Reagan in the last weekend of the campaign. While Reagan was speaking in suburban Cobb County, Clinton attended a rally in nearby Decatur.

For Clinton, the attention paid to Georgia served to divert Republican resources from other campaign venues. Most observers thought that Georgia would go Republican, despite polls that showed Clinton in the lead from the Democratic convention through late in the campaign.[10] When Bush was forced to shore up his base of support in places like Georgia, it prevented him from reaching out to voters in traditionally competitive or pro-Democratic states.

Symbolizing the competitiveness of Georgia for the first time in a decade, Atlanta was the site chosen for the 1992 vice-presidential debate. Dan Quayle, Al Gore, and H. Ross Perot's running mate, James Stockdale, met at Georgia Tech on October 13. Only about 500 voters were able to attend the debate, but it focused media attention on the role of Georgia in the election.

For many Georgia voters, the most important race in the fall of 1992 was hardly political. The Atlanta Braves baseball team was on its way to a second consecutive World Series appearance, and the team's success did not go unnoticed by the candidates. George Bush made the Braves' come-from-behind play-off victory over Pittsburgh into a rallying cry for his campaign. The former Yale first baseman told supporters across the South that "It isn't over until [Francisco] Cabrera swings," and "You've got to take a position. I am for the Braves." He likened Clinton to a Little League manager who wanted to run a

major league baseball team.[11] Cabrera appeared with Ronald Reagan on his visit
to Georgia, while former baseball great Hank Aaron campaigned with Clinton.[12]

The Perot Factor

The independent candidacy of Texas billionaire H. Ross Perot contributed an
element of uncertainty to the 1992 presidential election. Although he received
only 13.3 percent of the popular vote in Georgia, Perot captured the attention
of many Georgians during the campaign. A poll conducted in early June showed
Perot with a slight lead over George Bush, with Clinton in third place.[13]

At the end of May, Representative Newt Gingrich advised Republican congressional candidates to withhold pledges of support for Bush in the event of electoral
college deadlock. As House Republican whip and the only Republican in the
Georgia congressional delegation, Gingrich's apparent vote of ''no confidence''
stunned the Bush campaign.[14] One Republican congressional candidate endorsed
Perot before the July 21 primary, but finished out of the running in a multican-
didate race.

In Georgia, Perot supporters were required to collect 137,182 signatures to
place their candidate on the general election ballot. The feat was accomplished
on June 27, and the signatures were certified on August 31. Perot was not even
a candidate at the time. He was unable to regain momentum upon reentering the
race.

EXPLAINING THE OUTCOME: HOW DID CLINTON WIN GEORGIA?

For the first time in years, a Democratic candidate campaigned heavily throughout Georgia. Where did Bill Clinton get his victory? An analysis of county-level
election returns reveals that Clinton, as most Democrats do, did very well in the
counties with a high percentage of black residents. As a first step in explaining
the Georgia vote, we follow the lead of Abramowitz and Davis and utilize
regression analysis to ascertain how the vote breaks down county by county.[15]
Our dependent variable is the share of the vote that went for the Republican
candidate in 1992. Our independent variables are the same as those used by
Abramowitz and Davis to analyze the 1988 election, except they are updated
with current information.

The regression equation presented in Table 4.2 demonstrates that the findings
from 1988 are largely supported. Although there are differences, one is struck
by the similarity across years. The Republican base, although diminished since
1988, is located in the same general area. Bush was strongest in the areas that
supported Richard Nixon and George Wallace in 1968. Bush also did well in
the areas that are experiencing increases in population. The relative strength of
the variables indicates that while each seems relatively equal in importance,
traditional Republicanism is the most important of the four. There are, however,

Table 4.2

Regression Analysis of the 1992 Republican Presidential Vote in Georgia Counties

Independent Variables	B	S.E.	Beta
Black population	-.14	.04	-.32
Population growth	.17	.04	.32
Traditional Republicanism	.30	.09	.39
Racial conservatism	.17	.07	.30
Constant	26.57		
Adjusted R^2 = .58			

Note: The dependent variable is the percentage of the vote for George Bush in 1992. All the estimated coefficients are significant at the .01 level. Black Population is measured by the percentage of black population in each county; Population Growth is measured by the percentage change in population from 1980 to 1990; Traditional Republicanism is measured by the Nixon share of the vote in 1968; Racial Conservatism is measured by the Wallace share of the vote in 1968. N = 159.

Sources : Data compiled by the authors. Presidential vote by county data provided by the Georgia Secretary of State. Black population and population growth are from the current census report. Traditional Republicanism and racial conservatism data are from America Votes.

some differences worth noting. First, the magnitude of the coefficients has decreased since 1988. Second, the explanatory power of this equation is substantially less than it was for the 1988 election (adjusted $R^2 = .70$).

We are fortunate that a poll of potential Georgia voters was taken approximately four weeks before the election. The fall 1992 Georgia poll, with 590 respondents, asked a number of questions that are relevant for the study of presidential voting in the state.[16] Unfortunately, because this poll was conducted before the election (October 12–21, 1992), we have no way of ascertaining whether these people actually showed up on election day. Also, a substantial number of people were undecided in their presidential preference at the time of the survey.

Taking these caveats into consideration, we can look at the way in which Georgia voters intended to cast their ballots. The potential voters stated their preferences as follows: 39.3 percent for Clinton, 29.5 percent for Bush, 6.25 percent for Perot, and 25.0 percent undecided. From these poll results, it would appear as though the last-minute deciders went for Bush and Perot for the most part, with a much smaller portion opting for Clinton.

More interesting than the overall results is how various groups in Georgia intended to vote. Table 4.3 shows vote intention by party identification. We can see that the Democrats had slightly better success in holding their partisans than did the Republicans. The difference between the two parties is slight, and it is noteworthy that the difference is so small. In a recent survey of party activists, Democratic precinct committee members were surprisingly willing to admit they had defected from their party in the 1988 presidential election, while Republicans

Table 4.3
Presidential Vote Intention in Georgia by Party (in percent)

Candidate	Democratic	Independent	Republican
Bush	5.3	25.2	62.9
Clinton	65.5	36.3	4.0
Perot	4.1	7.4	7.3
Undecided	20.5	27.4	23.4

Note: N = 414.
Source: Fall 1992 Georgia Poll.

Table 4.4
Presidential Vote Intention in Georgia by Ideology (in percent)

Candidate	Liberal	Moderate	Conservative
Bush	13.5	28.0	71.6
Clinton	81.1	61.1	22.9
Perot	5.4	10.9	5.5

Note: N = 321.
Source: Fall 1992 Georgia Poll.

overwhelmingly supported their party.[17] Table 4.3 also shows that Clinton held a lead among political independents, a group among which Republicans must win if they are to do well in Georgia.

Clinton appears to have done a reasonably good job of holding the Democratic coalition together. Table 4.4 shows vote intention by ideology. Clinton was able to hold a tremendous lead among liberals, but more important, he also held approximately a two-to-one lead among the much more numerous bloc of moderates. Even among conservatives, Clinton was able to get the support of over 20 percent. From this it would appear as though Clinton was able to piece together the coalition that has worked well for southern Democrats running for statewide office: overwhelming support among liberals and solid support among political moderates.

The demographic breakdown of vote intention, presented in Table 4.5, shows a fairly familiar picture. Bush did comparatively well among the white segment of the population. This is one of the few groups of voters George Bush won. But even here, his victory was fairly small. That, combined with the overwhelming support Clinton received in the black community (over 90 percent),

Table 4.5
Presidential Vote Intention in Georgia by Demographics (in percent)

Demographic Characteristic	Bush	Clinton	Perot
Race			
White	47.1	44.2	8.8
Black	1.8	92.7	5.5
Gender			
Male	42.7	44.9	12.4
Female	35.4	60.8	3.8
Marital Status			
Married	46.9	43.5	9.6
Not married	26.8	66.9	6.3
Age			
18-29	38.2	52.7	9.1
30-39	36.7	54.1	9.2
40-49	40.3	56.5	3.2
50-59	41.5	43.9	14.6
60+	41.3	51.3	7.5
Education			
Less than high school	20.0	71.4	8.6
High school	43.5	48.2	8.2
Some college	44.8	45.7	9.5
College	36.4	56.6	7.1
Income			
Less than $5,000	20.0	80.0	0.0
$5,000-9,999	8.3	75.0	16.7
$10,000-14,999	29.4	58.8	11.8
$15,000-19,999	27.8	66.7	5.6
$20,000-24,999	44.8	48.3	6.9
$25,000-34,999	35.8	54.7	9.4
$35,000-49,999	33.8	50.8	15.4
$50,000-74,999	48.3	48.3	3.3
$75,000 and over	60.9	30.4	8.7

Note: Each row totals 100 percent (may vary slightly because of rounding); N = 305-336.
Source: Fall 1992 Georgia Poll.

shows us that for a Democrat to win the state of Georgia, that Democrat needs to be relatively competitive among the white electorate and have overwhelming support in the black community. The statewide returns show that even with the overwhelming support of the black community, Clinton was only able to eke out a narrow victory. The gender gap appeared to be alive and well in 1992 in Georgia. Clinton scored a narrow victory among men (2.2 percentage points), but among women, Clinton had a victory of landslide proportions (25.4 percentage points). There also appears to be a marriage gap. Bush had a narrow victory among married individuals, but Clinton scored an impressive victory among the unmarried population. Among the various age groups and education levels, Clinton scored a victory across the board. When we turn to income, we can see that Clinton was able to do very well up to the highest-income group. From the lowest-income group through $49,000, Clinton won. Among those who make between $50,000 to $74,999, Clinton and Bush were in a dead heat. Only among those making $75,000 and above was Bush able to gain a victory.

What issues were on the minds of voters in Georgia? Not surprisingly, the voters of Georgia were not terribly different from the voters across the nation. After being asked if a number of issues (economy, health care, abortion, environment, family values, and education) were important to them, voters were asked to name the single most important issue in determining which presidential candidate they would support on November 3. Of those who stated they were going to vote and had an issue preference, just over 50 percent named the economy. Of those who named the economy, Bill Clinton won the votes of slightly over three-fifths.[18] Less than 5 percent picked any of the remaining issues listed above. Despite the small number of respondents selecting any of the remaining issues, Clinton and Bush appear to have done reasonably well in emphasizing issues that were important to their core constituencies.[19] Clinton won among those selecting health care and education. Bush won among those selecting abortion and family values. The candidates split evenly (one person for each candidate) among those selecting the environment as the most important issue that determined their vote. In short, among those voters caring about any issues mentioned, the economy was the most important, and Clinton won this group quite convincingly.

Republicans are no longer active at only the presidential level in Georgia. While narrowly losing the state of Georgia in the presidential election, the Republican Party did remarkably well in other races. First, the Republicans won two statewide races, one for the U.S. Senate (Paul Coverdell) and the other for the Public Service Commission (Bobby Baker), although both required runoff elections. The Republicans also increased their share of the U.S. House delegation, moving from just one of ten members to four of eleven. At the state legislative level, the Republicans, while still clearly in the minority, have improved their position considerably. In a 180-member house of representatives, the Republicans went from thirty-four to fifty seats. In a fifty-six-member senate, the Republicans went from eleven to thirteen seats.[20]

So that we can ascertain whether presidential elections are atypical of statewide races in Georgia, we ran a similar regression for the runoff election for U.S. senator. We found that the same coalition of support that exists for Republican presidential candidates also exists in this senatorial election. Given that the county vote for Bush and Coverdell correlates at .86, this is not terribly surprising. Of greater interest is the apparent decision by many voters to select candidates of the same party in both races, as well as for other offices further down the ticket.

CONCLUSION

The election of 1992 showed that Georgia is not locked up as a part of either party's coalition. The presidential election was very close, with Clinton winning with a 16,000-vote margin. Elections below the presidential level show that Georgia is becoming a two-party state. For the first time in years, Georgia voters were able to select a slate of party candidates that were ideologically consistent and distinct on issues of public policy. Looking at the trends in the state over time, we would expect the next gubernatorial election to be highly competitive, especially if Governor Miller holds to his promise of not seeking a second term. The U.S. House delegation seems to be very competitive currently. Even the seats that the Democrats were able to hold on to have become much more competitive over the years. Twenty years ago, the Democrats won these seats without serious opposition. Today, of the seven seats won by the Democratic candidates, four were won with less than 60 percent of the vote. Like many of its southern neighbors, Georgia is clearly a state in transition at both the national and the local levels.

NOTES

The authors gratefully acknowledge the assistance of Douglas Hanson.

1. Alan I. Abramowitz and Wendy Davis, "Georgia: Ripe for the Picking—Presidential Politics in the Peach State," in *The 1988 Presidential Election in the South: Continuity Amidst Change in Southern Party Politics*, ed. Laurence W. Moreland, Robert P. Steed, and Tod A. Baker (New York: Praeger, 1991), 51–72.

2. Abramowitz and Davis, "Georgia," 51–72.

3. Mark Sherman, "Miller Wants Georgia Out of Super Tuesday," *Atlanta Journal and Constitution* (27 September 1991), A11.

4. A. L. May and Mark Sherman, "Clinton Comes South Preaching Unity as Miller Blasts Rival," *Atlanta Journal and Constitution* (20 February 1992), A10; Gwen Ifill, "In the South to Shore Up Support in Home Base," *New York Times* (20 February 1992), A11.

5. *Atlanta Journal and Constitution* (4 March 1992), A11.

6. *Atlanta Journal and Constitution* (4 March 1992), A12.

7. *Atlanta Journal and Constitution* (4 March 1992), A11.

8. Jeanne Cummings and Christina Cheakalos, "Buchanan Says Bush Backs Porn," *Atlanta Journal and Constitution* (27 February 1992), A6; Ben Smith III, "Buchanan Invokes Confederate Forebears in Bid for South's Votes," *Atlanta Journal and Constitution* (26 February 1992), A5.

9. Lyle V. Harris, "Georgia's GOP Vote 'Awesome,' " *Atlanta Journal and Constitution* (4 March 1992), A11; Charles Walston, "Black Vote Goes Solidly for Clinton," *Atlanta Journal and Constitution* (4 March 1992), A10.

10. See, for example, *Wall Street Journal* (21 October 1992), A18. For poll results, see *Atlanta Journal and Constitution* (23 September 1992), A8; (25 September 1992), C5; (10 October 1992), A1; (24 October 1992), A1.

11. Tom Baxter, "Behind in His Last Game, Bush Swings for the Fences," *Atlanta Journal and Constitution* (21 October 1992), A1; *Atlanta Journal and Constitution* (22 October 1992), A8.

12. After the Braves lost the World Series to Toronto, Clinton told reporters that he would not have bunted into the last out of the final game. "I believe if I were going down in the World Series, I'd want to go down swinging," he said. Lest he offend

baseball fans, he admitted that he knew less about baseball than Braves' manager Bobby Cox, however [*Atlanta Journal and Constitution* (26 October 1992), A7].

13. *Atlanta Journal and Constitution* (24 June 1992), A5.

14. Charles Walston, "Gingrich: Hold Off on Bush," *Atlanta Journal and Constitution* (30 May 1992), A1; Mark Sherman, "Georgia Candidates Ponder Their Course for a Hung Election," *Atlanta Journal and Constitution* (1 June 1992), A6.

15. Abramowitz and Davis, "Georgia," 51–72.

16. The fall 1992 Georgia poll was conducted and made available by the Survey Research Center at the University of Georgia. They are not responsible for any interpretations presented here.

17. Brad Lockerbie and John A. Clark, "Party Activists in Georgia" (Paper delivered at the 1992 Citadel Symposium on Southern Politics, Charleston, S.C., 5–6 March 1992).

18. These figures are from the 1992 Georgia poll cited in note 16. What is surprising is that the next most popular option, with slightly over one-third, was "other." People responded with something other than the items listed previously. Among this group, Bush scored a victory.

19. The issue mentioned most frequently after the economy is education, with 4.2 percent (13 people) selecting it as the most important issue.

20. *Atlanta Journal and Constitution* (5 November 1992), C10.

5

Louisiana: The Continuing Saga of Race, Religion, and Rebellion

CHARLES D. HADLEY

The themes developed for Louisiana state politics with respect to the 1988 presidential selection process were those of race, religion, and the Republican Party. Race played out in conjunction with the national Republican Party's orchestrated purge of blacks from the voter rolls immediately before the U.S. Senate race, which Democrat John Breaux went on to narrowly win over Republican W. Henson Moore in a runoff election. Religion played out in the capture of the Republican State Central Committee by religious fundamentalists. Both themes played out in the contest for the Eighth Congressional District seat and on center stage in the Republican presidential selection process. They remained on stage for the 1991–1992 state and national elections.[1]

The 1992 presidential contest provided Louisiana the vehicle to make Republican political opportunist and Nazi sympathizer David Duke as invisible as his former Invisible Empire, the Ku Klux Klan. Duke came into full bloom politically when he won a seat in the Louisiana House of Representatives as a Republican in a 1989 low-turnout special election. He defeated the entire Louisiana political establishment, Republicans and Democrats alike, in taking advantage of the state's unique open elections system that pits against each other the two candidates with the most votes regardless of political party, if any. Duke, literally a made-for-media candidate, won this election in the glare of the national and international news media that moved him to celebrity status; he had convinced sufficient numbers of voters to send a message, a not-so-subtle message against affirmative action and welfare. Embraced by his Republican legislative colleagues, accepted by the party leadership, and shunned by the national Republican Party, Duke brought paralysis to what was once a well-organized respected Republican state party.[2]

With known politicians lining up to run against him in his redrawn legislative district mandated by the 1990 census, he ran for governor and pushed his celebrity status to its zenith when he edged incumbent Democrat-turned-Republican Governor "Buddy" Roemer out of the 1991 runoff election with the help of Congressman Clyde Holloway, who was the officially endorsed Republican candidate. Seventy-two percent of the registered voters or 52.3 percent of the voting-age population participated in the election in which Edwards, Duke, Roemer, Holloway, and eight other candidates combined respectively earned 34, 32, 27, 5, and 2 percent of the votes cast. In another national and international media extravaganza, Duke entered the gubernatorial runoff against former Governor Edwin W. Edwards as much from outside the state on "Larry King Live," "Phil Donahue," "The Today Show," and "Meet the Press" as within the state.[3]

Louisiana voters received an intense and sustained anti-Duke media barrage from a united business community, the tourism and hospitality industries, and prominent people from all walks of life—professional sports stars, military personnel, and old political adversaries, including former Republican Governor David C. Treen and even President George Bush, among others. Voter registration increased by an unprecedented 35,054 whites and 32,243 blacks. Runoff election participation, moreover, rose to 78.7 percent of registered voters or 58.9 percent of the age eligible, an increase in every registration category, especially among voters aged eighteen to twenty and blacks (respectively 13.6 and 13.1 percentage points). Left between a rock and a hard place, citizens, many out of sheer fear, took to heart the bumper sticker "Vote for the Crook. It's Important" by handing a 61 to 39 percent victory to three-term former Governor Edwards, who survived a near-yearlong federal trial during his third term, after which Roemer snuffed out his 1989 reelection bid. Duke soon after took his message, national media exposure, and successful fund raising into the national political arena to challenge President Bush from the right.[4]

THE CAMPAIGN

Primary Phase

When David Duke chose not to enter the New Hampshire primary, he not only left conservative newspaper columnist Patrick J. Buchanan an opportunity for a head-to-head contest with President Bush, but also let Buchanan carry his message against affirmative action, the welfare system, and immigration. Once Buchanan, who was not burdened with a questionable past, became the carrier of the message from the right, Duke could not take it back, even in Louisiana. After New Hampshire, moreover, he failed to get on the ballot in the next four primaries, in some instances due to organized opposition from the Republican elected and party officials, for example, in Georgia. Ironically, it took threatened legal action by the American Civil Liberties Union to secure him a ballot position in South Carolina, his first opportunity to contest a primary. Given these circumstances, his election strategy became Super Tuesday in Louisiana and the rest of the South, excluding Florida.[5]

Duke failed to live up to the expectations created by his Louisiana electoral support and intense media attention. He no longer was the object of intense national and international media attention. Though he explored the possibility of applying for federal matching funds with the Federal Election Commission, he even found himself unable to raise the $5,000 from twenty states ($100,000) in amounts of $250 or less necessary to qualify for federal matching funds. Campaign contributions like those that poured into his gubernatorial campaign from outside Louisiana evaporated, a fact that attests to an unease with Duke's background compounded by the unexpected embarrassment when his contributors were interviewed and/or saw their names and contribution amounts published in home town newspapers around the country. Buchanan, of course, benefited because he was a legitimate conservative, period.[6]

Moreover, Louisiana Republican Party Chair William Nungesser, to the consternation of President Bush and Louisiana elected officials, dropped a bombshell when he unexpectedly acted on his own, though he represented the party, to endorse the candidacy of Buchanan in mid-April. Consequently Secretary of State Fox McKeithen, a Republican, attempted to counter the endorsement by establishing the Republican Elected Officials Organization as a "think tank" and fund-raising entity to rival the Republican State Central Committee headed by Nungesser. Said McKeithen, "This was an attempt to bring people back together. . . . We want to have some input."[7]

Buchanan, perhaps given his Louisiana endorsement and the obvious sympathy for his views among voters, campaigned harder there than any other candidate, making four campaign sweeps that culminated in New Orleans with an evening of live television interviews and late campaign appearances at four hotels. President Bush, in contrast, dispatched Louisiana native, former Congressman, and then White House Deputy Chief of Staff Henson Moore and Secretary of Housing and Urban Development Jack Kemp to the state. Joined by Secretary of State McKeithen, former Republican Governor Treen, and Congressman Richard Baker, they made a last-minute campaign sweep around the state, appearing in New Orleans, Lafayette, Alexandria, and Monroe. Buchanan focused on the dissatisfaction of conservative voters with the political establishment and emphasized that he was in the campaign through the end, that he was not just a protest candidate. Duke held a lackluster rally in his home territory, Kenner, where he railed against his usual whipping boys—affirmative action, welfare, and taxes. Countered Moore, if voters are "tempted to vote for [Buchanan and Duke] to send a message, my message to them is don't bother. The president long ago got the message. He understands." Kemp appealed directly to Buchanan, "Look Pat, it's time to stop bashing President Bush," foreign countries, foreign trade, immigrants, the poor, and minorities.[8]

The following day, President Bush received 61.9 percent of the vote, his lowest Super Tuesday showing, and all of the available delegates to the Repub-

lican National Convention in an election contest participated in by 32.9 percent
of registered Republicans. The president, in effect, locked up his renomination
on Super Tuesday. David Duke, on the other hand, failed to break into double
digits; in fact, he received fewer votes, 11,955 or 8.8 percent, than when he ran
as a Democrat four years earlier (23,390). Therein was his problem; Duke was
closed out of his north Louisiana conservative white Democratic base because
the presidential nomination required closed primary elections. Buchanan, who
received 36,525 Republican votes or 27.0 percent, credited himself with ter-
minating Duke: "I just finished interring the political career of David Duke in
a bayou in Louisiana." Duke, however, claimed success: "I've won because
the others are talking about my issues," a contention publicly shared by Republican Party Chair Rich Bond in an ABC-TV interview. Said Bond about
Buchanan's campaign strategy, it was "basically [to] hijack David Duke's message on race and religious tolerance and put a jacket and tie on it and try to
clean it up." Though he evaporated with a total vote of less than 2 percent and
no delegates, Duke did not officially withdraw until April 22.[9]

In direct contrast to the tumultuous Republican contest, the Louisiana Democratic political establishment—from Governor Edwards, Lieutenant Governor
Melinda Schwegmann, State Treasurer Mary Landrieu, and other statewide
elected officials, to state legislators and their leadership and New Orleans Mayor
Sidney Barthelemy—closed ranks around Arkansas Governor Bill Clinton very
early in the campaign. With united statewide support reinforced by three campaign swings through the state, Clinton received 69.3 percent of the vote and
all but one of the Louisiana delegates to the Democratic National Convention,
one delegate being awarded to Tsongas to Clinton's fifty-nine, in an election
participated in by 25.9 percent of the registered Democrats, about one-third of
whom were black.[10]

General Election Phase

The Democrats. The presidential general election campaign began in Louisiana
shortly after the Democratic National Convention. Clinton came to Lake Charles
and New Orleans on July 29 for campaign rallies that included the Louisiana
Superdome (the site of the 1988 Republican National Convention, which nominated President Bush) and a fund raiser at New Orleans' Fairmont Hotel. It was
the first time a candidate for president had campaigned in Lake Charles since
John F. Kennedy in 1960. For Louisiana with its nine electoral college votes,
it was the beginning of unprecedented attention not witnessed since 1876 when
a disputed electoral college vote helped elect Republican Rutherford B. Hayes
over Democratic candidate Samuel J. Tilden.[11]

Clinton began his day in a heavily unionized Lake Charles airplane hangar,
addressing more than 2,000 people assembled to hear him. Positioned as a
mainstream Democrat, he focused on the middle class concerns of health care,
jobs, education, crime, and the cost of housing. Later, it was symbolism at the

Louisiana Superdome. Clinton stood on the spot where George W. Bush was nominated for president and focused on the familiar. Where were the promised 15,000 new jobs? Where was the kinder gentler nation? Clinton went on: ''When George Bush stood here four years ago and said, 'Read my lips. No new taxes,' what he meant was ''No new taxes for the rich.' '' The issues were trust, broken promises, bad economic policy, and a failure on the part of the president to assume responsibility. Later, he was welcomed to the University of New Orleans' Lakefront Arena by a crowd of about 4,000 that included Lieutenant Governor Schwegmann, State Treasurer Landrieu, and Congressman William Jefferson, among others. Speaking to the enthusiastic crowd, Clinton invoked memories of Presidents Franklin Delano Roosevelt, Harry S. Truman, and John F. Kennedy and focused on presidential responsibility.[12]

The fund-raising dinner ($5,000 per couple) followed by cocktails ($500 per couple) was expected to clear $250,000 for the Victory Fund of the Democratic National Committee. The Democratic political establishment was present; people had to be turned away, given limited space. Among the notables were Louisiana Democratic Party Chair Jim Brady; Democratic National Committee Secretary Kathy Vick; Congressman Jefferson and his predecessor, Lindy Boggs; Mayor Barthelemy; Speaker Pro Tem of the Louisiana House of Representatives Sherman Coplin; U.S. Senator John Breaux, State Treasurer Landrieu; Attorney General Richard Ieyoub; and, representing the state, Lieutenant Governor Schwegmann. Business and labor leaders also were in abundance: Louisiana AFL-CIO President Victor Bussie; Greater New Orleans AFL-CIO Secretary-Treasurer Peter Babin; First Commerce Corporation Chair and CEO Ian Arnof; First Commonwealth Securities, Inc., Director Norbert Simmons, and mortgage banker Laurance Eustis III attended, among others. It was a stellar cast on any dimension.[13]

Next was a two-day campaign swing over September 8 and 9 from Shreveport to Baton Rouge and New Orleans by vice–president candidate Al Gore. Gore ridiculed President Bush's ''war on drugs'' at a Shreveport high school, and then went on to Baton Rouge where he was warmly greeted at the airport by Governor Edwards and accompanied on a shopping tour through the downtown area with State Treasurer Landrieu and Attorney General Ieyoub. At Lloyd's Po-Boy restaurant, Gore discussed the poor condition of the economy—increased unemployment and small-business foreclosures as well as decreased real wages: ''In the last four years we've had the worst performance since the Great Depression.'' Later in the day, Gore was in New Orleans at a public elementary school where, greeted by 250 children, he congratulated a teacher who was nominated for a teacher-of-the-year award. He then went on to discuss the drug problem with students who participated in an after-school program sponsored by the police department. Gore then left after appearing on the ''Larry King Live'' show in conjunction with the National Association of Broadcasters meeting in New Orleans.[14]

Two days later, Democratic National Committee Chair Ron Brown was in

New Orleans appearing on the same show with his counterpart, Republican National Committee Chair Rich Bond, after having come to Louisiana a day earlier to stump for the Clinton/Gore ticket at historically black Southern University in Baton Rouge. Brown told the students, "We expect to carry Louisiana in 1992. . . . We have a ticket that's a [s]outhern ticket and I think that will have considerable influence on voters' decision. But more than that, it's a dynamic, young, aggressive ticket that has boundless energy." From New Orleans, Brown went on to a rally in Lake Charles.[15]

In mid-September, State Treasurer Landrieu, who was co-chair of the Louisiana Clinton/Gore campaign, and Lieutenant Governor Schwegmann, among others, organized Women for Democratic Victory. The new organization planned to recruit women to support the ticket by holding a series of luncheons around the state on October 2, the goal being "to sign up" an additional 200,000 women by November 3. Said Schwegmann, "If you want a change, vote for the newcomer—not the incumbent." Public Service Commissioner Kathleen Blanco, moreover, noted that most of Louisiana's female elected public officials favored Clinton.[16]

In mid-October, two Clinton/Gore bus caravans were organized, the first by the Congressional Black Caucus under the leadership of Congressman Jefferson, who represents New Orleans, and the second by U.S. Senators John Breaux and J. Bennett Johnston. Clinton and Gore and their wives joined the first caravan in Baton Rouge, where they spoke to a crowd of about 900 at Southern University, the alma mater of Congressman Jefferson. At Southern, Clinton emphasized the continuing struggle for equal rights: "I got in this race because I don't want 30 years of civil rights struggles to come apart at the seams because of the economy . . . I ask all of you to go out and vote. Your whole life is on the line." After traveling to New Orleans, the candidates spoke at historically black Dillard University, where they were greeted by a crowd of about 1,000 waiting in the rain. They then attended a public rally at Woldenberg Park on the New Orleans riverfront, where both Clinton and Gore emphasized the future and the need to change, to change administrations. A week later, Clinton flew back to Louisiana to attend a *fais do-do* (cajun fest) in Lafayette, the center of the depressed oil and gas industry, with U.S. Senators Breaux and Johnston, Governor Edwards, State Treasurer Landrieu, Congressman Jefferson, and others. Clinton focused his remarks on the revitalization of the oil and gas industry and the need for sacrifice.[17]

The Republicans. Playing a traditional role for a president during a national emergency, President George Bush twice in the same week inspected the devastation sustained and the recovery from Hurricane Andrew by residents of southwest Louisiana. The president and his wife, Barbara, accompanied by Governor Edwards, traveled to Jeanerette, where they spent two and a half hours talking with sugar cane farmers, helping pass out bags of food to the needy, generally expressing concern, and promising quick action from relevant federal agencies. Those affected were of two minds: One hurricane victim reported, "I think it was for votes,'' while Governor Edwards, an early Clinton supporter, related, ''There's too much suffering and too many problems for us to look at why things are being done. . . . I think the president would have come . . . two weeks after the election.''[18]

The following week, Vice-President Dan Quayle's wife, Marilyn, a member of the Federal Emergency Management Agency (FEMA) board, came to Baton Rouge on an ''apolitical'' trip to defend criticized slow action by FEMA and to boost its employees' morale and was accompanied by Governor Edwards. She also traveled to Morgan City to talk with children, stressing the importance of education, at a recently reopened elementary school. Moreover, that same day, though attention was scant by the statewide news media, Secretary of Agriculture Edward Madigan inspected the sugar cane crop damage and spoke with cane farmers.[19]

Within a week of each other at the beginning of October, First Lady Barbara Bush and Mrs. Quayle staged campaign blitzes of Louisiana. Mrs. Bush, in Baton Rouge, countered the trip by Al Gore by criticizing his view that offshore oil drilling should end, saying ''[Oil] exports are up in your state tremendously, thanks to George Bush.'' She also visited an elementary school where she ''fielded'' questions from its fifth graders; she indicated that she was ''trying to make literacy a family word. By reading and by learning, we'd have less crime, less drugs, less people homeless, less AIDS and less pollution.'' Later in the day she visited a New Orleans Catholic school where she hugged children, continuing to stress the importance of education. She also visited a senior citizen center where she talked with those who lived there. Mrs. Quayle's three-day Louisiana campaign included stops in Monroe, Alexandria, Hammond, Slidell, and New Orleans. In Monroe, she attended a $25 per plate fund-raiser with seventy-five Bush/Quayle supporters, a senior citizen center in Hammond, private receptions by supporters in Slidell, and a coffee with Lawyers for Bush-Quayle '92 in New Orleans. During the campaign blitz, her public comments focused on family values, ''tax and spend'' Democrats, and inflation control.[20]

President Bush was out of the Rose Garden and back to Louisiana for the official signing of the National Energy Policy Act of 1992 amid a crowd of oil and gas workers in Maurice on October 24. During his three-hour Louisiana stop, he flew into Lafayette, where he was greeted by about 1,000 well-wishers, and went to Acadiana High School to tell a crowd of about 2,000 that the legislation to be signed in Maurice would create 45,000 jobs for hard-pressed Louisiana. In so doing, he stressed the importance of the nine Louisiana electoral college votes: ''Louisiana is a priority. I must and will win this state.''[21] Pat Buchanan made a trip to New Orleans three days later to speak at a luncheon fundraiser with some 125 Bush/Quayle supporters and to campaign for his former nemesis President Bush; his theme, ''The economy of Louisiana is going to be in deep trouble if this pair of environmental extremists get into the White House along with the liberal Democratic Congress on Capitol Hill.''[22]

The final week of the campaign proved to be a full court press by the Bush/

Quayle team. First, Mrs. Quayle gave a cancer awareness speech at the LSU Medical Center, only deviating for a moment to criticize Clinton's health care plan. Two days later her husband, Vice President Dan Quayle, flew into New Orleans, spoke to about 500 supporters in Kenner, and left, all within 90 minutes. Finally, President Bush himself touched down at the Baton Rouge airport on his way to Houston for his sixth visit to Louisiana and gave an upbeat 20-minute speech to some 4,000 assembled at the airport. In so doing, he focused on now familiar themes of Clinton's draft avoidance, trust, family values, the Louisiana oil economy, and jobs. Said Bush, "The question is, who do you trust with your kids? Who do you trust with your country?" He went on to note that "You can't be all things to all people in this job. . . . You don't try and waffle and be on all sides of the issues."[23]

H. Ross Perot. The Louisiana Perot campaign started small and quietly with an Alexandria meeting among some fifty volunteers, the upshot of which was Louisiana for Perot, Inc. Total seed money was $5,000 for the duration of the campaign. From that small beginning, the Perot organization expanded to Louisiana's eight largest cities and all sixty-four parishes (counties), an organization of some 150 full-time and 1,000 part-time volunteers. By the time of Perot's surprising "withdrawal" in the midst of the Democratic National Convention, his Louisiana network had collected some fourteen times the necessary 5,000 signatures—70,000—to place his name on the November ballot. Volunteers came from all walks of life and with varieties of political experience, lifelong Republicans, Democrats, apoliticals, blacks and whites, young and old. The one thing they had in common was commitment to Perot as an instrument for change in what had come to be perceived as politics as usual. Said one Republican activist who was a member of Women for Bush in 1988, "I don't think [Perot] wants to be a politician. I think he wants a challenge. . . . It's about the job." For others, Perot was the answer to Clinton and Bush. Said another, "The thing I like about Mr. Perot is he's not into blaming, he's into taking charge and getting things done." Many supporters were even more committed, more enthusiastic when he reentered the campaign. The shared feeling was "We're going to show the Democrats and Republicans how it really should be done. This is a momentous time. A third party is being born." Without fanfare or campaign visits, the Perot volunteer army continued to work hard on his behalf out of the media glare.[24]

THE ELECTION RESULTS

Toward Judgment Day

Approaching the general election, Louisiana voters were the object of a full court press by both the Clinton/Gore and the Bush/Quayle candidates, their spouses, and other surrogates. In fact, Bill Clinton spent two campaign days, Al Gore two more, and both with their wives another day. Ron Brown spent another two campaign days, for a total of seven. In the aftermath of Hurricane

Andrew, President Bush spent two campaign days, while Vice-President Quayle's wife, Marilyn, a FEMA director, spent one. President Bush returned for two additional campaign days during the general election period, Vice-President Quayle one and his wife another four, Barbara Bush one day, and Pat Buchanan one day, for a post-Andrew total of twelve campaign days. The respective candidates and/or their surrogates appeared to chase through Louisiana on each other's heels during the nine weeks after the Republican National Convention.

In a poll conducted by the Survey Research Center at the University of New Orleans, 7–15 October 1992, Clinton led Bush and Perot 40 to 35 and 8 percent, respectively, among all voters surveyed. Even among the 17 percent who were "undecided," Clinton led Bush 16 to 11 percent. Calculating the "undecideds" into the voter preferences, Clinton was besting Bush 43 to 36 percent, with Perot at 8 percent and the firm undecideds at 13 percent. Interestingly, white voters preferred Bush to Clinton 47 to 31 percent (Perot, 9 percent) and blacks, Clinton to Bush 73 to 9 percent, with 4 percent going to Perot. Analyzing the poll for 1988 Bush voters and Reagan Democrats, respectively, Clinton picked up 24 percent of the former and 42 percent of the latter. Within two weeks of the presidential election, Clinton had every reason to look for a Louisiana victory.[25]

Here At Last

Setting the context for the approaching presidential election, Louisiana significantly boosted its pool of registered voters even though it lost population between 1980 and 1990 and lost one of its congressional seats. After decreasing from 1984 to 1988 and again between 1988 and the 1991 gubernatorial elections, whites managed to surpass their 1988 registration level for the 1992 presidential election, as shown in Table 5.1. Even more important for the Democratic candidates, the number of black registered voters climbed 8.7 percent between 1988 and 1992; their proportion of registered voters increased, as well. The proportion of blacks and whites registered to vote, moreover, reached near parity, separated by only two percentage points.

With the highest voter turnout on record, 78.5 percent of registered (60.1 percent voting age population [VAP]) Louisiana voters weighed in on November 3 to turn over the state's nine electoral college votes to Democrats Clinton and Gore, who garnered 45.6 percent of the votes cast to the incumbent Republican's 41.0 and Perot's Prudence, Action, Results Party's 11.8 percent. Another eight candidates together received 1.6 percent. In the "final judgment," 81.5 percent of the state's white registered voters and 71.0 percent of its blacks participated, both in relative proportion to their voter participation in the congressional primary elections held a month earlier. While the female-male gender gap was about the same in both elections (4.6 versus 4.8 percentage points more female from one election to the next), the real difference in the turnout of registered voters was among those under age thirty-five, their turnout increasing 8.2 percentage points

Table 5.1
Louisiana Voter Registration by Race, 1980–1992

Race/Year	Number Registered	Percent Increase	Percent of Voting Age Population	Percent of Total
Blacks				
1980	465,005	14.4	60.7	23.1
1984	560,732	20.6	65.7	24.8
1988	582,504	3.9	66.8	26.1
1991P	593,329	1.8	71.1	27.3
1991G	625,429	5.4	75.0	27.9
1992	633,049	1.2	75.9	27.6
Whites				
1980	1,550,397	13.5	74.8	76.9
1984	1,701,211	9.7	76.3	75.2
1988	1,637,432	-3.9	72.5	73.9
1991P	1,564,832	-4.6	74.4	72.0
1991G	1,599,488	2.2	76.0	71.4
1992	1,639,233	2.5	77.9	71.5

Note: P = Primary election; G = General election.
Sources: Calculations by author. Data from State of Louisiana, Commission of Elections, "Report of Reg-
istered Voters" [close of voter registration preceding the election](Baton Rouge, 1980-1992); U.S.
Bureau of the Census, Statistical Abstract of the United States (Washington, D.C.: Government Printing
Office, 1986), 257; U.S. Bureau of the Census, "Projections of the Population of Voting Age for States:
November 1988," Current Population Reports, Series P-25, No. 1019 (January 1988), 9; Bureau of
the Census, 1990 Census of Population, General Population Characteristics, Louisiana (Washington, D.C.:
Government Printing Office, May 1992), 85.

from 21.1 to 29.3. Voter dropoff occurred among those aged 35–44, 45–54,
55–64, and 65 + as age increased, the respective percentages being 22.7, 17.1,
13.4, and 17.3. Conventional voter turnout wisdom was stood on its head![26]

Politics and Elections: Collective Impact

Because Louisiana lost one congressional district as a result of the 1990 census,
the Democrats, who controlled the office of Governor and both houses of the
legislature, had license to wreak havoc on incumbent Republicans—and they
did so. First, in agreement with the U.S. Department of Justice, the legislature
created a new black-majority congressional district and structured the other districts such as to force two incumbent Republicans, Richard Baker (elected) and
Clyde Holloway, to run against each other, automatically eliminating one, while
Democrat Ned Randolph, who garnered 30.2 percent of the three-way vote,
attempted to eliminate both of them in a close contest. It also forced another
incumbent Republican, Jim McCrery (elected), to run against conservative incumbent Democrat Jerry Huckaby. To add some additional spice to the congressional contest in southwest Louisiana, incumbent Jimmy Hayes (elected) was
challenged by his brother Fredric. United States Senator Breaux and the re-

maining four incumbents had only token opposition. The new majority black district drew eight candidates and ended up in a runoff between state senators Cleo Fields (D–Baton Rouge) and Charles D. Jones (D–Lake Province), a mismatch won by Fields with 73.9 percent of the vote.[27]

The State Republicans

While state Republican Party Chair Nungesser's endorsement of Buchanan over President Bush precipitated a mutiny among Republican elected officials, he survived a late-April attempt to oust him from his position by refusing to honor the motion. He was backed by the Republican State Central Committee on a sixty-seven to fifty vote even though he was the only state party leader in the country not to endorse the president and elected Republican officials wanted him out. Adding to state party woes, three members of the Republican State Central Committee bolted the party to endorse Clinton a week before the election. Said one conservative member rhetorically, "Is this the same Billy Nungesser [state Chair] that endorsed Pat Buchanan? . . . Clyde Holloway against [incumbent Governor] Buddy Roemer in the governor's race? . . . He is part of the problem with the state party." Said a moderate, "A vote for Clinton says that we do not endorse the Republican Party allowing itself to become captive of the extreme right. Nor do we endorse the use of negative character attacks."[28]

Of the 169-member Republican State Central Committee (expanded from 140), fifteen "ultraconservatives" lost seats as did nineteen other members, though ultraconservatives were estimated to still hold 50 seats for the new four-year term. According to Secretary of State McKeithen, who was newly elected, "The evangelicals lost this election. . . . The fundamentalists still have some influence but not as much as they used to have." State Representative Quentin Dastugue (R–Jefferson), also newly elected, claimed that "We elected 100 of 169 . . . members, people who are in line with mainstream thinking, . . . people whose priority is winning elections." State representative Garey Forster (R–New Orleans) noted that the influence of the religious right stemmed from Nungesser cutting "deals with them to keep his job . . . and that polarized the party." Nungesser, on the other hand, admitted that elected officials made gains on the state central committee, but called it a wash. Yet the state party continued to breed dissention. When the newly elected Republican State Central Committee met to elect officers, the controversial Nungesser and the Republican National Committeeman, two of the top three positions, were replaced with members of the religious right, David Duke supporters![29]

With all of the state Republican Party turmoil, however, its voter base continued to expand, as shown in Table 5.2. Republican voter registration increased from 16.4 percent in 1988, to 18.3 percent for the 1991 Edwards-Duke gubernatorial runoff election, to its highest point, 19.1 percent, for the 1992 presidential election. Conversely, Democrats lost ground, sliding from 75.2 percent in 1988 to 71.3 percent for the presidential election.

Table 5.2
Louisiana Voter Registration by Political Party, 1980–1992

Year	Total Number	Percent Democratic	Percent Republican	Percent Other
1980	2,015,402	86.6	7.4	6.0
1984	2,262,101	80.6	11.3	8.1
1988	2,231,857	75.2	16.4	8.4
1991P	2,172,378	73.3	18.2	8.5
1991G	2,240,264	72.9	18.3	8.8
1992	2,292,129	71.3	19.1	9.6

Note: P = Primary election; G = General election. Over 99 percent of those in the category "Other" are registered as independent.
Sources: Data from State of Louisiana, Commission of Elections, "Report of Registered Voters" [close of voter registration preceding the election](Baton Rouge, 1980-1992).

CONCLUSION

The 1992 presidential election in Louisiana commanded the attention of voters as did the gubernatorial election a year earlier, both elections encouraging high levels of voter registration and participation. In both instances, the candidates generated interest either by the unprecedented media attention focused on a gubernatorial contest between a former Klan leader and Nazi sympathizer and the discredited former three-term governor or by the unprecedented attention given the state by the presidential candidates, their spouses, and their surrogates in search of nine electoral college votes. Race baiting took the form of anti-affirmative-action/anti-welfare political messages espoused by Duke in the gubernatorial election. In the state Republican Party, far-right religious fundamentalists, whose principal litmus test was anti-abortion, helped destroy the incumbent Republican governor supported by the national Republican Party. They went after President Bush as well, with their endorsement of conservative commentator Pat Buchanan, who carried the same Duke message without the Duke baggage. Wounded during the primary phase of the presidential selection process, the president went on to lose the election in Louisiana to challenger Bill Clinton, who worked harder to win Louisiana than any presidential candidate since 1878.

NOTES

1. Charles D. Hadley, "Louisiana: Race, Republicans, and Religion," in *The 1988 Presidential Election in the South: Continuity Amidst Change in Southern Party Politics*, ed. Robert P. Steed, Laurence W. Moreland, and Tod. A. Baker (New York: Praeger, 1991), 73–94.

2. See, for example, the very personal account by Elizabeth A. Rickey, "The Nazi and the Republicans: An Insider View of the Response of the Louisiana Republican Party to David Duke," in *The Emergence of David Duke and the Politics of Race*, ed. Douglas Rose (Chapel Hill: University of North Carolina Press, 1992), 59–79.

3. See Douglas D. Rose and Gary Esolen, "DuKKKe for Governor," in *The Emergence of David Duke and the Politics of Race*, ed. Douglas Rose (Chapel Hill: University of North Carolina Press, 1992) 197–241; Tyler Bridges, "Edwards vs. Duke in Runoff: Edwards Leads; Roemer Loses Out," *New Orleans Times-Picayune* (20 October 1991), 1, A–4. Voter turnout was calculated from Department of Elections and Registration, *State Wide Post Election Statistical Report for the Election of 10/19/91*, 1.

4. For a good summary of the events surrounding the gubernatorial runoff campaign, see "4 Weeks: The Campaign the World Watched," *New Orleans Times-Picayune*, reprinted from the October 20 to November 17, 1991, issues of *Times Picayune*. Turnout figures are from Department of Elections and Registration, *State Wide Post Election Statistical Report for the Election of 11/16/91*, 1, 7.

5. Rhodes Cook, "Wilder's Exit from Race Leaves Questions About Black Vote," *Congressional Quarterly Weekly Report* (11 January 1992), 66; Rhodes Cook, "Duke Fading," *Congressional Quarterly Weekly Report* (15 February 1992), 369.

6. Cook, "Duke Fading," 369; the campaign contribution fact is underscored by Duke's plea for personal donations long after he dropped out of the presidential contest. He wrote, "This letter is not about a campaign. It concerns my ability to remain an effective public spokesman for the principles we believe in. It may even affect whether I live or die." He went on to note that "a personal gift is not a campaign contribution, so *any gift you make is completely private*, not public and reportable to any agency or entity whatsoever. You can make a personal gift of up to $10,000 without it being reported to the IRS or paying any 'gift tax.' " [Emphasis added by author.] Cited in Tyler Bridges, "Duke Pleads for Money from Followers," *New Orleans Times-Picayune* (14 August 1992), 1, A–8.

7. Ed Anderson, "La. GOP Chief Expects Mutiny," *New Orleans Times-Picayune* (23 April 1992), B–6.

8. Lisa Frazier, "Last-minute Pitches Made by GOP Rivals," New Orleans *Times-Picayune* (10 March 1992), A–6.

9. Secretary of State, *Proclamation of Election Returns, Presidential Preference Primary* [March 8, 1988], (24 March 1988); Secretary of State, *Proclamation of Election Results, For Democratic and Republican Presidential Nominees* [March 10, 1992], (20 March 1992); Department of Elections and Registration, *State Wide Post Election Statistical Report for Election of 3/10/92*, 1. Calculations are by the author. Tyler Bridges, "Duke's Swift Ascent Matched by Fast Fall," *New Orleans Times-Picayune* (11 March 1992), 1, A–6; Douglas Jehl, "Buchanan Urges Halt in GOP Contributions," *New Orleans Times-Picayune* (11 March 1992), A–12. Rhodes Cook, "Duke Out of Race: 'My Role Is Over,' " *Congressional Quarterly Weekly Report* (25 April 1992), 1086.

10. Lisa Frazier, "Low Turnout of La. Voters Helps Bush and Clinton," *New Orleans Times-Picayune* (11 March 1992), 1, A–8; Department of Elections and Registration, *Report for Election of 3/10/92*, 1. For an overview of the nomination phase, see Charles D. Hadley and Harold W. Stanley, "Surviving the 1992 Presidential Nomination Process," in *America's Choice: The Election of 1992*, ed. William J. Crotty (Guilford, Conn.: Dushkin, 1993), chapter 3.

11. Jack Wardlaw, "Demos Hope to Lure State Back to Fold," *New Orleans Times-Picayune* (29 July 1992), 1, A–7.

12. Michael Kelly, "Clinton Accuses Bush of Dodging Responsibilities," *New York Times* (30 July 1992), A20; Tyler Bridges, "Demo Candidate Speaks at Dome," New Orleans *Times-Picayune* (30 July 1992), 1, A–10.

13. Frank Donze, "Deep Pockets Support Party," *New Orleans Times-Picayune* (30 July 1992), 1, A–10. Louisiana corporations and their chief executives contributed considerable funds to the Republican National Committee; the top eleven contributors alone gave $380,000 in amounts ranging from $5,000 to $75,000. Meanwhile, the largest Democratic National Committee contribution at the time was $2,120. See Bruce Alpert, "La. Businesses Flood GOP with 'Soft Money,' " *New Orleans Times-Picayune* (8 September 1992), 1, A–7.

14. Peter Nicholas, "Campaigns Discover La. in Toss-up Year," *New Orleans Times-Picayune* (10 September 1992), 1, A–8.

15. Peter Nicholas, "Brown: Demos Can Carry La., " *New Orleans Times-Picayune* (11 September 1992), A–7; Coleman Warner, "Party Chairmen Grapple in N.O.," *New Orleans Times-Picayune* (12 September 1992), A–2.

16. "Women Campaign for Clinton," *New Orleans Times-Picayune* (22 September 1992), B–4.

17. Jack Wardlaw, "Clinton Caravan Bound for N.O.," *New Orleans Times-Picayune* (15 October 1992), B–3; Ed Anderson and Colleen McMillar, "Clinton, Gore Court N.O. Voters," *New Orleans Times-Picayune* (17 October 1992), 1, A–4; John McQuaid, "Clinton Assured in Visit to La.," *New Orleans Times-Picayune* (28 October 1992), 1, A–10.

18. Peter Nicholas, "Bush Visits Win Praise, Complaints," *New Orleans Times-Picayune* (2 September 1992), 1, A–14.

19. Peter Nicholas, "Edwards, Mrs. Quayle Trade Taters," *New Orleans Times-Picayune* (9 September 1992), 1, A–8; Bruce Alpert, "Hurricane Aid Package May Increase," *New Orleans Times-Picayune* (9 September 1992), 1, A–8.

20. Joan Treadway and Ed Anderson, "Young, Old Meet Barbara Bush," *New Orleans Times-Picayune* (1 October 1992), 1, A–8; "VP's Wife Stumps in La.," *New Orleans Times-Picayune* (7 October 1992), B–4.

21. Ed Anderson, "South La. Crowds Cheer for Bush," *New Orleans Times-Picayune* (25 October 1992), 1, A–12.

22. Lisa Frazier, "Buchanan Stumps for Bush in La.," *New Orleans Times-Picayune* (27 October 1992), A–5.

23. Carlos A. Campos, "Mrs. Quayle Stumps at Med Center," *New Orleans Times-Picayune* (31 October 1992), A–6; Frank Donze, "Kenner Supporters Get Quick Visit with Quayle," *New Orleans Times-Picayune* (2 November 1992); B–1; Ed Anderson, "Bush Says He'll Carry Louisiana," *New Orleans Times-Picayune* (3 November 1992), 1, A–6.

24. Frank Donze, "Orleans Camp Hears Siren Call," *New Orleans Times-Picayune* (14 June 1992), 1, A–2; Ed Anderson, "Perot Stays on Ballot in State," *New Orleans Times-Picayune* (21 August 1992), B–1; Lynne Jensen, "N.O. Headquarters Back in Business," *New Orleans Times-Picayune* (2 October 1992), A–3.

25. Susan E. Howell, *Louisiana Presidential Election Survey* (unpublished technical report, 21 October 1992), 1–3.

26. "Voters Set a Record in Election," *New Orleans Times-Picayune* (10 November

1992), B–2; Secretary of State, State of Louisiana, *Election Proclamation* [for the election held November 3, 1992] (21 November 1992); Department of Elections and Registration, *State Wide Post Election Statistical Report for Election of 11/03/92*. Calculations are by the author.

27. Secretary of State, State of Louisiana, *Election Proclamation* [October 3, 1992] (15 October 1992); Secretary of State, State of Louisiana, *Election Proclamation* [November 3, 1992] (16 November 1992).

28. Ed Anderson, ''State GOP Chief Survives Attempt to Replace Him,'' *New Orleans Times-Picayune* (26 April 1992), B–4; Ed Anderson, ''GOP Stalwarts Dispute Party, Back Clinton,'' *New Orleans Times-Picayune* (28 October 1992), B–1.

29. Ed Anderson and Jack Wardlaw, ''Moderates Win State GOP Elections,'' *New Orleans Times-Picayune* (8 November 1992), B–1, B–2; Ed Anderson, ''State GOP Elects Officers,'' *New Orleans Times Picayune* (15 November 1992), B–1, B–2; Iris Kelso, ''GOP: Spreading the Blame Around,'' *New Orleans Times-Picayune* (12 November 1992), B–7; and Iris Kelso, ''The GOP's Reshuffle at the Top,'' *New Orleans Times-Picayune* (19 November 1992), B–7.

6

Mississippi: Friends and Neighbors Fight the "Liberal" Label

STEPHEN D. SHAFFER

By the 1980s, the two-party system had become deeply embedded in Mississippi federal elections. Narrowly supporting regional native son Jimmy Carter in 1976 and then barely ousting him in 1980, Mississippians reflected the national trend by easily supporting Reagan's reelection in 1984 and Bush's subsequent presidential bid in 1988. The parties split control of the Congress, as Trent Lott joined Thad Cochran in 1988 to give Republicans both U.S. Senate seats, while Democrats retained all five U.S. House districts.[1] Competitive two-party politics in state and local elections became more evident in the state elections of 1991, as Republicans elected their first statewide candidates since Reconstruction—construction company executive Kirk Fordice as governor and state senator Eddie Briggs as lieutenant governor.

The 1991 state elections vividly illustrated one important role of a competitive party system—providing alternatives for voters dissatisfied with the status quo. Democrat Ray Mabus had been elected governor four years earlier as a reform-oriented advocate of education, but his ambitious education reform plans fell victim in 1990 to the economic recession as well as to government gridlock despite a heavily Democratic legislature. The legislature killed Mabus's education funding plan based on legalizing a lottery, introducing video poker, and raising user fees for various government services, while Mabus rejected legislative leaders' alternative plan to raise taxes to help education. Public dissatisfaction with recession-induced budget cuts and lack of progress in reforming education contributed to the defeat of Mabus as well as the long-time presiding officer of the senate, Democratic Lieutenant Governor Brad Dye.

"For years, my hero has been Ronald Reagan," proclaimed long-time Republican Party activist and conservative ideologue Kirk Fordice.[2] Referring to environmental extremists as "tree buggers" and metaphorically threatening to "call out the National Guard" rather than support any tax increase, even if required to do so by a U.S. Supreme Court case charging an underfunding of traditionally black universities, Fordice's rhetoric gave Mississippians their first view of an outspoken conservative Republican as a statewide officeholder.[3] As the recession lingered into 1992, the Democratic-controlled legislature raised the sales tax to prevent additional cuts in elementary, secondary, and higher education and passed a bond program for university projects, twice overriding Fordice's vetoes. In a speech to the state Republican convention, Fordice charged that the legislature contained "a number of pseudo-Republicans running up and down the aisles" and proclaimed that it was "time to send them home. Even more important, we need to fire some liberal Democrats."[4] Fordice urged repeal of the sales tax increase, prompting education supporters to urge voters to "repeal the repealers" in the special 1992 legislative elections called after court-ordered redistricting.[5] As Fordice dropped plans to roll back the tax hike, his conservatism nevertheless led black leaders to conclude that a backlash in the black community would generate votes for the Democrats in November.[6]

THE CAMPAIGN: UNIFYING NOMINATION BATTLES

Conservative challengers to Bush's renomination, Pat Buchanan and David Duke, flocked to Mississippi before the Super Tuesday primaries, viewing the reputedly conservative state as a last chance to bolster their sagging nomination hopes. They were countered by a state Republican Party leadership unified behind Bush that staged a February rally in Jackson designed to stimulate turnout and minimize support for the president's Republican challengers. First Lady Barbara Bush, his son George Walker Bush, and Vice-President Dan Quayle all campaigned in the Magnolia State. Four days before Super Tuesday, President Bush himself visited Jackson, and from the steps of the Capitol, he thanked 8,000 supporters who "stood with me" during Desert Storm and asked them to "reject the ugly politics of hatred that is rearing its head again" as well as the "big spenders who control the United States Congress."[7] Bush's subsequent victory margin of 72 percent was higher than in any other Super Tuesday state, dwarfing Buchanan's 17 percent and Duke's 11 percent. Especially interesting was the fact that 45 percent of Mississippians who voted that day chose the Republican primary, an increase from the 31 percent who voted in the state's 1988 Republican presidential primary, suggesting a continued growth in Republican sentiment in the Magnolia State.[8]

Meanwhile, state Democrats were more united than they had been in decades, as Clinton amassed over 200 endorsements from prominent Mississippi Democrats such as his state co-chairs, black Congressman Mike Espy and former Governor William Winter, as well as Secretary of State Dick Molpus, Attorney General Mike Moore, Treasurer Marshall Bennett, Auditor Steve Patterson, and House Speaker Tim Ford.[9] Hoping to repeat Jesse Jackson's 1988 plurality victory in Mississippi's Democratic presidential primary, Jerry Brown brought his populist campaign to some of the state's black churches and universities. Attacking elite politicians who listen only to millionaires and act like "little kings," but who forget the prophecy that "those who are first shall be last and those who are last shall be first," Brown mocked those who had provided a government " 'of the $1,000 givers,' . . . 'for the $1,000 givers,' . . . 'by the $1,000 givers.' "[10] Clinton himself came to Mississippi to attend a $250-a-plate breakfast with over 250 state Democrats and to visit a largely black classroom where he emphasized economic issues and called for racial brotherhood. Clinton easily carried Mississippi, garnering 74 percent of the vote to only 9 percent for Brown and 7 percent for Paul Tsongas (the remainder supported other candidates or were uncommitted).[11]

Both state delegations at the national convention stressed their candidates' themes that would play best in Mississippi. State Democrats reiterated that the party had "inalterably shifted more to the middle" and nominated someone who had firsthand knowledge of the state and its economic problems. Enthusiasm ran so high that Democrats planned a coordinated campaign in Mississippi with links established between the presidential race and the local elections.[12]

Meanwhile, Republicans launched a blistering attack on the Democrats as the "tax increase" party that would "cut defense to almost a crawl" and that espoused a moral code consisting of "anything goes." Stressing the anti-politician mood that had helped elect him as governor, Fordice claimed, "Americans are not going to be snowed by a glib, blow-dried professional politician like Bill Clinton." Recalling a sign he had seen at the Neshoba County Fair, Fordice said, "This guy had put up a little poster with the American flag and it said, 'George Bush served this and pointed an arrow up to the flag and [Clinton] didn't.' " Announcing the state's thirty-four votes for Bush, Fordice described Mississippi as "a beautiful state bounded on the west by that small state with a failed governor and on the north by a state that has a senator from Washington, D.C."[13]

As early as August, both parties had already established the themes that they would stress until election day.

THE CAMPAIGN: A PARTISAN GENERAL ELECTION WAR

State and local Democrats had been amassing a war chest through the year with such fund-raising events as a "Beans and Greens" dinner in Starkville in February, a Tupelo fund-raiser in July, and a Democratic Unity fund-raising dinner in West Point in June.[14] At a Labor Day rally in Starkville, the state Clinton/Gore campaign director, Lisa Walker, attacked Bush's use of his incumbency: "He's been flying around the country the last few days giving away things in a bigger giveaway than Publisher's Clearinghouse." She also read from a letter written by Clinton: "President Bush likes to say things are bad, but they could be worse. I like to say things are bad, but they could be better." At a Mississippi State University rally in October, former Oktibbeha County Chairman

Bill Collins proclaimed that "It's time to place the torch of leadership into the hands of a younger generation," while state senator Amy Tuck Powell said, "We have hope from a gentleman from Hope, Arkansas."[15] In mid-October the Clinton/Gore campaign held a series of regional rallies, spearheaded by a Meridian fund-raising barbecue attended by numerous state and local elected officials. Touring Columbus, Greenwood, and Jackson by bus with four other members of the Congressional Black Caucus, Espy attacked Bush: "He lied to us first when he said, 'Read my lips: No new taxes.' Now we're telling him, 'Read our lips: No new term.' " Espy also appeared on "The Today Show" to defend Clinton after the latter's criticism of black rapper Sister Souljah, labeling his gubernatorial record "absolutely perfect, just about perfect, on racial issues."[16]

Jesse Jackson visited Mississippi on two occasions to increase black voter registration. Claiming that black apathy had helped elect conservative Kirk Fordice, the reverend in speeches in Jackson in February concluded, "In Louisiana we stopped Duke, but in Mississippi you did less than your best and got ice." Comparing the right to vote to the rod that Moses held in his hand over the Red Sea, Jackson preached, "You drop the rod; the rod turns into a snake." In late July at voter registration drives in West Point and Greenville designed to help elect more black legislators, Jackson told cheering churchgoers, "Hands that once picked cotton can pick legislators. . . . Don't just complain about the governor. Run for governor." Jackson stressed economic issues and the fact that both races were "unemployed and malnourished together. Whether you're black or white, hunger hurts." Saying that "We don't need a man in the White House that can't spell potato," Jackson concluded that "It's time to send Bush and Quayle back to living private lives." Some Republicans feared that Democrats would benefit from a new mail registration law passed by the overwhelmingly Democratic legislature.[17]

Meanwhile, Republicans also promised a vigorous campaign, aided by the publicity accorded their statewide and federal officeholders. Responding to the Gore selection, Fordice charged that he embodied the "left-wing, tax-and-spend, big-government thinking that has stifled the United States Congress." At the Republican convention, Senator Cochran claimed that Clinton was "big trouble for American business" because of his proposals for "higher taxes and more regulations and controls." At a county fund-raising dinner, Lieutenant Governor Eddie Briggs touted the last twelve years of Republican leadership when the Berlin Wall and communism fell, so that "we can all go to sleep without the overriding fear of a nuclear attack." He charged that Clinton would take America back to "the misery index of Jimmy Carter, back to when our people were held hostage and our flag was being burned." At an October rally of 250 state Republicans, Fordice blasted Clinton's statement that if he had met KGB agents on his 1969 Moscow trip, he was not aware of it: "To me, that sounds like 'I didn't inhale.' "[18]

In the face of an aggressive state Democratic campaign effort and polls showing a dead heat in Mississippi, Bush and Quayle, accompanied by their spouses, made Gulfport their first stop after the national convention. Deflecting attacks on Quayle's inability to spell "potato," Fordice jokingly introduced Quayle to the crowd of 20,000 as "the national spelling champion." Quayle promised, "We won the Cold War, and with a new Congress, we'll win the domestic war." Expressing his pleasure at being in a town with such "strong family values," and chiding those "smart talking heads on television" who had written off his election chances, Bush lit into Clinton and the Democratic-controlled Congress. Arguing that Americans should "watch out for your wallet" when Clinton talked about $220 billion in new "investment," Bush termed it "Elvis economics, because by the time he is finished, American workers will all be checking in to the Heartbreak Hotel." The Republican president promised a Harry Truman come-from-behind victory, blasting the "gridlocked Congress" for blocking his jobs, education, and energy programs. Claiming that "I've ridden stationary bikes that can move faster than the U.S. Congress," Bush asked voters to "clean house, to clean the House."[19]

Less than two weeks later, immediately after the television Emmy awards, Quayle was again in Mississippi. Shouting to a Columbus high school crowd, "Murphy Brown, you owe me big time," the vice-president charged that Clinton had raised taxes 138 times in Arkansas and would raise taxes as president. Quayle then called for a strengthened American family by "letting parents choose where their children go to school," evoking cheers from the crowd that included students from three private schools, and by "getting criminals off the street" and "putting victims' rights ahead of criminals' rights." The vice-president also stressed the trust issue: "Who do you trust? The governor of Arkansas who said America was the mockery of the world or the president who led us in Desert Storm?"[20]

As the presidential race in Mississippi remained neck and neck, Bush became the first president since 1902 to visit the impoverished and heavily black Mississippi Delta. Speaking to 5,000 supporters at an airport hangar in Greenville, Bush urged Mississippians to look across the river for evidence of his opponent's "lousy" record as governor, citing his alleged neglect of Arkansas' environmental, health care, crime, and educational problems. Prior to his speech, police had escorted out of the crowd a Clinton supporter wearing a chicken costume and a sign reading "No debate about it. He's Chicken George." Commenting on Clinton's claims that Bush was afraid to debate him, the president responded, "Who is he to call me afraid, for heaven's sake?" Praising Mississippi as "one of the most patriotic of states," Bush added, "No, I'm not going to bring up the draft issue, but let me simply say that I am proud that I wore the uniform of the United States of America, and I am proud that I served."[21]

In the face of polls showing a tight race in the Magnolia State, national Democrats in mid-October acceded to requests by Mississippi partisans to personally campaign. Introducing Albert Gore to a rain-soaked crowd at Mississippi State University, Winter employed a "friends and neighbors" approach by stressing the vice-presidential nominee's family ties to the state, given his numerous relatives scattered across north Mississippi and the naming of Gore Springs after one of them. Gore himself stressed the ticket's southern roots: "Our part of the country is ready to provide leadership for our country." Then he attacked the Republican ticket for the economic problems facing the United States: "Unemployment is up. Real wages are down. The budget deficit is up. Consumer confidence is down. Everything that should be down is up. Everything that is up should be down. [Republicans] have it upside down, but we're going to turn it right side up." Playing on college students' concerns about job opportunities after graduation, Gore promised an expanded student loan program that could be repaid through community service and drew laughs when he claimed that "If George Bush went to Hollywood and made a movie, they'd have to call it, 'Honey, I Shrunk the Economy.' And of course the sequel would be, 'Honey, I Blew Up the Deficit.' "[22]

Sensing an opportunity to carry normally Republican Mississippi, Clinton himself visited Jackson the Wednesday before the election and addressed a crowd of 10,000. Accusing Bush of trying to shut down the Iuka, Mississippi, solid rocket motor program, Clinton blasted his opponent: "Mr. Bush has run out of energy, ideas and vision. He ought to be run out of Washington because all he does is appeal to the worst in us." Clinton blasted Bush for belittling his southern roots: "To hear him tell it, if you're the governor of a small Southern state, you shouldn't be able to run for president." Attacking the honesty of Bush's campaign ads, Clinton cautioned the audience that Bush had even told Mikhail Gorbachev "not to pay any attention to what he would say during the presidential campaign." Some Bush supporters infiltrated the crowd and began chanting "four more years," and one demonstrator even carried a large color picture of an aborted baby. Aggressively countering Clinton's speech was a "truth squad" of Fordice, the secretaries of labor and transportation, and three other nationally known Republicans. Attacking the media, Fordice made an election night prediction: "When George Herbert Walker Bush begins to surge ahead you will see their lips come out and little tears will begin to form because they have lost another chance to put a liberal, Democrat, draft-dodger, philanderer as the commander-in-chief of this greatest country in the entire world." Addressing a group of veterans protesting against Clinton, Fordice reportedly charged, "Why doesn't slick Willie just tell us what he was doing in Moscow? He had business with the enemy."[23]

National surrogates from both parties' campaigns entered the fray by visiting Mississippi and promoting their presidential hopefuls. The Bush/Quayle effort was backed by visits from Marilyn Quayle, Agriculture Secretary Edward Madigan, Education Secretary Lamar Alexander, and Federal Railroad Administrator and Mississippi native Gil Carmichael, while the Clinton/Gore ticket was boosted by Hillary Clinton, Tennessee Governor Ned McWherter, and Ohio Senator and former astronaut John Glenn.[24]

Meanwhile, H. Ross Perot's campaign was relatively invisible. Earlier, political observers had speculated that Perot might take votes away from the more conservative Bush, permitting Clinton to squeak by in the state. One major effort had been merely getting his name placed on the ballot, which was finally accomplished after Perot named Admiral James B. Stockdale as his running mate. Perot's temporary withdrawal from the race appeared to reduce his credibility among voters, as some felt that he let them down and that they could not trust him. Jackson attorney James Smith, chief of Perot's state campaign, pledged to travel across the state pushing his cause and recruiting poll workers after Perot reentered the race, but both parties attacked the independent. State Bush/Quayle Chair Clarke Reed charged that Perot "cannot win one electoral vote. He's like a spoiled kid with a lot of money," while a Clinton spokeswoman claimed that Perot's supporters were "really turned off when he dropped out."[25]

One interesting U.S. House race that was heating up was in the First Congressional District in northern Mississippi, after eighty-two-year-old Democrat Jamie Whitten "temporarily" stepped aside as chair of the powerful Appropriations Committee at the request of Democratic leaders concerned over his job performance after a month-long hospitalization for prostate surgery and blood pressure problems. Senator Cochran pointed out that Whitten had not really given up his power, but had simply delegated to another congressman the duty of presiding at meetings, illustrating how some Republicans were reluctant to go after the powerful Democrat. Fordice, on the other hand, pushing for term limits, argued that "Anyone that's been in Congress for 51 years obviously is at least to a degree out of touch with the people that they're supposed to be serving." Espy strongly defended Whitten, pointing out that his position as committee chair had given Mississippi more power in and benefits from Congress. Fordice responded, "We are still last aren't we?" and argued that "Espy and other entrenched incumbents will do just about anything they can to preserve their position." Espy shot back that "Without [Whitten] the question is how much worse would we be in Mississippi," and Whitten himself pointed out that "When the governor visited in February it was to call on my energy, experience and position to save the [advanced solid rocket motor] project at Yellow Creek." The project survived after a conference committee chaired and reportedly "strong-armed" by Whitten in late September provided the funds.[26]

Former Tupelo Mayor Clyde Whittaker, calling himself a "progressive conservative," waged the most aggressive Republican campaign that Whitten had faced in his career, outspending the incumbent by $196,769 to $156,151. Sensing a possible upset, U.S. Representative Guy Vander Jagt, chair of the National Republican Congressional Committee, flew to Tupelo the week before the election with a $50,000 donation for Whittaker, calling Whitten the "biggest spender in the world."[27] Meanwhile, Whitten effectively emphasized his incumbency asset of constituency service. At a dedication of the Jamie L. Whitten Historical Center at Fulton on the Tennessee-Tombigbee Waterway, a state conservationist echoed many Mississippians' view of Whitten: "Never have so many owed so much to one man." The conservative *Memphis Commercial Appeal* proclaimed it the "End of Era: Whitten's Time Is Over," but both the *Jackson Clarion-*

Ledger and the Tupelo-based *Northeast Mississippi Daily Journal* applauded the senior congressman's service to the state and urged his reelection. With the slogan "Stand Up for Our Congressman, Jamie Whitten, He Stands Up for Mississippi," the Whitten campaign ran numerous newspaper advertisements, including eight-page inserts in newspapers across the district the week before the election, stressing the federal programs that he had brought into "every county in our district."[28]

Both newspapers with statewide circulation endorsed presidential candidates that reflected their normal ideological leanings, with the *Memphis Commercial Appeal* enthusiastically pushing Bush and the *Jackson Clarion-Ledger* giving Clinton a weak nod. The Memphis paper applauded Bush as the more conservative candidate, who favored "market-based solutions to public problems" and "less regulation, less taxation, and less spending," while Clinton's more "statist bent" favored "old-fashioned income redistribution, massive spending on public works and social programs, and newfangled industrial policy designed in Washington." Acknowledging the "troubled aspects about all three candidates," the *Jackson Clarion-Ledger* termed Clinton a "moderate from the South" who "is like us" and pointed out that the United States needed an "Operation Domestic Storm" and an "activist administration on the economy" that Clinton would provide. A leading newspaper in north Mississippi, the *Northeast Mississippi Daily Journal*, reversed its Bush endorsement of four years ago and pointed out that "changing times call for a change in leadership and direction." Terming Clinton a "leader in the education reform movement nationwide," it praised his plans to retrain U.S. workers, promote workfare instead of welfare, invest in new technologies, and work closely with the private sector to promote economic development.[29]

In the last week of the campaign, state and local officials of both parties promoted their presidential hopefuls with rallies and ads in local newspapers. The state Republican Party shored up its core support by mailing to party supporters two fliers attacking Clinton. Sporting the picture of a middle-aged white man talking about the mistake he had made in voting for another allegedly moderate southern governor, Jimmy Carter, who brought the country "21 percent interest rates, 13 percent inflation, and four years of misery," one flier urged a "Vote Against Higher Taxes on Working Families." Accusing Clinton of backing "Mario Cuomo on the Supreme Court . . . Gay and Lesbian Rights Bill . . . Statehood for Washington D.C." among other liberal issues, the second flier also urged a vote "against bigger government and for basic values."[30] A Democratic rally and unity dinner in Tupelo included Espy, former Governors Winter and Allain, and state officeholders Patterson, Bennett, and Molpus, while Espy, Patterson, Molpus, and state Democratic Chair Ed Cole attended a rally in Yazoo City promoting turnout. Republican Senator Lott and Railroad Administrator Carmichael crisscrossed the state, urging support for the president.[31]

Elements of the Christian right weighed in against a Clinton presidency. Calling Clinton a "neo-pagan" who would "help destroy three centuries of

Christianity in America,'' one pamphlet placed on many Jackson churchgoers' windshields claimed: ''To vote for Clinton is to help him promote rebellion against God. And for God's people to follow Clinton is sin.'' The Saturday before the election, forty members of Parents Against Clinton gathered at the state Capitol and charged that the Democratic nominee and platform posed a ''threat to our children's future'' by favoring condom distribution in schools, public funding of abortions, and guaranteed civil rights for homosexuals, among other issues. One advertisement in the *Jackson Clarion-Ledger* the day before the election, paid for by Concerned Christian Citizens, was entitled ''Christian Beware'' and accused Clinton of violating specific Bible passages by supporting ''abortion on demand . . . the homosexual lifestyle . . . and giving condoms to teenagers in public school without parental consent.'' Former Democratic Governor Mabus termed the pamphlet ''pure desperation by a campaign that has absolutely nothing to say,'' while Clinton's state campaign manager, Lisa Walker, dismissed Parents Against Clinton as ''part of the Republican effort to bring up the character issue and frighten people.''[32]

RESULTS AND ANALYSIS: THE PRESIDENTIAL RACE

On election day, Mississippi was the only state in the nation to give Bush a majority (though a bare one) of the vote, 50 percent, while Clinton was held to 41 percent, only 2 percent more than Dukakis had garnered in the state in 1988, and Perot registered only 9 percent, his weakest showing in the nation (except for the District of Columbia). The Democrat carried only thirty of Mississippi's eighty-two counties, including all eighteen won by Dukakis in 1988. Especially strong in the poverty-stricken Delta, Clinton carried twenty-one of the twenty-four counties across the state that contained black population majorities. Unlike the successful Carter campaign of 1976, however, Clinton lost most of the white-majority counties in tradition-bound northeast Mississippi that Carter swept. Republicans claimed that they had limited conservative defections to Perot by pointing out that the independent had no chance of winning, and state Bush/Quayle chair Reed applauded Mississippi's deviation from the national results: ''We're saner. We're smarter. We know a liberal when we see one.'' Democrat Winter observed that voters were caught up in a sound-bite campaign where ''symbols and a kind of simplistic, superficial, flag-waving leadership mask what the issues are'' and concluded that many Mississippians had ''voted against our own economic and educational interests.'' One columnist perceived a more fundamental partisan shift in the election results, with the Democratic base in the state of 40 percent facing an uphill electoral struggle against a Republican base of 50 percent.[33]

One important explanation for Bush's convincing victory in Mississippi is that his moderate conservative image more faithfully mirrored the views of Mississippians compared to Clinton's more moderate liberal image. In an April 1992 poll conducted by Mississippi State University (MSU), the typical Mississippian

Table 6.1
Mississippi Perceptions of Candidate Ideologies (in percent)

Group	Very Liberal	Somewhat Liberal	Moderate	Somewhat Conservative	Very Conservative	Do Not Know
	1	2	3	4	5	
Entire population						
Adults (Mean = 3.5)	4	13	31	28	19	5
Bush (Mean = 3.5)	3	13	23	36	12	13
Clinton (Mean = 2.6)	11	25	20	14	2	28
Likely voters						
Voters (Mean = 3.5)	2	12	35	30	19	2
Bush (Mean = 3.5)	2	12	23	42	11	10
Clinton (Mean = 2.5)	14	27	22	13	1	23

Note: cell entries reflect all adults' and likely voters' own ideological positions and their perceptions of the candidates' positions. Values in parentheses are means, with ideology coded from 1 for "very liberal" to 5 for "very conservative"; "did not know" responses have been omitted from the analysis. The results were weighted or adjusted by demographic characteristics such as education, race, and gender to ensure a representative sample. The population sample yields a sample error of plus or minus 4 percent, while the sample of likely voters, determined by people's responses to three political knowledge, interest, and vote likelihood questions, yielded a sample error of 5 percent. For entire population, N = 558; for likely voters, N = 373.
Source: Mississippi State University poll, conducted 1-13 April 1992 by the Survey Research Unit of the Social Science Research Center at Mississippi State University.

perceived Bush's philosophy as somewhere between "moderate" and "somewhat conservative," virtually identical with their own position, while Clinton was viewed as somewhere between "somewhat liberal" and "moderate." (See Table 6.1.) State Republicans proceeded to reinforce this "liberal" image of Clinton's throughout the campaign, while Democrats continually stressed their candidate's "moderate" posture and southern roots. Perhaps state Republicans were more aggressive and successful than Democrats. Certainly, the visibility that the media provided to Governor Fordice's attacks on Clinton's "liberalism" may have helped reinforce this "somewhat liberal" image of Clinton's. But even if perceptions remained essentially unchanged after April, Bush's more moderately conservative posture would have helped him among the state's elec-

Table 6.2
Party Identification in Mississippi, 1982–1992 (in percent)

Group	1982	1984	1986	1988	1990	1992	Change
Voters and non-voters							
Democrats	53	44	44	45	46	39	- 1 4
Independents/apoliticals	32	40	31	34	28	31	- 1
Republicans	15	16	25	21	26	30	+ 1 5
	100	100	100	100	100	100	
Democratic advantage							
(% Dem minus % Repub)	38	28	19	24	20	9	na
Likely voters only							
Democrats	48	43	44	46	37	34	- 1 4
Independents/apoliticals	35	40	30	30	32	29	- 6
Republicans	17	17	26	24	31	37	+ 2 0
	100	100	100	100	100	100	
Democratic advantage							
(% Dem minus % Repub)	31	26	18	22	6	-3	na

Note: Survey question was as follows: "Generally speaking, do you consider yourself a Democrat, Republican, Independent, or what?"
Source: Statewide public opinion polls of adult Mississippi residents conducted by the Social Science Research Center at Mississippi State University.

torate. A related factor aiding Bush was his longstanding popularity in Mississippi. Even in the face of the lagging economy in April, 13 percent of "likely voters" in the MSU poll rated Bush's performance as excellent, 40 percent as good, 29 percent as fair, and only 16 percent as poor (with 2 percent offering no opinions). A September Mason-Dixon poll concluded that Mississippi was the only state in the nation where a majority of voters rated Bush's job performance as excellent or good.[34]

Another likely source of Bush's victory in the Magnolia State is the growing strength of the Republican Party. By 1992 among all adults, the Democratic advantage over the Republicans on the basic concept of psychological attachment to a political party was down to single digits. (See Table 6.2.) Indeed, among likely voters, Republicans actually outnumbered Democrats, and while the differences was statistically insignificant, it constituted the first Republican plurality among likely voters in the history of statewide academic polling. Especially noteworthy were Republican gains among the 64 percent of the state's population that was white. In 1981 and 1982, Democrats had outnumbered Republicans among all adult whites by a two-to-one margin, but whites became evenly divided between the parties in the 1986–1990 period.[35] By 1992, Republicans outnumbered Democrats among adult whites by 45 percent to 29 percent, and only the overwhelming Democratic margin among blacks gave the party of Andrew Jackson their advantage in the entire population. Among whites, the Republican label garnered a majority of the preferences of self-identified conservatives, college graduates, and those with annual family incomes exceeding $40,000. (See Table 6.3.) Democrats retained an advantage over Republicans (though not a majority) among self-identified liberals and moderates, those over sixty years old, and families with incomes under $20,000.

RESULTS AND ANALYSIS: OTHER RELEVANT ELECTIONS

Other election results suggested that Mississippi had simply become a more competitive two-party state rather than an emerging Republican bastion. Mississippians reelected all five of its all-Democratic U.S. House delegation with anywhere from 59 to 81 percent of the vote, as incumbency was so potent that even Whitten received nearly 60 percent of the vote in his narrowest victory ever. In the face of the Bush landslide, Republican numbers in the state house rose from twenty-three to twenty-seven and in the state senate from nine to thirteen, but Democrats still held 76 percent of the seats in the 122-member house and 52-member senate. Furthermore, court-ordered redistricting led to greater legislative gains for a more liberal group, blacks, whose numbers in the state house rose from twenty-one to thirty-two and in the state senate from four to ten. House Speaker Ford concluded that the increased number of women (from fourteen to nineteen in both chambers combined) and blacks would lead to a greater emphasis on social needs such as Medicaid, mental health, and the environment, while victorious civil rights attorney Carroll Rhodes predicted the possibility of "a lot of progressive legislation." Meanwhile, Fordice's personal endorsement of fifteen to twenty Republican legislative candidates and his fund-raising efforts for some of these angered Democrats, prompting at least one to call for a Democratic caucus to be established so that the party could "defend ourselves" and force partisan Republicans to "pay a price."[36]

A ballot measure repealing the constitutional ban on a lottery may have inadvertently helped Bush. Despite polls initially showing broad public support for a lottery, supporters appeared to run out of steam after the bitter legislative fights necessary to secure the two-thirds margin in each chamber in order to send the amendment to the voters and offered no organized support for the lottery in November. Lottery opposition was spearheaded by CARE—Citizens Advocating Responsible Economics—which included Governor Fordice and former Democratic Governors Bill Waller and Bill Allain. Pointing out the regressive nature of the lottery as well as moral concerns, CARE organized meetings across the state and ran newspaper ads in which prominent Mississippians criticized lotteries. State Baptists and Methodists came out strongly against the lottery amendment, both political parties in some counties joined forces to oppose it, and the *Northeast Mississippi Daily Journal* editorialized against it. On election day, the lottery narrowly passed with only 53 percent of the statewide vote. At the county level, support for the lottery and Clinton's candidacy appeared related

Table 6.3

Group Differences on Party Identification Among Mississippi White Voters and Nonvoters (in percent)

Characteristic	Democrat	Independent	Republican
Ideology			
Liberal	42	22	36
Moderate	39	34	27
Conservative	18	23	59
Years lived in state			
15 or fewer	23	29	48
Over 15 years	30	26	44
Race			
White	29	26	45
(Black)	(74)	(20)	(6)
Age			
18-35	27	26	47
36-60	22	29	49
61 and over	47	20	33
Education			
Less than high school graduate	36	24	40
High school graduate	34	29	37
Some college or college graduate	21	26	53
Family income			
Under $10,000	36	33	31
$10,000-19,999	50	17	33
$20,000-29,999	30	33	37
$30,000-40,000	25	32	43
Over $40,000	16	21	63
Gender			
Male	23	30	47
Female	35	22	43
Congressional District			
1st	39	19	42
2nd	23	35	42
3rd	29	25	46
4th	23	24	53
5th	26	29	45

Note: Percentages total 100 percent across each row.
Source: Mississippi State University poll, conducted 1-13 April 1992 .

with a Pearson R correlation of .38, as both scored well in black-majority areas such as the Delta.[37] To the extent that the anti-lottery campaign may have enticed the religious right to the polls, it may have diminished Clinton's vote in the state.

CONCLUSION

Certainly such unique factors as a lottery ballot measure that mobilized the religious right—as well as an aggressive campaign by a highly visible, conservative, and partisan governor, the first Republican governor since Reconstruction—may help explain Bush's strong showing in the Magnolia State. Yet Democrats clearly have cause for concern—if they are unable to carry the state with two "moderate" southerners on the ticket at a time when an incumbent Republican is plagued by a stagnant economy, when will they be able to carry Mississippi in a national election? A successful Clinton administration that hugs the centrist mainstream of the nation could be an important element in a Democratic presidential comeback in the Magnolia State, where competitive two-party politics is clearly here to stay.

NOTES

The author gratefully acknowledges funding support from Mississippi State University and its Social Science Research Center, as well as the valuable graduate assistance support provided by Robert Lord, Denise Keller, and Kellei R. Bishop.

1. See Stephen D. Shaffer, "Mississippi: Electoral Conflict in a Nationalized State," in *The 1988 Presidential Election in the South: Continuity Amidst Change in Southern Party Politics*, ed. Laurence W. Moreland, Robert P. Steed, and Tod A. Baker (New York: Praeger, 1991), 95–118.

2. *Northeast Mississippi Daily Journal* (Tupelo) (19 August 1992), B8.

3. *Jackson Clarion-Ledger* (18 January 1992), B1.

4. *Starkville Daily News* (10 May 1992), B1.

5. *Jackson Clarion-Ledger* (31 July 1992), B1.

6. *Jackson Clarion-Ledger* (5 July 1992), G3 (Joe Atkins column).

7. *Jackson Clarion-Ledger* (17 February 1992), B1; (5 March 1992), B1; (7 March 1992), B1; *Memphis Commercial Appeal* (7 March 1992), A8.

8. *Northeast Mississippi Daily Journal* (26 July 1992), C1; *Jackson Clarion-Ledger* (11 March 1992), B1.

9. *Memphis Commercial Appeal* (2 March 1992), A1.

10. *Delta Democrat Times* (8 March 1992), A6; *Jackson Clarion-Ledger* (9 March 1992), A3.

11. *Meridian Star* (28 January 1992), B1; *Memphis Commercial Appeal* (28 January 1992), A8.

12. *Jackson Clarion-Ledger* (12 July 1992), A1, A15; (17 July 1992), A6.

13. *Starkville Daily News* (21 August 1992), A2; *Jackson Clarion-Ledger* (16 August 1992), A17; (17 August 1992), A1; (20 August 1992), A1, A11.

14. *Northeast Mississippi Daily Journal* (29 July 1992), B2; *Starkville Daily News* (25 February 1992), B1; (14 June 1992), B1.

15. *Northeast Mississippi Daily Journal* (9 September 1992), B3; *Reflector* (Mississippi State University) (13 October 1992), A1.

16. *Jackson Clarion-Ledger* (18 June 1992), A6; (16 October 1992), B3.

17. *Memphis Commercial Appeal* (8 February 1992), B1; (29 June 1992), B4; (27

July 1992), A5; *Jackson Clarion-Ledger* (8 February 1992), B1; (27 July 1992), B1; *Starkville Daily News* (27 July 1992), A1, A10.

18. *Northeast Mississippi Daily Journal* (7 October 1992), B8. *Jackson Clarion-Ledger* (10 July 1992), B1; (23 August 1992), A14; (19 October 1992), B1.

19. *Memphis Commercial Appeal* (22 August 1992), A1, A16; *Northeast Mississippi Daily Journal* (22 August 1992), A1, A9, A13; *Jackson Clarion-Ledger* (22 August 1992), B1.

20. *Northeast Mississippi Daily Journal* (1 September 1992), A1, A15; *Starkville Daily News* (1 September 1992), A1, A10.

21. *Jackson Clarion-Ledger* (23 September 1992), A1; *Memphis Commercial Appeal* (23 September 1992), A1, A8; *Starkville Daily News* (23 September 1992), B1.

22. *Jackson Clarion-Ledger* (17 October 1992), A1; *Northeast Mississippi Daily Journal* (17 October 1992), A1, A7; *Starkville Daily News* (17 October 1992), A1, A12.

23. *Jackson Clarion-Ledger* (28 October 1992), B1; (29 October 1992), B1; (1 November 1992), G8 (Bill Minor column); *Starkville Daily News* (29 October 1992), A14.

24. *Jackson Clarion-Ledger* (16 April 1992), B1; (6 October 1992), A1; (7 October 1992), A1; *Northeast Mississippi Daily Journal* (8 October 1992), A1, B1; (9 October 1992), B1; *Starkville Daily News* (24 September 1992), B1.

25. *Jackson Clarion-Ledger* (7 June 1992), G3; (17 July 1992), G1; (30 August 1992), B1; (2 October 1992), B1: *Northeast Mississippi Daily Journal* (12 August 1992), B5.

26. *Northeast Mississippi Daily Journal* (3 October 1992), B1; (7 October 1992), B1; *Jackson Clarion-Ledger* (11 June 1992), B1; (7 October 1992), B1.

27. *Northeast Mississippi Daily Journal* (29 October 1992), B1; (31 October 1992), B2; *Jackson Clarion-Ledger* (8 October 1992), B3.

28. *Northeast Mississippi Daily Journal* (27 August 1992), A1, A9; (27 October 1992), A12; (31 October 1992), insert; *Memphis Commercial Appeal* (25 October 1992), B8; *Jackson Clarion-Ledger* (2 November 1992), A8.

29. *Memphis Commercial Appeal* (11 October 1992), B10; *Jackson Clarion-Ledger* (1 November 1992), G6; *Northeast Mississippi Daily Journal* (26 October 1992), A12.

30. Distributed by Mississippi Republican Party/Victory '92.

31. *Northeast Mississippi Daily Journal* (30 October 1992), B6: *Jackson Clarion-Ledger* (2 November 1992), B1; *Starkville Daily News* (1 November 1992), A5.

32. *Jackson Clarion-Ledger* (28 October 1992), B3; (1 November 1992), B1; (2 November 1992), A4.

33. *Jackson Clarion-Ledger* (4 November 1992), A7; (5 November 1992), A7; *Northeast Mississippi Daily Journal* (10 November 1992), A10 (Guy Land column); *Party Lines: News of the Mississippi Republican Party* (November 1992), B1 (published by state Republican Party, Jackson, Miss.).

34. *Northeast Mississippi Daily Journal* (14 October 1992), A1.

35. See Stephen D. Shaffer, "Party and Electoral Politics in Mississippi," in *Mississippi Government and Politics: Modernizers Versus Traditionalists*, ed. Dale Krane and Stephen Shaffer (Lincoln: University of Nebraska Press, 1992), 90–91, for the demographic sources of public partisanship in the 1980s. A study of changes in public partisanship in the 1980s and the impact of Reaganism is provided in Stephen Shaffer, "Changing Party Politics in Mississippi," in *The South's New Politics: Realignment and Dealignment*, ed. Robert H. Swansbrough and David M. Brodsky (Columbia: University of South Carolina Press, 1988), 189–203.

36. *Northeast Mississippi Daily Journal* (5 November 1992), B3; (12 November 1992),

A8 (Bill Minor column); *Jackson Clarion-Ledger* (5 November 1992), A9; *USA Today* (5 November 1992), A9.

37. *Northeast Mississippi Daily Journal* (12 October 1992), B3; (24 October 1992), B1; (2 November 1992), A5, A12; (5 November 1992), A7; (6 November 1992), B3; *Jackson Clarion-Ledger* (23 September 1992), B1; (18 October 1992), 1; *Memphis Commercial Appeal* (13 June 1992), B8.

7

South Carolina: Republican Again

LAURENCE W. MORELAND

In 1992, many South Carolina Democrats thought they saw indications that the long presidential drought their party had endured might finally come to an end. True enough, they had entertained that same hope in 1988, only to see Michael Dukakis write the state off from the outset of the campaign and ultimately take less than 38 percent of the vote. But, in 1992, the political situation was different from the Reagan era, which had generated three straight presidential victories in the state, including two landslides; in 1992, two southerners—Bill Clinton and Al Gore—on the Democratic ticket, a vulnerable George Bush on the Republican ticket, and wild card H. Ross Perot on a third ticket all combined to conjure up prospects of a competitive race, perhaps even reversing the long trend of presidential Republicanism in the state. That trend was an impressive one: Beginning in 1964 (and excepting only 1976 when former Georgia Governor Jimmy Carter headed the Democratic ticket), South Carolina had voted Republican in presidential races with an almost certain regularity. In the process, South Carolina became part of the Republican presidential "lock" on the South, and, indeed, it emerged as one of the most Republican states in the country in terms of presidential politics. Thus, the cautious summer optimism of Democrats was countered by the Republican view that "if George Bush can't carry South Carolina, he can't win anywhere."

POLITICAL CONTEXT

Recent Party History

The state's recent political history has been a dynamic one.[1] Since the early 1960s, the Republican Party has evolved from an extraordinarily weak political organization to a highly competitive party; indeed, there is at least some prospect that the Republican Party might become the majority party in the state in the 1990s. Republican strength has been built primarily in the suburban areas of the state's metropolitan districts; twelve of the state's counties fall into Standard Metropolitan Statistical Areas (SMSAs), roughly centered on three clusters of cities: Charleston-North Charleston on the Atlantic coast, Columbia-Florence-Augusta stretching across the midlands, and Greenville-Spartanburg in the uplands. The Republicans have been less successful in penetrating the rural areas of the state—which are largely poor and much more heavily black than the suburban areas.

African Americans are concentrated in the central cities and in the rural areas of South Carolina and, as elsewhere in the nation, have continued to be overwhelmingly Democratic in their party identifications and voting patterns. Dukakis in 1988 generally carried black precincts with margins ranging from 90 to 95 percent. On the other hand, white South Carolinians, at least in presidential contests, largely deserted the Democratic Party in the 1980s: Walter Mondale in 1984 and Michael Dukakis in 1988 each carried only about 20 percent of the white vote (the Dukakis white vote may have slipped to as low as 7 or 8 percent in some counties).[2] At the presidential level, and increasingly so at lower levels, the result of these voting patterns has been that the party system has demonstrated a tendency to become more and more racially polarized.

In the 1980s, one consequence of factors such as an invigorated state Republican Party and highly popular Republican leaders such as Ronald Reagan, Governor Carroll Campbell, and U.S. Senator Strom Thurmond was that, along with Republican presidential voting, identification with the Republican Party surged among white South Carolinians (who constitute approximately 75 percent of registered voters). An August 1990 survey by Ayres and Associates, a Columbia polling firm, indicated that 54 percent of the whites identified themselves as Republicans, 31 percent as independents, and only 15 percent as Democrats. With regard to younger voters, the survey data suggested a forbidding future for the Democrats: Among registered voters eighteen to thirty-four years of age, only 7 percent of whites identified with the Democratic Party, compared with 64 percent identifying with the Republicans.[3]

The tendency toward racial polarization in the state has been accompanied by each of the parties becoming internally more ideologically homogeneous (particularly the Republicans) and externally more ideologically distinctive from the other party, at least at the organizational level. A survey of delegates to the 1992 state party conventions indicated that 96 percent of the Republicans described themselves as "conservative"; for the Democrats, 66 percent described themselves as "liberal" (with 14 percent describing themselves as "middle-of-the-road" and 21 percent as "conservative").[4]

Finally, many white South Carolina voters have continued to split their ballots between parties. In 1988, for example, Democratic U.S. Representative Liz Patterson was reelected to a second term in the Fourth Congressional District even though Republican George Bush easily carried the district with nearly 70 percent of the vote. At the state and local levels, a large bloc of whites—about 30 percent—have voted relatively independently, casting their votes for particular candidates without allegiance to either party. By the early 1990s, this group of white independents held the key to the direction the state's partisan politics would take.

The 1990 Elections

In 1990, incumbent Republican Governor Carroll Campbell (who, as the U.S. representative from the Fourth Congressional District, had won the governorship in 1986 with just 51 percent of the vote) scored a landslide victory (70 percent, carrying forty-three of the state's forty-six counties) over black state senator Theo Mitchell; Campbell's popularity had been such that potential Democratic candidates stronger than Mitchell had been frightened off. In addition to the governorship, Republicans in 1990 for the first time won three other statewide constitutional offices (secretary of state, agriculture commissioner, and super-intendent of education). In the General Assembly, Republicans obtained their highest proportions ever in each house (34 percent in the lower house and 24 percent in the upper house).

While the state's recent political history clearly favored the Republicans in 1992, political analysts were still unsure whether the increasing success of the Republican Party reflected only favorable short-term trends or whether it indi-cated that the Republican Party was on the brink of attaining a stable majority status.[5] Regardless of the answer to that question, at least in the short run, Republicans in the state clearly held the advantage as the 1992 campaign began.

THE CAMPAIGN

In recent South Carolina presidential politics, the real contest typically occurs in the presidential primaries rather than in the general election in November. The state's Democratic and Republican presidential primaries occur just before the South-wide Super Tuesday primaries and are therefore taken as something of a bellwether by the media. Candidates in both parties typically give the state a fairly high campaign priority in the hope of building the momentum that will propel them into the regional primaries just a few days later. Candidates, can-didates' wives, and various surrogates regularly visit the state during the primary season, and the state's presidential political scene has both vitality and visibility. On the other hand, the general election campaign—at least at the presidential level—has been a relatively quiet, uninteresting, almost invisible affair, partic-ularly in 1984 and 1988. The state's small number of electoral votes (eight) and its reliability as one of the strongest Republican presidential states in the nation both have militated against much campaign activity: The Democrats, sure to lose, and the Republicans, sure to win, both pass over South Carolina on their way to more competitive and more important venues.

In 1992, the presidential campaign surprisingly did not closely follow the 1984 and 1988 pattern. The Democrats, with their all-southern ticket, hoped that it might spark at least a partial return to the glory years of the Democratic Party in the South. To that end, the Clinton/Gore campaign targeted five southern states (Arkansas, Tennessee, Georgia, Louisiana, and North Carolina), but did not include South Carolina. However, in South Carolina as in Florida and Texas, the Democrats did develop a campaign strategy designed to take advantage of the uncertainties of 1992 (particularly the Perot factor) and to cause George Bush to spend time and money in an area that a Republican presidential candidate normally would be expected to have locked up long before. As *The Carolina Report* observed, "this year the Democrats have a coherent presidential election strategy for the first time in recent memory."[6] That strategy was predicated on stimulating a high black turnout and holding rural voters plus making sufficient inroads on Republican strength in the urban areas in order to eke out a narrow statewide victory or, at least, to compel the Bush campaign to utilize resources in the state rather than elsewhere. Thus it was that South Carolinians were treated to a real presidential campaign in 1992.

Both parties began the 1992 campaign in South Carolina with high expectations. Democrats met on August 1, shortly after the Democratic National Convention, to introduce the state presidential campaign leaders and to organize Clinton/Gore committees in each of the state's six congressional districts.[7] The number of participants (500) was said to stun party leaders. "This is a tremendous thrill," said Democratic U.S. Senator Fritz Hollings as he watched former Governor Dick Riley attempt to bring the boisterous crowd to order, adding that "Four years ago there weren't enough to create disorder." Dwight Drake, a perennial Democratic activist, added that in previous years Democrats could have met in a phone booth "with room to spare."[8] As for Bill Clinton, he was no stranger to South Carolina as for a number of years he had vacationed at Hilton Head Island during New Year's, and the state's Democrats had given his candidacy a big boost in the 1992 presidential primary with 63 percent of the vote.

But even with such unusual enthusiasm among Democrats, a month later the campaign got off to a rocky start when Clinton, in what was seen as an effort to attract the male southern white vote (the "Bubba vote"), made a campaign stop on September 7 at the Darlington 500 stock car races in Darlington, South Carolina. Although there were a few Clinton/Gore signs in the crowd of 95,000, Clinton was roundly booed: "the fans were overwhelmingly hostile, booing the candidate, making obscene gestures and shouting for him to go home."[9] Overhead, a small plane displayed a banner proclaiming "No Draft Dodger for President."

The Republicans were enthusiastic, too, about 1992. Although Pat Robertson's Christian Coalition was as active in South Carolina as in any state in the country, and therefore continued to pose a potential threat to the traditional leadership of the party at all levels, its rumblings were held in abeyance during the campaign. And while some, such as Lee Bandy (the best-known political columnist in the state), expected even South Carolina to be in play during the race,[10] Republicans remained confident. "I'll work a little harder initially. But it'll all come back the way it should," prophesied Warren Tompkins, former executive director of the South Carolina Republican Party and senior southern advisor to the Bush/ Quayle campaign.[11]

Early opinion surveys indicated that in South Carolina, like elsewhere, Bush had undergone a long slide in popular preference since the success of Desert Storm in the Persian Gulf. In December of 1991, a Mason-Dixon poll indicated that 60 percent of the voters preferred Bush; just 26 preferred Clinton. The Bush percentage dropped to 55 percent by February, to 50 percent by July, and to 49 percent by mid-September; at the same time, the Clinton percentage grew to 31 percent by February, 40 percent by July, and 41 percent by mid-September. Ross Perot's percentages varied between 10 and 19 percent, ending at their lowest point (10 percent) as the campaign began in September.[12]

While Clinton did not actually set foot on South Carolina soil after his appearance at the Darlington 500, he did campaign on October 27 in Augusta, Georgia at an amphitheater on the banks of the Savannah River, just across from South Carolina. Over 5,000 people attended the rally, where Clinton was introduced by Georgia Senator Sam Nunn.[13] Just a few days earlier (on October 23), Al Gore had appeared at a rally at the University of South Carolina in Columbia. State senator Isadore Lourie, one of Clinton's South Carolina campaign chairs, publicly remained highly optimistic, declaring the state "competitive" and noting that "It's the difference between gloom and joy for the Democratic party. I go by headquarters, and they got more people coming out there in one hour than we had in a month in Dukakis headquarters. I sense the electricity of the 1960 campaign. It gives me a feeling of uplift."[14]

George Bush also campaigned in the state (his fourth best in 1988) in the closing weeks before election day. On a two-day train trip (October 20 and 21) beginning in Georgia, traveling across upper South Carolina, and ending in North Carolina, Bush spent the night in Spartanburg, South Carolina. On arriving in Spartanburg, Bush headed to the local Waffle House restaurant to contend that electing Clinton "would turn the White House into the Waffle House."[15] At a rally at the Amtrak station, which attracted 15,000 (including professional wrestler Ric Flair, another bow to the Bubba vote in the state), Bush focused his attack on the theme he was to sound repeatedly during the closing weeks of the campaign: "Who do you trust to be leader of the Free World?"[16]

Ross Perot's South Carolina campaign was as it was elsewhere—one wholly limited to national television advertising and limited grassroots organizing through his United We Stand, America organization. However, in South Carolina—and the South generally—Perot failed to create as high a level of excitement as his candidacy elicited in other regions, particularly the West.

With Perot in the race, newspaper opinion polls during the campaign suggested a narrow victory for Bush—or, with a little luck, a *very* narrow win for Clinton. By early October, the *Columbia State* had Bush barely leading (41 percent for Bush, 39 percent for Clinton, 10 percent for Perot, and 10 percent for other candidates or undecided).[17] By late October, some polls showed Bush pulling away; *Greenville News*, for example, had Bush at 38.5 percent, Clinton at 30.7 percent, and Perot at 10.4 percent, with a large 16.9 percent undecided.[18] However, a *Charleston Post and Courier* poll conducted at the same time had the race as still very tight, with Bush at 41 percent, Clinton at 38 percent, and Perot at 8 percent, with 13 percent undecided.[19]

In 1992, South Carolina was Bush's to lose. Although the economy in the state lagged, the recession was not as severe as elsewhere. Unemployment, for example, was at 6.3 percent (and dropping) by October, less than the national average of 7.5 percent.[20] As election day approached, Democrats maintained hope for what would have to be seen (increasingly so) as a surprise victory; at the same time, Republicans knew that a Democratic victory in South Carolina could only signify a national Republican electoral disaster, and that did not seem likely.

RESULTS AND ANALYSIS

As in 1988 (when the state ranked forty-ninth of the fifty states), South Carolinians were among the least politically motivated in the nation. In 1992, 44.4 percent of South Carolinians of voting age actually voted. While this was an increase of more than 5 percent over 1988's 38.9 percent, it was still less than the national average of approximately 54 percent, leaving South Carolina once again in forty-ninth place (only Hawaii ranked lower). However, if only registered voters are considered, the percentage of those voting in the presidential race rose to over 80 percent.[21]

At over 1.5 million (75 percent white, 25 percent nonwhite), the number of registered voters in 1992 set a new record, rising over 90,000 from 1988; however, the number of blacks registered to vote dropped by 3,000. Among registered voters, whites (at 82.6 percent) had a higher presidential election turnout rate than blacks (at 75.1 percent). Black turnout—together with the drop in black registered voters—was therefore a blow to the Democratic strategy, which depended in large part on stimulating a very large black turnout.[22]

Analysis: The Presidential Race

In 1992, for the sixth time out of the last seven presidential elections, the Republican ticket carried South Carolina. While Bush's margin was substantially reduced from 1988, he nevertheless won comfortably—for a three-man race—by taking 48.0 percent of the vote, with Clinton at 39.9 percent and Perot at 11.5 percent. (See Table 7.1.) Despite energetic major party campaigns in South

Table 7.1

Results of 1992 South Carolina Presidential, Senatorial, and Congressional Elections

Candidate (Party)	Percent of Vote	Vote Totals
President		
Bush-Quayle (R)*	48.0	577,507
Clinton-Gore (D)	39.9	479,514
Perot-Stockdale	11.5	138,872
Marrou-Lord (L)	.2	2,719
Phillips-Knight (US)	.2	2,680
Fulani-Munoz (UC)	.1	1,235
Total Presidential Vote		1,202,527
U. S. Senator		
Hartnett (R)	46.9	554,175
Hollings (D)*	50.1	591,030
Johnson (L)	1.9	22,962
Clarkson (A)	1.0	11, 568
Write-in	.1	703
Total Senatorial Vote		1,180,438
U. S. House of Representatives		
First District		
Ravenel (R)*	66.1	121,938
Oberst (D)	32.5	59,908
Peeples (A)	1.4	2,608
Write-in	.1	95
Total District Vote		184,549
Second District		
Spence (R)*	87.6	148,667
Sommer (L)	12.3	20,816
Write-in	.1	187
Total District Vote		169,670
Third District		
Bland (R)	38.8	75,660
Derrick (D)*	61.1	119,119
Write-in	**	85
Total District Vote		194,864

Table 7.1 (continued)

Candidate (Party)	Percent of Vote	Vote Totals
Fourth District		
Inglis (R)	50.3	99,879
Patterson (D)*	47.5	94,182
Jorgensen (L)	2.2	4,286
Write-in	**	63
Total District Vote		198,410
Fifth District		
Horne (R)	38.7	70,866
Spratt (D)*	61.2	112,031
Write-in	.1	189
Total District Vote		183,086
Sixth District		
Chase (R)	34.7	64,149
Clyburn (D)	65.3	120,647
Write-in	**	75
Total District Vote		184,871

Key: * = incumbent; ** = less than 0.1 percent of the vote; R = Republican Party; D = Democratic Party; A = American Party; L = Libertarian Party; US = U. S. Taxpayers Party; UC = United Citizens Party. *Source*: Compiled by the author from data provided by the South Carolina State Election Commission (Columbia, South Carolina).

Carolina (particularly in October), the percentages for all three candidates were very close to those of a Mason-Dixon poll conducted in the state in mid-September.

Nationally, the Clinton/Gore ticket in 1992 performed only marginally differently from the Dukakis/Bentsen ticket in 1988, typically running only a few points ahead or behind the 1988 Democratic proportion of the vote for various demographic groups. Indeed, Clinton won the race with 43 percent of the vote nationally, 3 percent less than Dukakis obtained in his losing effort in 1988. The real story therefore is that Clinton did not win by attracting large numbers of new Democratic votes; instead, he won as a consequence of the enormous reduction (15 percent nationally) in Republican votes. As Rhodes Cook has put it, "Only rarely could Clinton attribute his victory to a surge in the Democrats' share of the vote. Rather, it came from a dramatic drop in Republican support, accompanied by a large vote for independent Ross Perot. These numbers suggest the Perot vote was carved almost exclusively out of Bush's hide."[23] Of course, in a straight two-man Clinton-Bush race, Clinton might still have won: The 10 percent increase in the number of voters over 1988, the dynamics of a Perot-less campaign, and other factors might have combined to result in a Clinton victory.

South Carolina in 1992 mirrored national trends, but with a twist consistent with the state's recent electoral behavior. As was the case nationally, the Bush proportion of the presidential vote dropped dramatically—by nearly 14 percent from 1988 (from 61.5 percent in 1988 to 48.0 percent in 1992). At the same time, the Democratic share of the vote rose only marginally, from 37.6 percent to 39.9 percent, just a little more than a 2 percent increase. The difference between South Carolina and much of the rest of the nation, however, lay in the fact that Republicans not only had been habitually winning the state in presidential elections, but also had begun winning it by very large margins. Therefore, even a 14 percent drop for Bush still allowed him to claim the state, albeit with a bit under 50 percent of the vote.

South Carolina in 1992 not only remained one of the strongest states for Republican presidential candidates, but also improved its position from being the Republicans' fourth best state in 1988 to being that party's second best state in 1992; only Mississippi, at 49.7 percent, exceeded the Republican percentage in South Carolina.

As in other states in the South, Ross Perot's appeal was less strong in South Carolina than in much of the rest of the nation. Although Perot won 19 percent of the vote nationally, he ran substantially less well in South Carolina (at 11.5 percent). Indeed, Perot's ten worst states were all in the South, and only five states had a lower Perot proportion of the vote than South Carolina. (On the other hand, South Carolina was the best state for Howard Phillips and the U.S. Taxpayers Party, although Phillips won only about 2,700 votes, 0.2 percent of the total.)[24]

Race. Data obtained through exit polling help to delineate the nature of the Bush victory. In terms of race, the 1992 election looked very much like 1984 and 1988, with nearly all blacks voting Democratic, but with only a fifth or so of the whites doing so. Exit polling by Voter Research and Surveys indicated that 91 percent of black South Carolinians supported Clinton, with 7 percent for Bush and 1 percent for Perot.[25] Whites, on the other hand, gave 60 percent of their votes to Bush, 14 percent to Perot, and just 26 percent to Clinton. Even though Clinton won only a quarter or so of the white vote, that percentage nevertheless represented an improvement over Michael Dukakis's approximately 20 percent in 1988.

The 1992 presidential election points up the continuing problem of South Carolina Democrats with race. On the one hand, the Clinton/Gore ticket attempted to attract white middle-class voters by focusing on mainstream economic problems and by distancing the ticket from blacks (emphasizing welfare reform and displaying a coolness toward Jesse Jackson are but two examples). This approach did not work in South Carolina: The Democrats' proportion of the white vote remained dismally small (and, at the same time, the ticket failed to stimulate black enthusiasm, at least as reflected by voter registration figures).

Gender. South Carolina represented something of an oddity in 1992, at least on the matter of gender. During the Reagan-Bush years, Democrats generally fared better among women than among men, creating what has become known as the gender gap. The 1992 presidential election continued this phenomenon, as Clinton did better nationally among women than among men (46 to 41 percent, with Bush winning 37 percent of women).[26] In South Carolina, however, the reverse occurred: Bush won 52 percent of the votes of women and 44 percent of the votes of men; Clinton won 40 percent of each group; and Perot, as nationally, did better among men than women (16 percent to 8 percent).[27] While it is not wholly clear why South Carolina women gave a majority of their votes to Bush, explanations center on the very substantial strength of the religious right in the state and on the social conservatism of many South Carolina women who continue to prefer traditional roles for both genders, particularly as both George Bush and Dan Quayle have defined them.[28]

Geography. Of the state's forty-six counties, Bush and Clinton each carried twenty-three. While Clinton improved on the Dukakis performance (he had carried only twelve), the Republicans continued their domination of the state's urban centers. Of the twelve metropolitan counties (counties identified as falling within SMSAs), eleven supported the Republican ticket. (See Table 7.2.) Only in Richland County (where Columbia, the state capital, is located) did Clinton score a victory over Bush in the urban corridors (Clinton won 50.5 percent of the Richland vote). Richland County was also Dukakis's best urban county in 1988 at a little over 47 percent; not surprisingly, Richland had a substantial percentage of nonwhite voters (34 percent), the highest in the twelve urban-corridor counties.

Republicans continued to be strongest in the vote-rich upcountry urban corridor, a group of five counties that accounted for over a quarter of all presidential votes cast in the state. Although less strong in the midlands and the lowcountry corridors, Bush nevertheless scored victories in both of them. Even though he lost the largest county (Richland) in the midlands corridor by almost 10 percent, Bush more than made up for it with his overwhelming win in suburban Lexington County, which is adjacent to Richland County and which has only a very small proportion of nonwhite voters (7 percent in 1992; only two counties in the state had lower percentages). Bush carried Lexingon with over 60 percent of the vote (Clinton won barely over a quarter), continuing Lexington's reputation as one of the most Republican counties in the Deep South.

The continuing weakness of the Democrats in the state's urban centers prevents them from being genuinely competitive. Inasmuch as the urban centers aggregately contain nearly two-thirds of the voters, Democrats—unless they improve the performance of their presidential ticket in the urban corridors—would have to carry the smaller counties by extraordinary proportions, beating the Republicans by an impossible margin of three to one, to have a chance of winning statewide.[29]

As with other recent presidential elections, the Democratic ticket performed well in the counties outside the urban corridors; these are largely rural counties which, for the most part, tend to be racially less white, and the Republicans have put less effort in organizing there. In 1992, of the thirty-four non-SMSA counties, Clinton won two-thirds of them (twenty-two); in these nonurban Clinton

Table 7.2
1992 Presidential Vote by County and by County Proportion of Total State Vote in South Carolina's Three Urban Corridors (in percent)

Corridor	Bush	Clinton	Perot	Other	Proportion of State Vote*
Lowcountry (Charleston) Urban Corridor					
Berkeley County	50.9	35.3	13.1	0.7	3.0
Charleston County	48.0	40.6	10.5	0.9	8.3
Dorchester County	53.5	32.7	13.0	0.8	2.3
Totals for Corridor	49.5	38.0	11.5	0.9	13.6
Midlands (Columbia) Urban Corridor					
Aiken County	55.0	31.6	12.9	0.5	3.9
Florence County	50.8	39.9	9.0	0.3	3.3
Lexington County	60.5	26.5	12.5	0.4	5.8
Richland County	41.2	50.5	7.5	0.9	8.9
Totals for Corridor	50.2	39.2	10.0	0.6	21.9
Upcountry (Greenville-Spartanburg) Urban Corridor					
Anderson County	51.7	33.5	14.5	0.3	4.0
Greenville County	57.1	30.4	12.0	0.4	9.5
Pickens County	57.7	28.1	14.0	0.3	2.5
Spartanburg County	51.9	35.1	12.3	0.7	6.1
York County	48.7	36.3	14.7	0.3	3.7
Totals for Corridor	53.9	32.6	13.0	0.5	25.8
All Urban Corridors	51.6	36.2	11.6	0.6	61.3

* Each figure in this column represents the percentage of the total number of votes cast in the county as a proportion of all votes cast in the state.
Source: Calculated by the author from 1992 election statistics provided by the South Carolina State Election Commission (Columbia, South Carolina).

counties, nineteen of them had voting populations (actual 1992 voters) at least 30 percent black.[30] On the other hand, Bush carried only two counties where the proportion of black voters exceeded 30 percent (Barnwell County, 31.4 percent black voters; and Sumter County, 37.5 percent nonwhite voters). In the twenty-two nonurban Clinton counties, his proportion of the vote ranged from 44.9 percent (Darlington County; 32.7 percent black voters) to 62.5 percent (Allendale County; 56.2 percent black voters).

Analysis: Other Races

In other races, the South Carolina Republican Party continued its steady growth. While Republicans have yet to gain a clear parity with the Democrats, they moved yet closer in 1992.

State Legislature. In the state legislature, Republicans gained four seats in the state senate so as to reduce the Democratic margin from thirty-four/twelve to thirty/sixteen. In the state house of representatives, Republicans gained six seats, reducing the Democratic advantage from seventy-nine/forty-four to seventy-three/fifty (with one independent). While the Republican Party remains the minority party in both houses of the state legislature, it has nevertheless continued its unbroken string of incremental successes begun in the mid–1960s.

Even though gaining on the Democrats, the Republicans still saw the 1992 state legislative elections as something of a disappointment: Reapportionment had theoretically offered the prospect of major gains, but only if districts were drawn so as to concentrate blacks in a small number of districts, thereby creating new white districts susceptible to being picked up by the Republicans. However, when the legislature and the governor reached a stalemate, the federal court imposed a reapportionment plan that protected incumbents of both parties rather than offering opportunities for much in the way of major shifts.[31]

U.S. House of Representatives. Prior to the 1992 elections, the state's House delegation consisted of four Democrats and two Republicans; five of the six ran for reelection. Four of the incumbents—Republican Arthur Ravenel (First District), Republican Floyd Spence (Second District, who faced only a Libertarian candidate), Democrat Butler Derrick (Third District), and Democrat John Spratt (Fifth District)—faced unknown and underfinanced challengers. All four won easily; while the Republicans had a very easy time of it (Ravenel won with 66 percent and Spence with 88 percent), the Democrats, too, were hardly threatened (each won with more than 61 percent). (See Table 7.1.)

The fifth incumbent, Democrat Liz Patterson of the Fourth District (Greenville-Spartanburg), was finishing her third term. Although the district was otherwise overwhelmingly Republican (the seat had been previously held by Carroll Campbell, the state's Republican governor, and was regarded by Republicans as rightly "theirs"), Patterson was a conservative Democrat (her father was the late U.S. Senator Olin Johnston), who had worked hard at cultivating the district through a conservative voting pattern and conscientious constituent service. For a Democrat to win in such circumstances would never be a foregone conclusion, but Patterson, a savvy politician, was expected to squeak by once more, just as she had in her three previous victories. Thus, her narrow loss in 1992 to thirty-three-year-old Greenville attorney Bob Inglis was the only real surprise in the state's election results (in losing, Patterson still ran almost 15 percentage points ahead of the Clinton/Gore ticket in the district).

Inglis, running for public office for the first time, mounted an unusual campaign: Rather than launching a head-on attack (which his polling indicated would be a mistake against a woman he described as "a nice lady"), his campaign embraced a "stealth" strategy. Use of hundreds of volunteers going door to door, distribution of thousands of door hangers comparing the views of the two candidates just before the election (including distribution at 700 churches), the support of the Christian Coalition, and some degree of complacency on the part of the Patterson campaign (Inglis permitted the idea to spread that he was out of money and therefore dead in the water, although that was not the case) all combined for an Inglis victory. After the election, Patterson was angry, contending that the door hangers contained false information, wrongly stating, for example, that she favored abortion on demand and homosexual rights and had no opinion on controlling taxes.[32]

The sixth incumbent was Sixth District Democrat Robin Tallon who, very reluctantly, retired in 1992. The court-imposed reapportionment plan for the state created a new congressional district out of the heart of Tallon's old district, but the new district was a black-majority one (as mandated by the Voting Rights Act). After announcing that he planned to run and then suddenly withdrawing from the race just fifteen minutes before the filing deadline, Tallon was finally out of the race for good. The new district, 58 percent black, is a sprawling one, stretching from the North Carolina line almost all the way to Georgia and picking up along the way parts of Florence, Columbia, and Charleston. Jim Clyburn, state human affairs commissioner and one of the state's best-known and respected black politicians, easily won both the Democratic primary and the general election. His white opponent, little-known Florence city councilman and tax attorney John Chase, was largely cut off by the Republican establishment, who feared that a real race in the district by a white Republican might stimulate very large numbers of black voters, perhaps threatening Bush's chances and certainly making life more difficult for the party's U.S. Senate candidate.[33]

U.S. Senate. Aside from the presidency, the other statewide race in 1992 was the bid for reelection of the state's junior senator, Ernest F. (''Fritz'') Hollings. (The state's *very* senior senator is the legendary Strom Thurmond, born in 1902, who has served in the Senate since 1954 and who has given every indication of running for reelection in 1996.) Hollings, seventy years old and a twenty-six-year veteran in the Senate (modest accomplishments by Thurmond standards), was opposed by Tommy Hartnett, a former three-term congressman from Charleston. Hartnett had left the House of Representatives in 1986 to run for lieutenant governor as Carroll Campbell's running mate, but had lost that race (Campbell, of course, was elected to his first term as governor).

Regarded by Republicans as one of the most vulnerable Democratic senators in 1992, Hollings was weakened not only by the increasingly Republican leanings of the South Carolina electorate, but also by his vote against Desert Storm. Although not a strong candidate, Hartnett nevertheless received very substantial national Republican support and campaign direction as he sought to make an issue of Hollings's long-time incumbency; his endlessly repeated campaign slogan was ''if you want to change the Senate, ya gotta change the senator.'' In turn, Hollings tried to position himself as a Washington outsider fighting for taxpayers, not an easy task for a five-term incumbent; in his television ads, he complained that ''If those boys up in Washington cared half as much about your checkbook as they do their own, we could get this country moving again.'' In what for most observers was the nastiest campaign that South Carolina has seen

in living memory,[34] Hollings won an extraordinarily close race, winning just
50.1 percent (his weakest performance ever). The closeness of the race suggested
to many that if the Republicans could have persuaded popular GOP Governor
Campbell to have taken on Hollings, the outcome might have been very different.
Hollings squeaked out his victory by carrying all but five of the nonurban corridor
counties, by adding to them two of the largest of the twelve urban counties
(Charleston and Richland), and by running better than Clinton in the other urban
counties.

CONCLUSION

The 1992 elections held few surprises in South Carolina. The state voted once
again for the Republican presidential nominee despite, for the first time since
1980, a genuine Democratic campaign. The Clinton/Gore ticket was able to build
only marginally on the Dukakis showing of 1988 even though Dukakis had
conceded the state from the very beginning. In other races, too, the Republicans
either held their own or continued to show growing strength.

Despite two southerners on the Democratic ticket and the subsequent loss to
the Republicans of four southern states (Arkansas, Tennessee, Louisiana, and
Georgia), the South in 1992 retained its position as the Republican presidential
base, providing two-thirds of Republican electoral votes. In that context, South
Carolina has emerged as one of the most dependable anchors for that base.

The Democrats have been unable to staunch the hemorrhaging—the flight of
white voters—that has hurt them so badly in presidential races. In 1992, George
Bush was a wounded candidate, yet he still managed to attract twice as many
white votes as Bill Clinton did. This fact does not bode well for the Democratic
Party as the erosion of white voters, begun in the 1960s at the presidential level,
continues to move downward through other offices, particularly in the urban
counties. On the other hand, while the unexpected loss of a U.S. House seat
was a disappointment, Democrats did succeed in retaining their U.S. Senate
seat, albeit by a very narrow margin, and the victory of Jim Clyburn as the
state's first black member of Congress in modern times made South Carolina
political history.

While the Republicans have much to be pleased about, they, too, have their
problems. The religious right, which rumbled intermittently during the Bush
years, has begun to exert real strength within the state's Republican Party. Pat
Robertson's Christian Coalition is as well organized in South Carolina as anywhere, and its appetite is growing. Following the Bush defeat, Christian Coalition
supporters flocked to Republican precinct meetings in the early spring of 1993,
obtaining a majority of the delegates to the party's May convention. Growing
friction between traditional Republicans and the religious right within the party
led the retiring party chair, Barry Wynn, to call for a truce and a lowering of
voices as he urged a search for compromise on divisive issues such as abortion.
Wynn also called for Governor Campbell to use his influence and stature with

both groups to bridge the gap; otherwise, he contended, the party might well lose the governorship in 1994 when Campbell finishes his second (and last) term.[35] At the May convention itself (where Kansas Senator and potential 1996 GOP presidential candidate Bob Dole gave the keynote speech, urging unity), the Christian Coalition succeeded in sweeping the party's top offices, including state chair.[36] Wynn reacted by characterizing the Christian right takeover as the triumph of intolerance and as "un-Republican and un-American"; he urged his friends to forego contributions to the state Republican Party as long as it was controlled by the religious right (instead, he suggested contributions to individual candidates).[37] In this struggle for control of the state party, abortion continues to be both a key issue and a potent symbol. For example, among Republican Party activists at the 1992 state convention, about a third opposed the Christian Coalition's hard-line abortion position.[38]

Despite at least the appearance of internal divisions within his party, Governor Campbell has refrained from publicly taking sides and has dismissed conflict between traditional Republicans and the Christian Coalition as natural for an expanding party: "You go through growing pains like this and there's going to be conflict. That's part of the process."[39] Others, such as Furman University political scientist (and expert on the religious right) James Guth, agree: "after a few months, most of these people will be working together very well. The controversy won't have as negative an impact as some Democratic commentators would have us believe. The Christian right and regulars have gotten along better in South Carolina than in most other places."[40]

The mid–1990s should clarify, perhaps decisively, the future of South Carolina partisan politics. If the Republicans overcome their internal differences regarding the role of the Christian right, hold the governorship (with former state representative David Beasley, supported by those around Governor Campbell as well as by the Christian Coalition, or with folksy, moderate Congressman Arthur Ravenel as the likely nominee), and make further gains in the legislature, they will be on the way to becoming the majority party, almost certainly so by the end of the decade. On the other hand, if the Republicans quarrel rancorously among themselves over the social issues pushed by the religious right and if the Democrats regain the governorship with likely nominee Lieutenant Governor Mike Daniel or Charleston Mayor Joseph P. Riley, Jr., the Democrats may yet be able to breathe new life into a party that has increasingly faced hard times. But, of course, one factor is beyond the control of either Democrats or Republicans in the state, as each party—directly for the Democrats, inversely for the Republicans—may well suffer or prosper as the Clinton/Gore administration suffers or prospers.

NOTES

1. For a summary of the state's political history, see Robert P. Steed, Laurence W. Moreland, and Tod A. Baker, "South Carolina Party System: Towards a Two-Party

System," in *Government in the Palmetto State: Toward the 21st Century*, ed. Luther F. Carter and David S. Mann (Columbia: Institute of Public Affairs, University of South Carolina, 1992), 25–42; see also Laurence W. Moreland, Robert P. Steed, and Tod A. Baker, "South Carolina: Different Cast, Same Drama in the Palmetto State" in *The 1988 Presidential Election in the South: Continuity Amidst Change in Southern Party Politics*, ed. Laurence W. Moreland, Robert P. Steed, and Tod A. Baker (New York: Praeger, 1991), 119–140; and Laurence W. Moreland, Robert P. Steed, and Tod A. Baker, "South Carolina," in *The 1984 Presidential Election in the South: Patterns of Southern Party Politics*, ed. Robert P. Steed, Laurence W. Moreland, and Tod A. Baker (New York: Praeger, 1986), 123–156.

2. Moreland, Steed, and Baker, "South Carolina: Different Cast, Same Drama," 132.

3. For a general discussion of these surveys and other data, see Glen T. Broach, "Electoral Politics in South Carolina: The Changing Landscape" (Paper presented at the 1991 Annual Meeting of the South Carolina Political Science Association, Charleston, S.C., 20 April 1991).

4. Laurence W. Moreland, "Party Activists and State Parties in South Carolina: An Issue and Ideological Profile" (Paper presented at the 1992 Annual Meeting of the Northeastern Political Science Association, Providence, R.I., 12–14 November 1992).

5. Broach, for example, argues that despite the recent success of Republicans at the presidential level, continued Democratic strength in congressional and state and local elections should caution against the conclusion that there has been a realignment of voters' basic allegiances in favor of the Republicans. Instead it would be safer to speak of dealignment, where party preference means much less to the voter's choice in elections. Clearly South Carolina is not immune from these national trends and the re-election of most incumbent Democrats to the General Assembly in 1990 despite Campbell's landslide victory suggests that the same forces are at work in the Palmetto state (Broach, "Electoral Politics in South Carolina," 7).

6. *The Carolina Report* 7, no. 7 (19 September 1992): 1. *The Carolina Report* is edited by Glen Broach, professor of political science at Winthrop University (Rock Hill, S.C.) and is published monthly as a commentary on the state's politics.

7. "Clinton Rallies Party," *Columbia State* (2 August 1992), 1-B. *State*, published in Columbia (the state capital), offers the best political coverage of state politics of any newspaper in the state.

8. Both the Hollings and the Drake quotations are from "Clinton Rallies Party," *Columbia State* (2 August 1992), 1-B.

9. "Race Crowd Boos Clinton," *Charleston Post and Courier* (7 September 1992), 1-A.

10. Lee Bandy, "How Clinton Can Win S.C.," *Columbia State* (19 July 1992), 4-D.

11. *Columbia State* (19 July 1992), 4-D.

12. These Mason-Dixon polls were reported in "Bush Keeps S.C. Hold Despite Slip," *Charleston Post and Courier* (25 September 1992), 1-A.

13. "Clinton Courts Swing Vote," *Columbia State* (28 October 1992), 1-A.

14. "Gore Tires to Reclaim S.C.'s Vote," *Columbia State* (24 October 1992), 1-A.

15. "Riddles, Waffles on Bush's Menu," *Columbia State* (22 October 1992), 1-A.

16. "Bush Rides Rails for Southern Votes," *Charleston Post and Courier* (21 October 1992), 1-A, 9-A.

17. "Poll: Race Too Close to Call in S.C.," *Columbia State* (2 October 1992), 1-A.

18. *The Greenville News* (25 October 1992), 1-A.

19. "Bush's S.C. Lead in Danger," *Charleston Post and Courier* (27 October 1992), 1-A.

20. "Jobless Rate Dips in S.C.," *Columbia State* (28 October 1992), 7-B.

21. The percentage voting of the voting-age population was calculated by the Committee for the Study of the American Electorate, reported in the *Charleston Post and Courier* (5 November 1992), 1-B. The percentage voting of the registered voters was calculated from data provided by the South Carolina State Election Commission in Columbia.

22. These statistics were calculated from data provided by the South Carolina State Election Commission. South Carolina is one of the few states that maintain data on both registration and voting by race. See also *The Carolina Report* 7, no. 10 (14 November 1992): 1.

23. Rhodes Cook, "Republicans Suffer a Knockout That Leaves Clinton Standing," *Congressional Quarterly Weekly Report* 50, no. 49 (12 December 1992): 3810.

24. *Congressional Quarterly Weekly Report*, 51, no. 4 (23 January 1993): 191.

25. Reported in "White Voters Gave Bush His S.C. Win," *Charleston Post and Courier* (6 November 1992), 1-A.

26. Voter Research and Surveys exit poll, reported in "Bush Won S.C. Women," *Columbia State* (8 November 1992), 1-A.

27. "Bush Won S.C. Women," 1-A.

28. "Bush Won S.C. Women," 1-A, 15-A.

29. Democratic pollster Harrison Hickman, in a memo dated 20 November 1992 and prepared for the state's Democrats, in Lee Bandy, "A Dose of Reality for the Democrats," *Columbia State* (24 January 1993), 4-D. Even beyond the urban centers, Bush carried sixteen of the state's twenty most populous counties.

30. Statistics were calculated from data provided by the South Carolina State Election Commission in Columbia. As noted above, South Carolina is one of the few states that maintains not only registration data, but also voting data by race.

31. See Glen T. Broach, Philip H. Jos, and David S. Mann, "The General Assembly," in *Government in the Palmetto State: Toward the 21st Century*, ed. Luther F. Carter and David S. Mann (Columbia: Institute of Public Affairs, University of South Carolina, 1992), 82–84.

32. See "Shoe Leather, Secrecy, Christian Coalition Helped" and "Congresswoman Calls Tactics Irresponsible," *Greenville News* (5 November 1992), 1-A, 7-A.

33. "Tallon Abandons 6th District Race," *Columbia State* (26 June 1992), 1-A.

34. See "Hollings, Hartnett Ads Fling Accusations," *Columbia State* (28 October 1992), 1-B. For example, a Hartnett television ad contended that Hollings favored hiring quotas for gays. Hartnett eventually apologized for the ad—not to Hollings, but to homosexuals. See "Hartnett Apologizes to Gays over Ad," *Charleston Post and Courier* (24 October 1992), 1-A.

35. See "GOP Chief: Campbell Can Be Party 'Glue,' " *Columbia State* (23 April 1993), 3-B. See also "Abortion Shadows the GOP," *Columbia State* (3 May 1992), 1-B.

36. "Christian Right Wins State GOP," *Columbia State* (9 May 1993), 1-A. Repub-

lican Party Executive Director Mike Burton immediately resigned and cleaned out his desk upon election of the new Christian-Coalition-sponsored state chair, Henry McMaster.

37. "Withhold GOP Funds, Wynn Asks," *Charleston Post and Courier* (20 May 1993), 3-B. See also "Christian Right Doesn't Own State GOP, McMaster Says," *Columbia State* (20 May 1993), 1-B. Henry McMaster is the state Republican chair, newly elected with heavy Christian right support.

38. A survey of delegates to the 1992 state Republican convention indicated that 35 percent opposed a constitutional amendment to prohibit abortion, a key plank of the Christian right. Moreland, "Party Activists and State Parties in South Carolina."

39. Quoted in "GOP's Religious Right Might Rule Convention," *Columbia State* (8 May 1993), 1-B, 2-B.

40. Quoted in "GOP's Religious Right Might Rule Convention," 1-B, 2-B.

PART III

ELECTIONS IN THE RIM SOUTH

8

Arkansas: Ground Zero in the Presidential Race

DIANE D. BLAIR

The 1992 presidential election in Arkansas was so atypical an event that it may offer little reliable insight into the present and future political reality of Arkansas. With only six electoral votes, Arkansas had never previously been a significant presidential battleground. Candidates typically swung through Arkansas on the way to states with more primary delegates and richer electoral vote lodes, often making their obligatory single stop in Texarkana where the media coverage would reach Texas as well as Arkansas. Furthermore, although its conversion from solidly Democratic to reliably Republican in presidential contests came later than elsewhere in the South, three straight Republican victories in the 1980s (48 percent for Reagan in 1980, 61 percent for Reagan in 1984, and 56 percent for Bush in 1988) seemed to confirm its new coloration: reliably Republican rather than enticingly undecided.[1]

When Arkansas Governor Bill Clinton announced his bid for the Democratic nomination on October 3, 1991, in a highly produced event on the grounds of the Old State House in Little Rock, what had become the state's steady trajectory toward solid presidential Republicanism was thrown askew. It was by no means certain at the outset, however, what the ultimate consequences of the Clinton bid would be. In June 1991, a hypothetical match between President Bush and Governor Clinton produced overwhelming preference for Bush over Clinton, 65 to 27 percent, and Bush's favorable job performance rating seemed an impregnable 81 percent. An October 1991 poll taken immediately after Clinton's presidential announcement showed that Bush's lead had narrowed significantly, but the president was still favored 53 percent to Clinton's 40 percent in Arkansas.[2]

Further shadowing Clinton's potential presidential bid was a pledge he had made during a televised debate with Republican gubernatorial candidate Sheffield Nelson in the 1990 contest. When asked if elected for a fifth time whether he would pledge to serve the full term and not run for president, he had responded: "You bet. I told you when I announced for governor . . . and that's what I'm gonna do. I'm gonna serve four years. I made that decision when I decided to run."[3] So conscious was Clinton of that promise that he came close to passing up the presidential contest in 1992, even when he recognized that the absence of better-known party heavyweights provided an opening for a relatively unknown candidate from a small state to secure the nomination. Finally, however, he was persuaded that it was primarily his backers (rather than his perennial opponents) who had the right to either hold him to or release him from that pledge, and a series of meetings with those supporters around the state in August 1991 gave Clinton the psychological freedom to go forward. Interestingly, it was clear from the various scenarios sketched by Clinton at those meetings that he originally viewed this race primarily as a way to "escape obscurity" if he were ever to make a serious future bid for the presidency. Only laughingly did he tell his Fayetteville, Arkansas, audience, "I might mess around and win this thing."[4]

As developing events (Clinton's victory in the December Florida straw poll, Governor Mario Cuomo's announcement of noncandidacy, increasing attention to Clinton from the national media, and especially stronger signs of Bush's vulnerability) changed both the nature and the perception of Clinton's candidacy from a "positioning for the future" race to a serious quest for the presidency, Arkansans became increasingly excited and attentive. A home-state presidential candidate always ensures above-average news coverage and citizen interest. Several factors, however, guaranteed that the Clinton candidacy would be a dominating attention-getter in Arkansas throughout 1992.

First, what might have been a medium-sized story in a large state was a huge story in a small state. Little Rock television now reaches almost all of the state's population, and all its stations featured daily coverage of Clinton's election-related appearances and statements. Arkansas's only remaining statewide daily, the *Arkansas Democrat-Gazette*, was equally lavish in its coverage. Attention, it should be emphasized, does not equate with support; indeed, on a regular basis the editor (Paul Greenberg) and major columnists (John Robert Starr and Meridith Oakley) of the paper, which took over the venerable (and traditionally Democratic and pro-Clinton) *Arkansas Gazette* three days after Clinton announced his presidential candidacy, produced reams of anti-Clinton stories and commentary—and constant calls for his resignation. Still, Arkansas got an enormous daily dose of presidential politics for more than a year.

Second, the intensely personal nature of Arkansas politics meant that thousands of people felt intimately involved with the campaign, as though they were riding the campaign roller coaster with Clinton. Long before the national media began noticing and writing about FOBs (Friends of Bill, the nationwide network of school friends and other personal and political acquaintances that Clinton has attracted and cultivated over the years), thousands and thousands of Arkansans had developed a genuine personal relationship with Bill and Hillary Clinton. (A former Clinton chief of staff has estimated that more than half the people in Arkansas had met him personally.[5]) When the personal attacks on the Clintons began in earnest (charges of marital wrongdoing in January, charges of draft evasion in February, highly unflattering portraits of Hillary in March, insinuations of financial impropriety and self-dealing on both their parts), the Clintons' numerous Arkansas backers reacted with the outraged intensity of a family rallying around an unjustly accused member.

First a few, but eventually hundreds of Arkansans paid their own way, first to New Hampshire and ultimately to other states as well, to personally tell the "true" story of Bill and Hillary Clinton, to give witness to the Clintons' love for each other and their devotion to the well-being of Arkansas, and to buoy the spirits of the battered candidate. Hundreds of Arkansans who could not personally trek to New Hampshire took out a full-page ad listing their names and phone numbers in New Hampshire newspapers, offering to answer any questions asked. The Arkansas financial contribution was equally extraordinary, eventually ranking first in per capita contributions to presidential candidates in the 1992 cycle.[6] Furthermore, thousands of Arkansans volunteered, some on what became a nearly permanent basis, at Clinton's ever-expanding Little Rock headquarters, and each new round of Clinton bashing produced a new wave of angry pro-Clinton Arkansas activists.

Finally, as the campaign progressed, it became increasingly clear to the people of Arkansas that it was they themselves—their state, their lifestyle, their economic well-being, their educational attainments, their environment, indeed their intelligence in consistently reelecting Clinton—that was being questioned. Presumably, the citizens of any state would arise in patriotic defense against perceived slurs from "strangers," but for Arkansans, the slights, which began in the primary and then escalated into a major campaign theme in the general election, reopened sensitive psychic wounds of long duration. Arkansans are acutely aware of, and highly resentful and defensive about, the state's longstanding national reputation for poverty, provincialism, and general backwardness. The 1992 story, then, becomes the story not only of the presidential election *in* Arkansas, but also of the presidential election *about* Arkansas. For that reason, its telling needs the talents of a journalist or dramatist more than the analytical skills of a political scientist; but for the record, here is what happened and what it seems to suggest about contemporary politics in Arkansas.

THE PRIMARY NONCONTESTS

After its disastrous experiment with a caucus system in 1984, the Arkansas state legislature mandated a return to a presidential preferential primary for 1988 and simultaneously authorized Arkansas's participation in the common Super Tuesday date. While the preferential primary method was retained for 1992, Super Tuesday participation was not. To avoid the additional expense of a statewide primary for presidential candidacies only, Arkansas had pushed up the

Table 8.1
Presidential Primary Results in Arkansas

Candidate	Democratic Primary		Republican Primary	
	Vote	Percent	Vote	Percent
Jerry Brown	55,543	1 1	na	na
Bill Clinton	341,401	6 8	na	na
Lyndon LaRouche	14,126	3	na	na
Uncommitted	91,060	1 8		
Patrick Buchanan	na	na	6,568	1 3
George Bush	na	na	45,729	8 7

Source: Compiled by the author from 1992 *Arkansas Election Returns* (published biennially by the Arkansas Secretary of State, Little Rock).

date of its regular primary contest by nearly three months in 1988, but Democratic lawmakers were not satisfied with the outcome. The earlier primary meant decisions on filing had to be made early, back in December. Furthermore, the lack of significant statewide contests in the Democratic primary (since the governor and other elected officials now seek four-year terms in nonpresidential off years) had facilitated record turnout in the Republican primary. Hence, in March 1989, the Democrat-dominated state legislature mandated a return to the fourth Tuesday in May for state primaries, including the presidential preferential.[7]

There was never much doubt about the outcome in either the Republican or the Democratic presidential primary contest in 1992 in Arkansas. Whatever support Buchanan might have gotten at an earlier date had begun to dissipate by the time of the May 26 primary. Although Bush did not personally appear in Arkansas to campaign for his renomination, by late May Buchanan's race had run out of steam, and Bush easily carried all seventy-five counties with a decisive 87 percent of the Republican primary vote.

As for the Democrats, in a typically quixotic gesture, Jerry Brown made a campaign swing through Arkansas the week before the primary, addressing a Vietnam veterans group, calling attention to Arkansas poverty, and declaring the state an "environmental disaster."[8] The gesture received considerable media attention in Arkansas, but ultimately few votes. A Mason-Dixon poll taken the week before the primary indicated 71 percent of likely Democratic voters had a negative view of Brown, compared with 13 percent with a negative view of Clinton, and this assessment was closely reflected in the primary outcome, displayed in Table 8.1.[9] Interestingly, this poll, conducted 18–19 May, 1992, indicated that since June 1991, when Bush led Clinton by 65 to 27 percent, Bush had dropped 25 percent while Clinton had gained 23 percent to lead Bush 50 to 40 percent. In a match-up including Perot, Clinton dropped 9 percent,

Table 8.2
Primary Voter Turnout in Arkansas in Presidential Election Years, 1976–1992

Year	Democratic Primary	Republican Primary
1976	525,968	22,797
1980	415,406	8,177
1984	492,321	19,040
1988	497,506	68,305
1992	502,130	52,297

Source: Compiled by the author from 1992 *Arkansas Election Returns* (published biennially by the Arkansas Secretary of State, Little Rock).

primarily in the southwest area of Perot's boyhood, while Bush lost 12 percent, primarily in the northwest Arkansas area of his greatest strength.

While Bush's margin was the greatest ever received in Arkansas by a candidate in the Republican presidential primary, the Democratic primary suggested that not all of Clinton's home state, not even all Arkansas Democrats, enthusiastically embraced his candidacy. Still, Clinton's 68 percent was the biggest majority he had received in a Democratic primary since his 69 percent vote when he sought renomination for the governorship in 1980, and it was considerably better than his 54 percent Democratic primary win in 1990. Also, as Table 8.2 demonstrates, the steady upward trend in Republican primary voting had been, at least temporarily, halted. Furthermore, Republican numbers were still heavily concentrated in places of previous strength: Over three-fourths of the Republican primary vote came from the northwest Third Congressional District and from the state's most urban Pulaski County. In thirty-nine of Arkansas's seventy-five counties, fewer than 100 votes were cast in the Republican primary.

The lackadaisical Republican turnout was not for want of contests. There was in fact a sharp contest for the Republican nomination to challenge Democratic Senator Dale Bumpers for his seat, as well as a free-for-all in the increasingly Republican northwest Third Congressional District to succeed thirteen-term Republican Congressman John Paul Hammerschmidt. In both instances, the candidate with the strongest ties to the religious right won: Mike Huckabee, a Baptist minister, won the Senate nomination, and Tim Hutchinson, a graduate of Bob Jones University, founder of a Christian school, and also a Baptist minister, won the House nomination.

It was the Democratic primary that produced the sharpest clashes and biggest surprises, however. For the U.S. Senate, incumbent Dale Bumpers had no trouble securing a decisive 69 percent victory over State Auditor Julia Hughes Jones, a surprise candidate. Even in the "Year of the Woman," Jones drew little support from either the state Democratic organization or women's groups, who gave Bumpers high marks as a supportive senator. However, twelve-term Congressman Bill Alexander, revealed earlier to be among the top ten overdraft offenders, was trounced (40 to 60 percent) by political novice Blanche Lambert in eastern Arkansas's First Congressional District; and seven-term Congressman Beryl Anthony, member of the House Ways and Means Committee and former chair of the Democratic Congressional Campaign Committee, also slightly tainted by overdrafts and heavily opposed by both the state AFL-CIO and the National Rifle Association, was forced into a runoff where he was defeated by Secretary of State Bill McCuen. Only freshman Congressman Ray Thornton in central Arkansas's Second Congressional District was unopposed, meaning that regardless of the general election outcomes, Thornton would be the most senior member of the House delegation in the Congress.[10] For Arkansas, which once specialized in congressional seniority, this was a revolution indeed.

ARKANSAS IN THE SPOTLIGHT: THE CONVENTIONS

Arkansas's delegations to both the Democratic and the Republican National Conventions received extraordinary amounts of attention. Both arrived at their respective sites wearing buttons proclaiming "I'm from Arkansas, Ask Me About My Governor," but they did so with different motives and responded quite differently when asked.

For the Democrats, New York City provided unending opportunities to proclaim Clinton's accomplishments and attest to his personal virtues. Members of the Arkansas delegation happily found themselves feted at parties and featured in the news, and they, along with the "Arkansas travelers," were systematically employed by the Clinton campaign as "Arkansas ambassadors" to reach out to other state delegations and help build enthusiasm for the Clinton candidacy. It was with the travelers that the Clinton family, watching television in the Cellar Grill at Macy's, awaited the final delegate count, emotionally celebrated the outcome, and then strode as a group to the nearby convention hall to accept the nomination.

Earlier that week, on the eve of the Democratic convention's opening, Republican Chair Rich Bond held a press conference at which he announced that Clinton's record as governor of Arkansas (rather than questions of personal character) would be the attack focus of the fall campaign, used the phrase "failed governor of a small state" several dozen times, and listed Arkansas's low rankings in health, poverty, the environment, and other measures.[11] Governor Clinton responded strongly in his acceptance speech, bringing especially loud cheers from the Arkansas delegation at the foot of the podium when he thundered: "We took one of the poorest states in America and lifted it up. So I say to all of those in this campaign season who would criticize Arkansas, come on down, especially if you're from Washington."[12] Truly, there was never a finer time to be a Democrat from Arkansas. The decision to keep the national headquarters of the Clinton/Gore campaign in Little Rock, a decision made by Bill and Hillary Clinton against the advice of all their senior staff, further enhanced state pride and produced much favorable press about the economic boon that Clinton's candidacy was providing to Arkansas.

For the Republican delegation in Houston, the Arkansas connection was much more problematic. Bashing Bill Clinton could be done easily and enthusiastically. For example, the Sebastian County Republicans sold T-shirts reading "1992 Platform: Gennifer Flowers—NOT; Dodge the Draft—NOT; Smoke Dope (Inhale)—NOT; Eat Hillary's Cookies—NOT; Bill (Slick Willie) Clinton!" Arkansas Republicans also sold buttons reading "Smile If You Had an Affair with Bill Clinton" and cheerfully gave press interviews about Clinton's various sins of omission and commission during his five gubernatorial terms.[13]

When the convention began bashing not Clinton, but Arkansas, however, their cheer turned to concern as Wyoming Senator Alan Simpson described how Clinton had driven "Arkansas into the ground" and as keynote speaker Senator Phil Gramm of Texas derided Arkansas's fiftieth ranking in income, environmental policy, and law enforcement funding. The widely worn political button proclaiming Clinton to be the "Failed Governor of a Small State" was *not* popular in the Arkansas delegation. "That's not one of the best ones," stated Asa Hutchinson, co-chair of the state Republican Party, whose brother Tim, Republican nominee for the Third Congressional District seat, decided to skip the convention altogether.[14]

Some Arkansas Republicans attempted to distinguish between the state (many began wearing buttons saying "Arkansas Pride") and the governor or attributed its low rankings exclusively to him. Sheffield Nelson, the other Republican co-chair (and Clinton's gubernatorial opponent in 1990) made the distinction as follows: "I don't like the idea they're running down Arkansas, either. It's hard to leave the state alone when its indicative of the job that Clinton has done, but it's more an indictment against Clinton than it is Arkansas."[15] Even the most ardent Republicans, however, winced and objected when Marilyn Quayle, speaking to the Texas delegation, rhetorically asked, "Do we want our country to look like Arkansas?" (That her later apology, written as a letter to the editor of the *Arkansas Democrat-Gazette*, was inadvertently addressed to Little Rock, Arizona, prompted memories of President Bush's earlier gaffe referring to Arkansas as a place located somewhere between Texas and Oklahoma.)[16]

A "truth squad" led by Clinton's former Chief of Staff Betsey Wright held daily press conferences in Houston challenging the accuracy of the anti-Arkansas assertions, and the Clinton rapid response team issued a constant stream of rebuttals. Nonetheless, the hits on Arkansas continued as a major component of the Republican's fall campaign—a component that did not advance the party's electoral chances in Arkansas.

THE CAMPAIGN: "LOWEST OF THE LOW"

The first Republican surrogates to appear in Arkansas after the Houston convention, Senators Bob Dole (Kansas) and Don Nickles (Oklahoma) steered away from the Arkansas bashing, apparently at the behest of embarrassed Arkansas Republicans, and instead carefully lauded the state as "a great state with great people."[17] However, on September 16, three Republican heavy-hitters—Lynn Martin, secretary of labor; Sam Skinner, general chair of the Republican National Committee; and Michael Deland, chair of the Council on Environmental Quality—accepted the invitation to "Come on down" and see how Clinton had "lifted" the state. They came armed with a battery of statistics indicating Arkansas's low national rankings in health care, children's issues, crime, the environment, and education.

The invasion, however, turned into a rout. At each of their stops, well-prepared Clinton supporters and operatives far outnumbered the Republican contingent; ensured equal television time for their pro-Clinton, pro-Arkansas message; and distributed press packets challenging the Republicans' grim data and offering positives in their place about Arkansas's nation-leading job and income growth. At the Republicans' first press conference on the grounds of the State Capitol, Betsey Wright outmaneuvered former Republican Governor Frank White for control of the microphone and rebuked the "outsiders" for disparaging the people of Arkansas with their critical remarks.

At the second stop, in Pine Bluff, local citizens—including the Republican candidate for Congress, who had not been advised in advance of the visitation and was clearly unhappy with it—strongly advised the interlopers of their resentment. The Pine Bluff mayor heatedly explained to the national press that the Republican-selected news conference site, in front of what appeared to be a dilapidated building, was in fact a restoration project of an old theater scheduled to reopen as a performing arts center in two years. Some African Americans who had been lined up to recount their difficulties in obtaining financing from area banks dutifully did so, but also assured the national press that they did not blame Clinton for their fruitless efforts and that they in fact had always supported the governor and planned to support him for president.[18]

A foray into northwest Arkansas the following day, designed to compare the water quality in Arkansas's streams unfavorably to that in New York harbor, was greeted with a similar lack of enthusiasm by local citizens and politicians—including area Republican state legislators who distanced themselves from the national effort—and was denounced by the Arkansas chapter of the Sierra Club.

David Maraniss, in a *Washington Post* article entitled "GOP's Arkansas Foray Retreats in Confusion," detailed a long series of embarrassing Republican blunders. He concluded by noting that the largest sign seen on television, held directly over Secretary Martin's head throughout her Pine Bluff press conference, read: "GOP—Quit Lying About Arkansas."[19]

Although a Bush/Quayle campaign spokeswoman claimed that the Arkansas campaign swing had been a success and that a return engagement could be expected, none materialized. Rather, the next assault on Arkansas came from President Bush himself, who spent September 22, the day originally established for the first presidential debate, in a sixteen-hour fly-around to each of the six states surrounding Arkansas. Stopping briefly in Missouri, Oklahoma, Texas, Louisiana, Mississippi, and Tennessee, Bush regaled the airport audiences with horror stories of what "he's really done for the people of Arkansas, or put it this way, what he's done to the good people of Arkansas." Flying 2,500 miles in his daylong dash, Bush derided Clinton as "a man who has the gall to go around America and promise the moon, when on issue after issue, the sky has fallen in his own backyard." "He talks one way at home and delivers misery at home," Bush noted, strongly criticizing Clinton for everything from the absence of a state civil rights bill to "rivers so polluted the fish glow in the dark."[20]

Since the southern and border states surrounding Arkansas were all previous Bush states and were seen as essential for a 1992 Republican victory, the fly-around was probably a cost-effective way of raising doubts about Clinton's fitness for the presidency. In Arkansas, however, the renewed outrage and resentment were sufficient to cause the state's Republican candidates concern. Jay Dickey, seeking election in the Fourth Congressional District and needing Democratic crossover votes to do so, issued a press release stating: "When I'm asked whether I want the rest of the country to look like Arkansas, my answer isn't 'yes' it's 'heck, yes!'. If there is any criticism . . . let's leave it to those who live here, not those in Washington, D.C." Tim Hutchinson, the Second District Republican nominee, expressed his concern at a rally in Harrison, Arkansas, saying he did not think northwest Arkansas voters would blame him for Bush's Arkansas bashing, "but my concern is obvious. That's why I've spoken up about it." And Republican State Chair Asa Hutchinson, referring to the anti-Arkansas tenor of the national Bush campaign, acknowledged that "It's not playing well. . . . There's a lot of pride in this state and we're concerned about a negative reaction."[21]

These statements represent a complete turnabout from recent presidential campaign years when Arkansas Republicans enthusiastically wrapped themselves in the national mantle, while state and local Democratic candidates either politely went through the motions of national unity or carefully kept their distance. In 1992, while Arkansas Republicans were wary of being tied too closely to the top of the ticket, the attacks on Arkansas solidified and energized the state's Democrats.

Speaking to the Democratic state convention, Senator David Pryor invoked thunderous applause by referring to the GOP attacks: "They're not talking about just Bill Clinton. They're talking about you. They're talking about me. They're talking about Arkansas." And Clinton himself reminded the crowd of Marilyn Quayle's slurs on Arkansas and pled: "Send them a message on November 3."[22] At local Democratic rallies as well, Clinton's candidacy and the spate of Arkansas attacks it had invoked "stirred the speechmakers to return fire at the Republicans and to whip up enthusiasm for Democratic candidates for everything from justice of the peace to president."[23]

The determination to stand united against the Republican anti-Arkansas onslaught may also have inadvertently made it easier for Clinton to be absent as extensively as he was. In the early days of Clinton's candidacy, there was considerable speculation that neither the Arkansas voters nor the state's political establishment would tolerate an absentee governor and that his presidential bid would be torpedoed from the inside. Lieutenant Governor Jim Guy Tucker, who under the Arkansas Constitution immediately became the de facto governor each time Clinton left the state, had opposed Clinton in a bitter contest for the gubernatorial nomination in 1982 and had come close to challenging him in 1990. The legislature, though overwhelmingly Democratic, has never been particularly supportive of Clinton. Either the lieutenant governor or the legislature could have created embarrassing situations requiring Clinton to either leave the campaign trail or resign his governorship. After some early tests of stength, however, neither chose to do so, and the attacks on Arkansas seemed to solidify their resolve to do Clinton's candidacy no harm.

Despite warning signs from Arkansas Republicans, the Bush campaign intensified its attacks on Arkansas in the closing weeks of the campaign. Republican surrogates everywhere, such as actor Bruce Willis, described Arkansas as "synonymous with last in everything," and Bush himself, in the third and final presidential debate, said that what worried him most was for Clinton to "do to America what he did to Arkansas. . . . We do not want to be the lowest of the low." Radio ads targeted to particular audiences listed particulars of the state's shortcomings. And, finally, the last Bush/Quayle national television ad depicted Arkansas as the land that time forgot. Against grainy black-and-white images of weeds rustling in the wind, an abandoned field with a windmill, a lightning storm illuminating a dead tree in a desert with a vulture sitting in its barren branches, an ominous voice intoned, "And now Bill Clinton wants to do for America what he's done for Arkansas. America can't take that risk."[24]

The Clinton campaign churned out an endless supply of radio ads and fact sheets disputing the accuracy and relevance of the assorted attacks. They also responded vehemently to a last-minute half-hour "infomercial," entitled "Deep Voodoo, Chicken Feathers and the American Dream," in which H. Ross Perot mocked Arkansas's economic reliance on the poultry industry and suggested that a Clinton-led national economy would produce a nation of chicken pluckers. (In Perot's one Arkansas campaign appearance, on May 30, he had proudly claimed his close boyhood ties to Arkansas and had saved his derision for Bush.[25])

While the Clinton campaign's constant polls indicated that Bush's attacks were not significantly advancing the latter's candidacy, to the sensitive psyche of Arkansans, each new attack was salt in the wounds. Robert McCord, writing in the *Arkansas Times*, expressed the thoughts of many: "George Bush and the Republican Party owe the people of Arkansas an apology. They have vilified this state for the last four months. Much of what they have said was untrue, and all of it was unnecessary. George Bush was supposed to be running against a man, not a state."[26]

Even the *Arkansas Democrat-Gazette*, whose failure to endorse Clinton was pointed to by both Bush and Perot as proof of Clinton's failure in his own state, finally had enough. In a lead editorial entitled "Hands Off Arkansas," it also demanded an apology from President Bush: "Not for our sake, you understand. We know better. We live here. For his."[27]

No such apology was forthcoming. However, on election night, when President-elect Clinton claimed victory on the very site where he had begun his quest thirteen months previously and spoke with smiling deliberation as he thanked the people of "this wonderful, *small* state" for their support, the pain of the past year's drubbing was washed away in the jubilation of electoral success.[28]

RESULTS AND ANALYSIS

As official election returns reveal, a native son returned Arkansas to the Democratic presidential column with 53.8 percent of the popular vote—the largest percentage for Clinton in any of the fifty states in 1992. Bush's support in Arkansas dropped from 56.3 percent in 1988 to 35.6 percent in 1992, while Perot drew 10.6 percent. Bush, who had carried fifty-two of Arkansas's seventy-five counties in 1988, was reduced to six counties in 1992, fewer than Goldwater carried in 1964 or Nixon in 1968. As Figure 8.1 demonstrates, all of Bush's counties, and all but one of the counties in which his margin was 5 percent or more above his statewide average, were in the increasingly Republican northwest Third Congressional District. Perot also did best in this area, as well as in the southwest corner of the state, closest to his native Texarkana.

In what has become the familiar pattern, Clinton's strongest counties (in which his margin was 5 percent or more above his statewide average) were primarily in southern and eastern Arkansas, reflecting the areas of highest black population and strongest Democratic traditions. However, the so-called Rural Swing counties—a band of twenty-six counties running diagonally northeast to southwest across the state; counties that are disproportionately white, rural, and dry; counties whose swing against Clinton in 1980 caused Clinton's upset defeat and whose increasingly Republican presidential voting behavior had seemed the greatest source of future Republican victories—went solidly for Clinton in 1992. Indeed, some of the Rural Swing counties gave Clinton his biggest margins of victory.[29]

While Perot's presence obviously complicates any straightforward comparisons between the 1992 results and those from previous years, Table 8.3 makes certain relationships apparent. Obviously, Clinton's victory is in line with rather than a radical departure from the strength of other recent Democratic presidential candidates. His victory also correlates closely with Dale Bumpers' 1992 strength. Indeed, the political or electoral variables have a more powerful relationship to the 1992 outcome than do any of the demographic variables. While some of the strongest past patterns are evident (Clinton drawing more strength from areas of greatest black population, Bush doing better in the more rapidly growing and

Figure 8.1
Presidential Election Results in Arkansas Counties, 1992

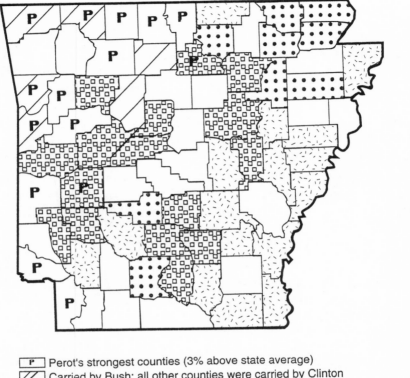

☐ P ☐ Perot's strongest counties (3% above state average)
▨ Carried by Bush; all other counties were carried by Clinton
Counties carried by Clinton:
▤ Rural Swing
⬚ Clinton's strongest counties (5% above state average)
⦙ Rural Swing and Clinton's strongest counties (5% above state average)
☐ Other Clinton counties

more prosperous areas), the demographic relationships are not so significant as in past presidential contests (i.e., Clinton's victory was more broadly based).

In terms of wins and losses, it was not a banner year for Arkansas's emerging Republicans. Despite a spirited challenge, Dale Bumpers returned to the Senate with a comfortable 60 percent victory over Reverend Mike Huckabee. Arkansas has yet to elect a Republican to the U.S. Senate. In House races, the Republicans were much more successful. Tim Hutchinson kept the Third District seat in the hands of the Republican party, and newcomer Jay Dickey, the beneficiary of

Table 8.3
Simple Correlation Coefficients (Pearson's *r*) Between the 1992 Clinton, Bush, and Perot Votes in Arkansas and Selected Variables

Variable	Clinton	Bush	Perot
Demographic variables			
Percent population growth, 1980-90	-.4267	.4164	.2901
Percent black population, 1990	.2970	-.2717	-.2391
Percent income growth, 1980-90	-.1137	.0651	.1387
Percent urban, 1990	.2488	-.0935	-.3948
Electoral variables			
Percent Democratic presidential vote, 1976	.5368	-.5283	-.3887
Percent Democratic presidential vote, 1980	.7507	-.6994	-.6025
Percent Democratic presidential vote, 1984	.7583	-.7057	-.5854
Percent Democratic presidential vote, 1988	.7614	-.7514	-.5089
Percent Democratic U.S. Senate vote, 1992	.8614	-.7971	-.6723
Percent for term limits amendment, 1992	-.6672	.5967	.5596

Source: Data on all 75 Arkansas counties compiled and analyzed by the author with the assistance of John Redfern.

strong leftover bitterness from the Democratic primary, captured the Fourth District seat. This was the first time in history (excluding the Reconstruction period) that a Republican had captured a congressional district in south Arkansas, and only the third time in history that Arkansas's congressional delegation would be split evenly between Republicans and Democrats. In the First and Second Districts, however, Republican candidates received only 30 percent and 20 percent of the vote, respectively.

State and local offices remain overwhelmingly Democratic. Midway in their four-year terms, none of Arkansas's elected executives were on the ballot, and all are Democrats. Despite the opportunities for change usually created by post-census redistricting, Republicans picked up only one seat in the house (for a total of 10 of the 100 seats) and one seat in the senate (for a total of five of the thirty-five seats). Of twenty prosecuting attorney districts, the one Republican candidate was not a lawyer. In short, despite references by Republican Chair Asa Hutchinson to "tremendous, tremendous record gains," this was not a significant growth year for the Republican party.[30]

There were several developments, however, indicating some strong prospects for Republican growth in the future. First, the fact that the only daily statewide newspaper left in the state, the *Arkansas Democrat-Gazette*, gave its editorial support exclusively to Republicans could eventually have as important a Republicanizing impact in state politics as the long-lived *Arkansas Gazette* had in giving the state its moderate-to-liberal Democratic flavor. As ex-*Gazette* writer John Brummett noted, "Now that we've endured a general election in Arkansas with only one statewide daily newspaper, we can reasonably conclude that the real winners of the vaunted newspaper war were the Republicans."[31]

Second, the enthusiastic adoption of a term-limitation amendment by 60 percent of the Arkansas electorate spells potential good news for the state's Republicans, who ardently advocated its adoption, and bad news for the Democrats, who ardently opposed it. While its imposed limits on U.S. senators and representatives are of dubious constitutionality and under challenge, the limits it places on state officials (state representatives limited to three two-year terms, state senators to two four-year terms, state elected executives to two four-year terms) will go into effect for terms starting in 1995; and it will clearly be easier for the minority Republican Party to make progress in a sea of open seats than against a barricade of advantaged overwhelmingly Democratic incumbents.

Third, as both Figure 8.1 and Table 8.3 suggest, Perot drew more heavily from traditionally Republican than traditionally Democratic geographic and demographic sources of support, support seemingly available to Republican candidates in the future. Strongly confirming this impression was the Perot organization's formal endorsement of Republicans Huckabee, Hutchinson, and Dickey in their 1992 congressional races.

On balance, however, it was a stronger and sweeter year for Arkansas Democrats. Not only had they been instrumental in providing the nation with its first victorious Democratic nominee in twelve years, but also they had helped to provide an alternative and more positive image of Arkansas than those of the past. As one writer noted:

At least for one wonderful evening in downtown Little Rock, the "lowest of the low" as one candidate had called this state, was clearly transformed into the "highest of the high". Arkansas has given the U.S. its 42nd president, and Bill Clinton has given the people of this state a measure of pride and self-respect that can come in no other way.[32]

The sense of state pride was so pervasive, in fact, that even in its defeat, the *Arkansas Democrat-Gazette* could not help exulting over "the day one Arkie beat two Texans."[33]

NOTES

1. The details of Arkansas's political conversion in presidential contests are related in Diane D. Blair, "Arkansas," in *The 1984 Presidential Election in the South: Patterns of Southern Party Politics*, ed. Robert P. Steed, Laurence W. Moreland, and Tod A. Baker (New York: Praeger, 1986), 185–207; and Diane D. Blair, "Arkansas: Reluctant Republicans in Razorbackland," in *The 1988 Presidential Election in the South: Continuity Amidst Change in Southern Party Politics*, ed. Laurence W. Moreland, Robert P. Steed, and Tod A. Baker (New York: Praeger, 1991), 143–164.

2. Mason-Dixon poll, reported in *Arkansas Democrat-Gazette* (9 October 1991), A1.

3. Quoted in *Washington Post* (15 July 1992), A26.

4. Recalled by the author and quoted in Brenda Blagg, "Voters Ratify Clinton's Early Campaign Disclaimer," *Morning News* (Springdale, Ark.) (10 November 1992).

5. John Brummett, "Arkansas: Up Close, Personal," *Arkansas Gazette* (15 May 1990), B1.

6. *Arkansas Democrat-Gazette* (29 December 1992), B1, citing National Library on Money and Politics. In the 1988 contest, 73 percent of direct contributions from Arkansas went to Bush; in 1992, 90 percent went to Clinton.

7. The consequences of Arkansas's Super Tuesday participation are discussed in Blair, "Arkansas: Reluctant Republicans," 146–148. By 1993, the state legislature was seriously considering a return to Arkansas's pre-1972 fourth-Tuesday-in-July primary date. The dates were changed then to accommodate Representative Wilbur Mills so he could retain his seat in the U.S. House of Representatives should his presidential bid fail.

8. "Brown Attacks Clinton Record on Environment," *Arkansas Democrat-Gazette* (17 May 1992), A1.

9. This poll was published in *Arkansas Democrat-Gazette* (21 May 1992), A1.

10. Congressman Thornton represented the Fourth District in the U.S. House from 1973 until 1979, serving on the Judiciary Committee that voted to impeach Nixon. He ran for the U.S. Senate in 1978 and lost to David Pryor.

11. "GOP to Focus on Clinton Record," *Arkansas Democrat-Gazette* (13 July 1992), A3.

12. Quoted in *New York Times* (16 August 1992), A19.

13. "State's Delegates in Houston Feeling Talkative About Clinton," *Arkansas Democrat-Gazette* (17 August 1992), A9.

14. "Delegates Grin, Bear Blasts at State," *Arkansas Democrat-Gazette* (21 August 1992), A16; "Republicans Defend State, Bash Governor at Convention," *Arkansas Democrat-Gazette* (19 August 1992), A11.

15. "Republicans Defend State," A11.

16. "Marilyn Quayle Explains Comments," *Arkansas Democrat-Gazette* (1 October 1992), A1; Ernest Dumas, "Bush Depicts a Sorry State," *Arkansas Times* (3 September 1992).

17. "Dole Advises Huckabee to Fly Balanced Budget," *Arkansas Democrat-Gazette* (23 August 1992), B1.

18. See "Clintonites Buzz Bush Team in Counterattacks at LR, PB," *Arkansas Democrat-Gazette* (17 September 1992), A1; and "Campaign Bottoms Out," *(Springdale) Morning News* (18 September 1992), A4.

19. *Washington Post* (17 September 1992), A1. See also the satirical editorial "C'mon Down" in *Spectrum* (22 September 1992).

20. "Encircling Arkansas, Bush Opens Harsh Attack on Clinton's Record," *New York Times* (23 September 1992), A1; "Sky Has Fallen in Arkansas, President Says," *Arkansas Democrat-Gazette* (23 September 1992), A1; "Circling Arkansas, Bush Seizes Media," *Arkansas Democrat-Gazette* (24 September 1992), A15.

21. Quotes from an Associated Press wire story by James Jefferson (25 September 1992). See also B. Drummond Ayres, Jr., "A Clinton Team Maps Plans to Get Out the Indian Vote," *New York Times* (25 September 1992), A18; and "Dickey Defends Pine Bluff's Quality of Life," *Arkansas Democrat-Gazette* (18 September 1992), A12.

22. "Clinton Co. Presents Bill to the Voters," *Arkansas Democrat-Gazette* (30 August 1992), A1.

23. "Bashing of State Gets Democrats Lathered," *Morning News* (Springdale, Ark.) (30 October 1992), A1.

24. "Bush Keeps Low Arkansas Statistics in Spotlight," *Arkansas Democrat-Gazette* (2 November 1992), A12; "Final Debate Puts Clinton on Defensive," *Arkansas Democrat-Gazette* (20 October 1992), A1; "New Bush Ad Blasts Clinton's Arkansas Record," Washington, D.C., Associated Press story (28 October 1992); "Perot Turns TV Guns on Clinton," *Arkansas Democrat-Gazette* (2 November 1992), A1.

25. "Perot Ready to Seek 'Dirty Job,'" *Arkansas Democrat-Gazette* (31 May 1992), A1.

26. *Arkansas Times* (5 November 1992), 25.

27. *Arkansas Democrat-Gazette* (29 October 1992), B8.

28. *Arkansas Democrat-Gazette* (4 November 1992), A15.

29. For detailed analysis of the Rural Swing counties, see Diane D. Blair, *Arkansas Politics and Government: Do the People Rule?* (Lincoln: University of Nebraska Press, 1988), 84–87.

30. "Republicans: Clinton's Coattails Clipped in Election," *Northwest Arkansas Times* (5 November 1992), A4.

31. "Republican Newspaper," *Arkansas Times* (5 November 1992). For the political influence of the *Arkansas Gazette*, see Blair, *Arkansas Politics and Government*, 271–272.

32. Jerry Dhonau, *Arkansas Democrat-Gazette* (5 November 1992), B11.

33. Editorial, *Arkansas Democrat-Gazette* (5 November 1992), B11.

9

Florida: A Muddled Election

WILLIAM E. HULBARY, ANNE E. KELLEY, AND
LEWIS BOWMAN

The 1992 electoral outcomes in Florida were mixed. George Bush won the state's twenty-five electoral votes, but he carried the state by less than two percentage points over Clinton. Bush received 40.8 percent of the popular vote, with Bill Clinton (39.1 percent) and H. Ross Perot (19.8 percent) dividing the rest—a large majority. Bush's narrow popular-vote victory was twenty percentage points below his margin in 1988 when Florida gave him the largest victory margin in the ten most populous states.[1]

In other 1992 Florida elections, the results also were mixed. Bob Graham was reelected to the U.S. Senate by a resounding thirty-one percentage points. Following the 1990 census, Florida received four new U.S. House seats; the Republicans gained three, and the Democrats only one, of these seats. However, Republican gains were less dramatic than expected in view of the Democrats' redistricting and incumbency problems.

The Republicans only gained three seats in the Florida house. This was less than expected, raising their representation to only 49 seats, while leaving the Democrats with 71 of 120 house seats. The Republicans gained one seat in the Florida senate, creating a partisan deadlock, twenty to twenty. Forced to compromise, senate Republicans and Democrats agreed to share power, selecting first a Republican and then a Democrat to successive one-year terms as president of the Florida Senate.[2] A very mixed electoral outcome indeed!

BACKGROUND

Florida has been overwhelmingly Republican in presidential elections during the post–World War II era. Only Harry Truman in 1948, Lyndon Johnson in 1964, and Jimmy Carter in 1976 carried Florida for the Democrats. From 1968 to 1988, Florida and Virginia were the southern "anchors of the Republican era."[3] Bucking this Republican trend, and the attraction of Perot, Clinton received 39.1 percent of the Florida vote, less than one percentage point more than Dukakis in 1988.

It seems bizarre that Bill Clinton and Al Gore were within two percentage points of winning Florida in 1992 unless several factors are considered: very high levels of voter discontent with Bush's economic and domestic policy; how diverse the Florida electorate had become; the impact of Ross Perot's presidential efforts in the election; and how much the growing political power of women means to elections. While scraping by to electoral victory in the state, even the largess George Bush promised in response to Hurricane Andrew was not enough to distract many from the major difficulties of his presidency. With Jeb Bush (one of the president's alleged influence-peddling sons) running his campaign, George Bush was barely able to overcome the widespread dismay of Florida voters faced with the prospect of George Bush in the presidency for four more years.[4]

TURMOIL IN THE 1992 CAMPAIGN ENVIRONMENT

Several issues during 1991 and 1992 heightened animosity among various interests in the state, making the 1992 election campaign especially acrimonious and chaotic. Controversy in the Democratic Party in 1991 about who controlled the party, who should be state party chair, and related issues set the tone for the politics of 1992. Governor Lawton Chiles was surprised when the state party chose Simon Ferro rather than the governor's own candidate for state party chair. This dispute continued through the year, disrupting the party's state convention in December because the governor refused to attend.[5]

Other events also showed how Florida's Democrats were no longer able to control their internal factionalism, much less control the state's politics generally. Throughout the twentieth century, Democratic-controlled legislatures (usually led by ruling "panhandle" Democrats) redistricted the state. Districts were gerrymandered to maintain substantial advantages for the Democrats in elections. More recently, as Republicans gained strength, arguments about redistricting have become more intense. In 1992, largely due to partisan politics and individual personal interests in the senate, the Florida legislature found it nearly impossible to agree on a plan. Cuban Americans (overwhelmingly Republican in Florida) and African Americans (overwhelmingly Democratic) demanded the application of the Voting Rights Act mandates. The Democrats lost control of the process, and a series of lawsuits moved the redistricting controversy into the federal courts where a panel of federal judges and their appointed consultants changed the political maps and quite probably the future course of Florida politics.

This reapportionment produced four new districts designed to enhance the election of minority candidates. As a result, three African Americans—two women, Corinne Brown of Jacksonville and Carrie Meek of Miami, and one man, Alcee Hastings of Fort Lauderdale (an impeached federal judge)—were elected to the U.S. House in 1992.[6] A second Hispanic, Lincoln Diaz-Balart of Miami, also was elected.[7] Redistricting state legislative districts went through similar gyrations and also yielded a number of new minority districts for Hispanics and African Americans.

A gubernatorial and legislative budget showdown further exacerbated tension in state politics and political parties.[8] In 1992, the governor and the legislature reached a standoff about restructuring the tax system, tax increases, and spending reforms. In late June, after several gubernatorial vetoes, it appeared the state would have no budget to start the new fiscal year and would have to close down many services. The arguments around these issues dragged through the election year and seemed to poison the electoral atmosphere even more.[9] The unwillingness of Democrats in the state legislature to support the Democratic governor illustrated the weakness of the party.[10]

CHANGES IN VOTER REGISTRATION

In the past decade, the Republicans increased their portion of registered voters from less than 30 percent to slightly over 40 percent. They added over 1.2 million, while the Democrats were adding less than 400,000.[11] By the summer of 1992, only slightly more than half of the registered voters in Florida were Democratic. The Democrats have been able to maintain their majority because over 90 percent of registered African Americans were registered Democrats. Registered whites were split evenly between the two major parties. Overall, other ethnic groups were slightly Republican in their registration.[12]

SUPER TUESDAY IN FLORIDA

Approaching Super Tuesday and the Florida presidential primary on March 10, George Bush's and Bill Clinton's cumulative nomination results were markedly different.[13] Bush had received 86 percent of the Republican delegates, while Clinton had received only 30 percent of his party's delegates.[14] The Florida Democratic Party's 167 delegates were particularly important to Clinton because he needed to separate himself from the Democratic field.[15] Bush's nomination appeared secure, but Florida's ninety-seven Republican delegates were important to show that challenger Pat Buchanan's support was too small to indicate significant discontent with Bush's first term.

Clinton counted on his state political contacts,[16] a strong campaign organization, and adequate campaign finance to carry the Florida primary. His campaign organization extended to each of the state's sixty-seven counties[17] and blanketed the state with television messages. Among Clinton's Florida challengers, only Paul Tsongas was a serious competitor.[18] Making little effort in other southern states on Super Tuesday, Tsongas engaged in an all-out struggle against Clinton in Florida; in the last week of the primary campaign, Tsongas spent over half a million dollars on Florida television. In response, Clinton focused on Tsongas, turning the campaign into a two-man race between the front-runners. Clinton was able to hone his message and establish himself as an outsider with a plan to change the economic system. In the final days of the primary campaign, he effectively used television and campaign speeches to attack Tsongas on a series of issues, including reductions in entitlement programs (Social Security and Medicare), proposed gasoline tax increases, capital gains tax-rate cuts, and being "soft on Israel."

Clinton's Florida campaign put Tsongas on the defensive. Polls taken just before primary election day showed one-third of the primary electorate still undecided and Tsongas losing strength.[19] On election day, previously undecided voters opted disproportionately for Clinton. He ran strongly throughout the state, receiving 51.7 percent of the vote and eighty-seven delegates. Tsongas and his strategists ran a sloppy campaign, squandering his strength and making him appear increasingly defensive. He received 34 percent of the vote and fifty-eight delegates, but carried only two counties. Although he took votes away from Clinton among highly educated, affluent white voters, Tsongas ran poorly among African Americans, senior citizens, and blue-collar workers. Jerry Brown finished a distant third, won no counties, and received only 12.3 percent of the vote and three delegates.[20]

The Democratic race dominated the Florida primary campaign. Loyal Republican leaders were expected to deliver Bush a strong Florida victory, and the Republican candidates were concentrating more of their efforts in Mississippi and Louisiana. In those states, Buchanan was trying to capitalize on the racial issues stirred up in recent elections. However, rhetorical code words such as "welfare," "civil rights," "affirmative action," "quotas," and "crime"— used in 1988 to overwhelm Dukakis—came back to haunt Bush in the Florida primary. Republican leaders fought to keep David Duke off the Florida ballot, and the court upheld their position. However, Bush's ordeal continued, as Pat Buchanan adopted many of Duke's ideas and came south to campaign against him. According to Kenneth Walker, "it is there that Bush is hamstrung. He has not been able to go negative on Buchanan without risking separating himself from the Southern good ol' boys he desperately needs in the general election. And, as president, he can't very well outflank Buchanan on the race issue without thoroughly disqualifying himself for the presidency."[21]

Bush had to turn to other issues. He tried "family, jobs, and peace," but had difficulty articulating what these policies meant (a recurring problem throughout the year). More important, he was forced to apologize for breaking his 1988 "no new taxes" pledge and pledged (anew) to veto any new taxes "the moment they hit my desk." He pressed for educational reform, vowed to get even tougher against Fidel Castro, and railed against "socialized medicine." Finally, Bush praised Reaganism, appealed to the religious right, and claimed a major role in the "defeat of communism." Countering Bush's defensive campaign, Buchanan attacked the president's handling of the economy and his betrayal of conservatives. With the state's high unemployment (8.7 percent), many felt Buchanan's attack on the president's inability to create promised jobs would hurt Bush in Florida. Buchanan also used Bush's own code rhetoric to press Bush on racial issues.

On Super Tuesday, President Bush received 68 percent of the Florida vote and won in each of the state's sixty-seven counties. Though Buchanan received 32 percent of the Republican primary vote, the Republican Party's congressional-district-winner-take-all formula gave Bush all ninety-seven Florida delegates.

THE PRESIDENTIAL GENERAL ELECTION CAMPAIGN

The national conventions set the tone and timing for each national campaign. In Florida, however, the presidential campaign had to contest for air time with tough battles in the statewide September primary and in the October primary runoffs. The presidential electoral campaign also had to overcome the divisiveness of these state primaries. Hurricane Andrew struck southern Florida severely on August 24, further complicating the primaries and the general election campaigns during the next few weeks.

Clinton strategists did not target Florida for prime campaign activities in the general election because initially they saw little chance of winning the state. To carry the state and its electoral vote, Clinton would have to win a vote more than eleven percentage points larger than that of Dukakis in 1988.[22] In fact, the swing vote needed to win Florida was larger than in any other populous state. Comparing the Clinton and Bush strategies, Merle Black observed that "What Bush really needs is to sweep the South to have any Electoral College chance ... Clinton doesn't need to sweep the South but to split it."[23] Consistent with this strategy, Clinton tried to create a biracial coalition, walking a fine line between "Bubba and Brother."[24] Early in the campaign, Clinton's strategists apparently decided this strategy was not likely to win in Florida and Texas because the necessary swing vote was too large; hence, these states did not warrant very much campaign funding or many campaign visits during the general election.

Bush strategists also had assumed Florida was safe. Bush had won Florida handily in 1988 without making a campaign visit to the state after Labor Day. By mid-October, considering the situation hopeless, Dukakis withdrew his campaign staff, conceding the state to Bush well before the election.

Imagine the surprise of strategists in both campaigns as they watched the 1992 race tighten in September and October! By mid-October Bush and Clinton were very close in the Florida polls, with some already predicting a Clinton victory.[25] In early October, when Clinton and Gore became aware of the possibility of taking Florida, they scheduled appearances and drew crowds in larger numbers than anyone expected. Clinton and Gore's strategists also had better communication and coordination in the state than other recent Democratic presidential campaigns. They were able to command considerable financing in October when it became clear Clinton had a chance. Many of these efforts late in the general election campaign evolved as Bush experienced more difficulty holding southern states than his strategists had expected.

The shifting strategies of the two campaigns were apparent in the candidates' Florida campaign appearances. President Bush did not visit the state after the March presidential primary until he returned September 9. National Democrats had ignored the state until Tipper Gore made a swing through Florida a few days after Bush's early September visit. Then, in October, both candidates made two major campaign trips through Florida. These late appearances suggest how close the race had become and how much the Republican incumbent's grip on Florida had weakened.

Nationally and in Florida, the outcome of the campaign had become so uncertain that President Bush could not afford to lose any significant bloc in his Florida coalition. On one swing through the state, in an effort to ensure retention of the Cuban-American vote in south Florida, Bush signed the Cuban Democracy Act, which he had opposed earlier. Courting the same constituency, Clinton had met with Jorge Mas Canosa, chair of the Cuban American National Foundation, to emphasize his support for this legislation, which had been introduced by Democratic Senator Bob Graham of Florida.

Continuing these campaign tactics, the president announced the transfer of National Oceanic and Atmospheric Administration (NOAA) aircraft to MacDill Air Force Base in Tampa in order to maintain that facility, which was threatened with closing. He also announced that he supported rebuilding Homestead Air Force Base (near Miami) at a cost of over one-half billion dollars and that he opposed further general cuts in military spending. Suddenly, and unexpectedly, Bush was opposed to offshore oil drilling in Florida *again*; he had opposed this during the 1988 campaign, but later supported legislation that would have permitted offshore drilling under certain conditions. Bush was single-minded and dogged in his drive to hold Florida's twenty-five electoral votes. Just as Tsongas accused Clinton of being "pander bear," one could see Bush, in danger of losing Florida, emerge as a real "Florida pander bear" himself. Responding to Bush's tactics, Clinton chastised Bush for his "empty" promises: "It's the same old story: George Bush will say anything to get elected. He said so himself."[26]

The Florida electorate was distressed and concerned about the economy under George Bush far in advance of Clinton's and Perot's attacks upon him as the inept keeper of the nation's economic well-being. For a year, there had been ample evidence of a dramatic drop in Floridians' support for the president. A poll in the state in November of 1991 found 63 percent of the residents reporting that the state's economy was getting worse; over half of the respondents said the next generation of Floridians would be worse off financially than the current generation; and 68 percent gave George Bush a grade of "C" or worse, with almost half giving him a "D" or worse.[27] As the primary neared in 1992, almost one-half of respondents in a statewide poll said they were worse off financially than they had been a year ago.[28] In the same poll, 42 percent said the economy was the one issue they would like to hear presidential candidates talk about.

By September, surveys of registered voters showed Bush's position so weakened in Florida that totally unanticipated efforts had to be made if Bush was to win the state. Responses showed "that Mr. Bush's high marks for his handling of the hurricane [were] severely undercut by dissatisfaction with his management of the nation's economy."[29] As the race tightened, the reentry of Ross Perot scrambled the campaign even more for strategists in both major parties. Some thought Perot would help Clinton in many southern states.[30] Another journalist was more uncertain, writing:

As for Perot, the poll indicates the majority of his supporters are Republican, and overwhelmingly white men. Perot polls strongest in the Panhandle, in Northeast Florida, and in the Orlando-Daytona area.

Overall, Perot has taken twice as many voters from Bush in Florida than from Clinton. . . . In many other states, Perot's recent surge has appeared to hurt Clinton more than Bush.[31]

On the eve of the election, the presidential contest in Florida was too close to call, and much of the confusion had to do with Perot. From its inception, the Perot phenomenon in Florida was hard to evaluate. One of the Perot movement's founders, Jack Gargan, was a Tampa financial planner. He founded Throw the Hypocritical Rascals Out (THRO) in May 1991 and played a role in setting up the efforts to draft Ross Perot to run for president. Perot visited Florida in November 1991 and proclaimed his familiar anti-incumbent message: "Nobody's taken out the trash in a long time. Nobody's cleaned out the barn."[32] By May 1992, his supporters had procured petitions with more than 230,000 signatures, four times the number required. On May 27, Perot officially qualified to be on the Florida ballot. Two days later Perot made his second trip to Florida, speaking to an estimated 7,000 in Orlando. Even though Perot was not an announced presidential candidate, he was so popular in Florida that an early June poll found he was the leading candidate with 34 percent (Bush—31 percent; Clinton—22 percent; undecided—13 percent).[33] The findings showed that Perot was drawing support from 28 percent of those who had chosen Bush in earlier polls, 31 percent who had chosen Clinton, and 59 percent who had been undecided. Among those choosing Perot, 69 percent thought he would be elected president in November, whereas only 63 percent of Clinton adherents thought their candidate would win. At that point, Perot was a real force in the Florida presidential campaign.

After Perot withdrew from the campaign in July some thought he would no longer influence the outcome. But when he returned to the electoral race, he found a substantial bloc of diehard supporters waiting, many of whom seemed to have little interest in politics other than his candidacy. Clearly he kept a substantial bloc of potential voters participating and continued to influence the outcome of the election.

In the 1992 campaign, much time was given to discussing Fidel Castro, family values, health care reform, the economy, term limits for public officials, and tax-and-spend liberals.[34] But the overriding issue in the campaign was the economy. A poll taken near the end of the campaign showed "Floridians' deep pessimism about the economy and their surprising willingness to pay higher taxes."[35] In this survey, almost one-fifth of the respondents thought they might get laid off from work within a year, and over one-half felt their children would not do as well financially as they had. Perot attacked this point over and over in his appearances, even asking younger persons in his audiences to stand and then lecturing the audience about the importance of ensuring the future for the nation's youth. His attack on the rise in the national government's deficit often focused on this argument. As in the nation, the Florida general election campaign kept returning to the overriding concerns about the performance of the economy and expectations about its future performance.

ANALYSIS OF ELECTION RESULTS

Several factors help explain the electoral outcome in Florida in 1992. The continuing attraction of Floridians to Republican candidates in statewide races, changes in voter registration and turnout, and Perot's third-party candidacy offer valuable insights. Several socioeconomic and demographic variables—including age, income, education, race, ethnicity, and type of household—also are helpful.[36]

Republican Electoral Strength

Although marginal and less robust than the victories of other recent Republican presidential candidates, Bush's 1992 success in Florida was not idiosyncratic. A strong partisan consistency is evident in statewide elections from 1980 to the present. Indeed, in view of the weak economy on a Republican watch and an unattractive Republican candidate, Bush's razor-thin win is a significant manifestation of emergent Republican strength in Florida presidential politics. His victory was only the most recent in a long series of Florida Republican electoral successes, a series that includes Reagan in 1980 and 1984, Bush in 1988, Paula Hawkins for the U.S. Senate in 1980, Bob Martinez for governor in 1986, and Connie Mack for the U.S. Senate in 1988. These Republican outcomes correlate strongly with Bush's 1992 victory in Florida. (See Table 9.1.) The counties that supported Republican presidential candidates and other statewide candidates most strongly during the 1980s were counties that gave Bush a larger share (and Clinton a smaller share) of their votes in 1992. Even in elections where Republican candidates lost, the correlations are strong and in the same direction.[37]

Differences from 1988 to 1992 in the Florida vote for each major party's presidential candidate were much larger for Republicans than Democrats. Compared to Dukakis in 1988, Clinton drew a similar share of the vote in 1992; the

Table 9.1

Correlations Between 1992 Florida Presidential Vote and Selected Political and Demographic Variables

Variable	Percent of vote for		
	Clinton	Bush	Perot
Recent statewide elections			
Percent voting for President:			
Reagan (R), 1980	-.56c	.53c	.11
Reagan (R), 1984	-.95c	.78c	.39b
Bush (R), 1988	-.95c	.84c	.29a
Percent voting for U.S. Senate:			
Chiles (D), 1982	.43c	-.38b	-.15
Hawkins (R), 1986	-.78c	.64c	.33b
Mack (R), 1988	-.81c	.83c	.08
Graham (D), 1992	.84c	-.74c	-.27a
Percent voting for Governor:			
Martinez (R), 1986	-.84c	.72c	.32b
Chiles (D), 1990	.67c	-.68c	-.08
Term Limit Amendment, 1992	-.48c	.42c	.17
Retention of Sup. Ct. Justice R. Barkett, 1992	.41c	-.24a	-.33b
Voter registration and turnout			
Percent registered Republican, 1992	-.28a	.28a	.04
Increase in Republican registration, 1988-92	-.46c	.45c	.08
Voter turnout (among registered voters), 1992	-.09	.24a	-.23
Increase in voter turnout, 1988-92	.13	-.08	-.10
Education and income			
Less than high school degree (percent), 1990	.19	-.28a	.11
Four-year college degree (percent), 1990	.05	.11	-.26a
Median household income, 1989	-.30a	.44c	-.19
Population below poverty level (percent), 1989	.38b	-.38b	-.09
Household type			
Percent married with children, 1990	-.32b	.39	-.08
Percent single parent families, 1990	.32b	-.11	-.39c
Percent non-family households, 1990	.35b	-.28a	-.17
Race and ethnicity			
Percent African-American	.60c	-.34b	-.52c
Percent Hispanic	.11	.03	-.25a
Percent white Hispanic	.15	.03	-.31a

Table 9.1 (continued)

Variable	Percent of vote for		
	Clinton	Bush	Perot
Age			
18-34	.08	.12	-.35b
35-49	-.16	.30a	-.23
50-64	-.16	-.10	.44c
65 or more	.06	-.22	.25a

Note: Table entries are Pearson's correlations (r); the units of analysis are Florida's 67 counties. Statistical significance is indicated as follows: a = significant at the .05 level; b = significant at the .01 level; c = significant at the .001 level.
Source: Compiled by the authors from census data and from election results provided by the office of the Florida Supervisor of Elections.

1988 and 1992 vote percentages for both Democratic candidates were within five percentage points in every Florida county. In contrast, Bush's share of the vote dropped substantially between the two elections. In 1992, his share of the vote was more than ten percentage points lower in every county and more than twenty percentage points lower in fifty-five of sixty-seven counties.

The Perot Factor

Did Ross Perot hurt George Bush or Bill Clinton more, or did he have no net effect?[38] Perot's candidacy can be linked to the decline in Bush's vote between 1988 and 1992. The correlation was quite strong ($r = .83$) between the size of the Perot vote and the decline in the Bush vote over the four-year period. The Perot vote also was associated with a declining Democratic vote from 1988 to 1992, but the correlation ($r = .40$) was less than half as large. Perot consistently attracted a larger share of the vote in those areas where Bush's vote declined the most between 1988 and 1992. Perot apparently attracted more 1988 Bush voters than voters who supported Dukakis.

Focusing on the 1992 election, a different and more ambiguous picture emerges. Perot's vote was correlated more strongly and negatively with Clinton's vote than it was with Bush's vote.[39] In areas (counties) where Perot's vote was higher, Clinton's was consistently lower. This was true of Bush's vote as well, but the relationship was weaker and less consistent. However, the 1992 Perot and Bush votes were similar in one respect. Perot's vote was associated with other recent statewide elections in a manner resembling that of the 1992 Bush vote. Although the correlations for Perot's vote are weaker (see Table 9.1), they. are consistently in the same direction as those for the 1992 Bush vote. Apparently, Perot voters tended to favor Republican candidates in the 1980s—but not in 1992.

We suspect that most of the Perot voters were swing voters, including many independents and Reagan Democrats. In the past, these swing voters were inclined to support Republicans (e.g., Bush in 1988), but found Bush and "business as usual" unacceptable in 1992. If Perot had not been an available candidate, we suspect that Perot voters would have voted disproportionately for Clinton, if only to protest the status quo.

Related Ballot Items

Two other items on the 1992 ballot shed additional light on the presidential election and the level of popular discontent with "politics as usual." First, Floridians overwhelmingly approved (76.8 percent) a term-limits amendment to the state constitution, limiting elected officeholders to no more than eight consecutive years in a given office.[40] Second, Floridians voted (60.9 percent) to retain Justice Rosemary Barkett on the Florida Supreme Court. Barkett's retention became a highly visible and partisan issue during the campaign; her opponents accused her of being pro-abortion, favoring gun control, and being soft on crime, while her supporters charged the opposition with gender bias.[41]

The votes on Justice Barkett and on term limits were closely related to the presidential vote (Table 9.1). Support for term limits was greater in counties that gave a larger share of their vote to George Bush and a smaller share to Bill Clinton. Support for term limits was also slightly greater in areas giving more support to Ross Perot, but the correlation was weaker than it was for the two major party candidates. Unlike the term-limit question, support for the retention of Rosemary Barkett was larger in counties that gave a larger vote to Clinton. Support for Barkett's retention was lower in areas that gave proportionately more votes to Bush and Ross Perot. In a state where lengthy incumbency has been more characteristic of Democrats than Republicans, the partisan distinctiveness of the vote on term limits was not surprising. But the results manifest important ideological distinctions as well. The Bush vote and the Perot vote shared some similarities; both were more conservative about social issues—more anti-abortion, more anti–gun control, and more sympathetic to law-and-order appeals— as well as more willing to curtail the power of incumbency through term limits. In these respects, the Clinton vote appeared to be distinctively different.

Party Loyalties and Voter Registration

In southern states with a long tradition of Democratic Party dominance, voter registration is sometimes a poor indicator of underlying partisan loyalty and partisan electoral outcomes. But as Florida's Republican Party gains strength and two-party competition becomes the norm, the state's partisan voter registration increasingly reflects underlying party preferences and election outcomes. Thus, Florida's 1992 presidential vote was fairly consistent with the distribution of party voter registration. Areas with a higher percentage of registered Republicans gave a larger share of their vote to Bush and a smaller share to Clinton (Table 9.1). Moreover, the correlations between major-party presidential vote and partisan voter registration were stronger (by 25 to 30 percent) in 1992 than in 1988.[42] Florida voters continued to make their vote choices and party registration more congruent with their underlying party loyalties. Unlike the two major-party candidates, there was no association between Perot's vote and partisan voter registration. Perot drew votes equally well in strongly Republican *and* Democratic areas; his persistent nonpartisan appeal appeared to be equally effective among disgruntled Democrats and Republicans.

Voter Turnout

Florida counties with higher voter turnout in 1992 tended to give George Bush a larger share of their votes (Table 9.1). Bill Clinton did almost as well in counties with higher turnout as he did in those with lower turnout; the association between turnout and the Clinton vote was negative, but quite small. Support for Ross Perot was generally lower in high-turnout counties and somewhat greater in low-turnout counties. This suggests a conclusion at variance with much of the popular wisdom surrounding the campaign. If Ross Perot motivated more people to become involved in politics and the campaign process, thereby stimulating higher turnout, the increased turnout did not appear to help him; on the contrary, it may have diminished Perot's share of the vote.

Florida is usually one of the states with the lowest voter turnout in the nation, and 1992 was no exception.[43] Only about 50 percent of Florida's voting-age population voted, compared to 55 percent nationally. But Florida, like the rest of the nation, also experienced an increase in turnout in 1992. Compared to the 1988 presidential election, turnout in Florida was up about five percentage points, an increase close to that reported nationwide. Did the increased turnout between 1988 and 1992 help some candidates at the expense of others? The correlations in Table 9.1, although small, suggest that Bill Clinton was helped somewhat by the increase in turnout, while Bush and Perot were hurt. Counties manifesting the largest increases in turnout between 1988 and 1992 gave Clinton a somewhat larger share of the vote. Counties with the smallest increases (or actual decreases) tended to give a larger share of their votes to Bush or Perot. Again, we see evidence that Perot did not benefit by mobilizing disenchanted Florida voters. Nor did George Bush. If any candidate benefited from the increased turnout, it was Bill Clinton.

The link between turnout and presidential voting choices suggests some interesting, if speculative, interpretations. Likely Republican presidential voters in Florida are also likely to be white, affluent, and fairly well educated. These voters tend to have consistently high rates of voter turnout. Thus, turnout in 1988 and 1992 would be associated with support for Bush (as it was in each election), but *changing* levels of turnout between 1988 and 1992 would not. As for the Democratic opposition to Bush, Dukakis in 1988 was hurt by his inability to mobilize likely Democratic voters in Florida, particularly nonwhites and less affluent, less educated voters.[44] These groups are the most likely to have fluctuating rates of turnout from election to election and displayed low turnout in

1988. In 1992, Clinton was more successful in mobilizing these likely Democratic voters. Thus, Clinton benefited more from increased turnout between 1988 and 1992 and was able to mount a more successful campaign against George Bush.

Affluence and Education

We expected the 1992 Florida presidential vote to be associated with differences in socioeconomic status (SES), particularly with measures of affluence, but also with education level. The election occurred in the midst of a long, widespread, and severe economic recession. Consequently, many workers were beset by feelings of economic insecurity, concern about a decline in their standard of living, and fear of losing their jobs. Responding to these fears, Clinton had made the economy and job creation the central theme of his campaign. We expected these themes to resonate especially well among those hardest hit by the recession, the less affluent and less well educated.

Our expectations were generally confirmed (Table 9.1). President Bush's share of the vote was highest in more affluent areas, counties with a higher median household income and a lower percentage below the poverty level. In contrast, Clinton received more of the vote in less affluent areas. Perot's electoral support was relatively independent of affluence, although he may have drawn slightly more support in less-affluent areas. However, it was Clinton, not Perot, who benefited most from economic discontent with the Bush administration and who received more support in less-affluent areas.

President Bush's share of the vote also was lower (and Clinton's somewhat higher) in areas with lower education levels, that is, in those counties where a greater percentage had less than a high school education (Table 9.1). Furthermore, Perot's share of the vote was significantly lower in areas with more college graduates. Clearly the recession hurt Bush and helped Clinton and Perot in a predictable fashion. President Bush drew more of the votes in areas where levels of affluence and education were higher, while Clinton (and Perot in some measure) drew more votes in less-affluent areas with lower levels of education.

Race and Ethnicity

In the 1992 presidential election, the Florida electorate divided along racial lines in much the same way it has in other recent presidential elections. As expected, Clinton's percentage of the vote was higher in counties with a larger percentage of African Americans (Table 9.1). In contrast, George Bush and Ross Perot fared poorly in counties with proportionately more African Americans. The particularly large, negative correlation between the Perot vote and the percentage of African Americans suggests that Perot was hurt even more than Bush by his failure to appeal to Florida's African-American voters.

Unlike the African-American vote, the vote of Hispanics was weakly (or not at all) correlated with the major-party vote. Clinton and Bush did equally well in counties with high and low percentages of Hispanic voters.[45] The results in Dade County (Miami), Florida's most populous county, were particularly interesting. Reagan and Bush had carried the county throughout the 1980s, and Republican strength rested largely on overwhelming support from the county's large and rapidly growing Hispanic population (49 percent in 1990, predominantly Cuban American). However, in 1992, Bush lost Dade County to Bill Clinton by a margin of 3.5 percentage points.

Like African Americans, Hispanic voters were not attracted by Perot's campaign. His share of the vote was lower in counties with higher proportions of Hispanic voters. The core of Perot's Florida support exhibited little racial and ethnic diversity and was limited largely to non-Hispanic whites.

Households and Family Values

Family values (and related issues such as sexual preference, abortion, and welfare reform) were prominent themes at the Republican National Convention and in the campaign speeches of Dan Quayle and representatives of the Christian right, who played a prominent role in the Bush campaign. Although President Bush downplayed these themes late in the campaign, they still appeared to divide the Florida electorate on election day. Counties with a higher proportion of traditional family households (male and female parents and their children) tended to give more votes to George Bush and fewer to Bill Clinton (Table 9.1). Conversely, areas with more nonfamily households and single-parent households tended to favor Clinton and gave a lower proportion of their votes to Bush. Like George Bush, Ross Perot also fared worse in areas with larger proportions of single-parent families and nonfamily households.

Age

The vote for the two major-party candidates generally showed a weak correlation with age (Table 9.1). As he did in other parts of the country, Clinton received a slightly larger share of the vote in counties with more young voters *and* counties with more older voters (those aged eighteen to thirty-four and those aged sixty-five or more). The Clinton vote tended to be lower in counties with more middle-aged voters (aged thirty-five to sixty-four). The Bush vote was also slightly higher in areas with proportionately more younger voters. Bush did particularly well in counties with more voters aged thirty-five to forty-nine, but he fared worst in counties with more voters aged sixty-five or more. Bush appeared to have the most appeal to those younger voters approaching middle age who were initially attracted to Reaganism in the 1980s. However, the youngest Florida voters (aged eighteen to twenty-five) found Clinton and Bush about equally appealing.

Compared to the vote for the two major-party candidates, Perot's share of the vote bore a strong association with age. The correlations in Table 9.1 indicate that Perot did much better in counties with higher percentages of older voters. He attracted a much smaller share of the vote in areas with more young voters. Perot may have hurt Clinton more than he hurt Bush by drawing away older voters who would have voted for Clinton in higher proportions had Perot not been in the race.

CONCLUSION

In the spring of 1992, Kevin Phillips characterized the evolving political year as immersed in "the politics of frustration,"[46] an apt metaphor for interpreting many aspects of the year's election in Florida. While not fully devolving into a pervasive radicalization of the nonideological center, as implied by Phillips's metaphor, the state's 1992 presidential election did take on significant aspects of "center extremism." Furthermore, the turbulent politics of 1991–1992 illustrates the difficulties of political parties in the state.

In this setting, the presidential incumbent won. George Bush carried Florida, while losing nationally and losing several southern states that had been part of the "Republican lock" on the presidency for several decades. Clearly, Florida has become a Republican stronghold in presidential elections. Aggregate analysis of the county data shows that Republican partisanship salvaged Florida's electoral votes for George Bush. His support tended to come from voters having a typical Republican profile. Thus, his support was greatest in counties that had more registered Republicans and rapidly increasing Republican voter registration; more support for term limits (sold as a device to get entrenched Democrats out of public office); and more voters who were white, better educated, and affluent and who lived in a "regular" nuclear family.

Like Bush, Bill Clinton drew heavily on a partisan electorate. He drew a larger share of the vote in almost exactly those counties where Dukakis did well in 1988 and where Mondale did well against Reagan in 1984. The strong associations between the Clinton vote and opposition to term limits and between the Clinton vote and support for the retention of a state supreme court justice perceived as "too Democratic" on policy issues also reinforce our view of the partisan nature of Clinton's support. The Clinton voter profile resembled that of the typical Democratic voter; he received his greatest support in counties with greater racial and ethnic diversity, lower education and income levels, and more voters in single-parent or nonfamily households.

Although he may have hurt Clinton more, Perot captured frustrated Florida voters from both parties. He tended to draw heavily on older whites with less than a college education; he also drew more votes in areas with fewer single-parent households. Much of Perot's early appeal stemmed from his call to "get the rascals out of office"; thus, it is not surprising that Perot supporters were more likely to favor term limits and disproportionately favored ousting an incumbent state supreme court justice perceived as too progressive. Similarly, his call to the frustrated drew more support from long-term Republican registrants and less from more recent Republican registrants.

Perotism muddled Florida's electoral outcome, but the frustrations producing Perotism did not stop the process propelling development of substantial two-party politics in the state. In the United States, independent political movements and developing third parties often have pushed the major parties to broaden their agendas and deal with the frustrations of particular eras. The political pressures generated by these confrontations, in turn, have brought additional participants into the political arena and have forced the major parties either to incorporate them or to see them participate in new, more viable parties. At this critical juncture, the skepticism of Perot and his adherents toward Florida's major parties may encourage these Democrats and Republicans to align their participants, candidates, issues, public officials, and activists so as to conduct the people's business on a more responsive basis. In the short run, the 1992 election had the positive outcome of electing a Florida congressional delegation of much greater diversity. From a long-term perspective, the 1992 election in Florida may serve as a catalyst, facilitating the partisan sorting process[47] that the state's two major political parties have been undergoing for the past two decades.

NOTES

1. Having carried Florida by nearly a million votes in 1988, Bush carried it by less than 100,000 votes in 1992.

2. Ander Crenshaw from Jacksonville became the first Republican senate president in more than a century. Although net partisan change in the legislature was small, turnover in legislative seats was high. Nearly a third of incumbents did not seek reelection, and after the election, almost 40 percent of the Florida house and nearly half of the Florida senate were new members.

3. Rhodes Cook, "Constructing a Republican Map: Lessons, Solace From 1976," *Congressional Quarterly Weekly Report* (22 August 1992), 2516.

4. See Thomas Petzinger, Jr., and Edward T. Pound, "Bush Sons Jeb and Neil Have Walked a Fine Line Between Business Career, Exploitation of Name," *Wall Street Journal* (23 October 1992), A16; and Curtis Lang, "Party Favors: For Jeb Bush, Politics and Business Are Inseparable," *Village Voice* (23 June 1992), 35–37.

5. Later a similar controversy developed about who would lead the Florida Democratic delegation to the national presidential nominating convention.

6. This meant that Florida, which had had no African-American representative in the Congress for 116 years, would no longer be the largest state in the nation without an African-American representative.

7. In 1989, Ileana Ros-Lehtinen, a Cuban American, was the first Hispanic from Florida to win a seat in the U.S. House of Representatives.

8. Confrontation over the antiquated tax structure in Florida seems to grow more volatile each electoral cycle. With no personal income tax, the state has to depend on sales taxes for four-fifths of its tax revenues.

9. Larry Rohter, "Tax Fight in Florida May Halt Services," *New York Times* (29 June 1992), A8.

10. During the year, electoral system changes also were proposed with varying degrees of seriousness. Florida considered changing the traditional winner-take-all allocation of electoral votes to a system awarding one electoral vote to the winner of each congressional district and the remaining two electoral votes to the statewide winner. See George Will, "Winner-take-all Helps Preserve the Two-party System," *St. Petersburg Times* (11 June 1992), D2. Elections supervisors also advised changing the double primary (runoff) system. See Michael Sznajderman, "Elections Supervisors Work to Kill Double System of Primaries," *Tampa Tribune* (29 July 1992), B1. Nothing came of these proposed changes, but they illustrate the volatility of the electoral system itself in a period of substantial transition for the state.

11. *Congressional Quarterly Weekly Report* (7 September 1991), 2445.

12. With their negative perceptions of the Republican Party, African Americans continued to give the Democrats an advantage in voter registration, but left them open to charges of being a haven for special interests. Offsetting this liability for the Democrats were the visibility and the policy demands of Cuban Americans and the religious right in the Republican Party.

13. Recently Florida's closed presidential primary has become more important in national politics for several reasons: The state's growing bloc of convention delegates in each party; its emerging importance to Republican candidates as one of the pillars of their "southern strategy"; and its centrality to the Super Tuesday primaries.

14. Derived from data in *Congressional Quarterly Weekly Report* (7 March 1992), 562.

15. Clinton was coming off a solid primary victory in Georgia the previous week. There he put together a biracial coalition that gave him nearly 60 percent of the vote; he survived strong personal attacks and ran well among a variety of constituencies. However, white and black voter participation declined from the 1988 primary election. Clinton forces feared that voters were unenthusiastic about their candidate and unsure whether he could be competitive in the November general election. See *Congressional Quarterly Weekly Report* (7 March 1992), 559.

16. Clinton, Lieutenant Governor Buddy MacKay, and U.S. Senator Bob Graham had been among the early members of the Democratic Leadership Council. Both MacKay and Graham endorsed Clinton early, and MacKay eventually chaired Clinton's Florida general election campaign.

17. David E. Rosenbaum, "The 1992 Campaign: Florida," *New York Times* (29 February 1992), 8.

18. Other aspirants provided less opposition for Clinton and Tsongas than expected. After suffering a series of early setbacks, Bob Kerrey and Tom Harkin withdrew the week before the Florida primary; Jerry Brown made little effort in Florida, concentrating his efforts in Michigan and Illinois where primaries were scheduled the week following Super Tuesday.

19. For data on relevant polls and the primary results, plus some related interpretation, see Elizabeth Kolbert, "From Florida, a Cautionary Lesson of Perception," *New York Times* (12 March 1992), A13.

20. Differing from the Republicans, the Democrats utilized a proportional representation formula that enabled the Democratic losers to receive delegates.

21. Kenneth Walker, "Buchanan, Bush, and Southern Strategy," *USA Today* (10 March 1992), A9.

22. See the estimates in "American Survey—Into the Swing," *Economist* (12 September 1992): 25–26.

23. Quoted in Rhodes Cook, "Democratic White House Hopes Shine by Southern Lights," *Congressional Quarterly Weekly Report* (3 October 1992), 3087.

24. Quoted in Cook, "Democratic White House Hopes," 3087.

25. *New York Times* (15 October 1992), A10.

26. Quoted in *St. Petersburg Times* (2 November 1992), 3A.

27. See Kart Loft, "Gauging the Mood: What Floridians Think," *Tampa Tribune* (1 November 1991), Metro–1.

28. The data in this section are from a February 23–27 *St. Petersburg Times*–Eyewitness News Poll reported in *St. Petersburg Times* (1 March 1992), 2A.

29. See Larry Rohter, "Survey Shows Bush Weak in Republican Stronghold," *New York Times* (17 September 1992), A1.

30. See the discussion by Robin Toner, "Contest Tightens as Perot Resurges and Clinton Slips," *New York Times* (25 October 1992), 1.

31. Michael Sznajderman, "Clinton-Bush Race Too Close to Call, Poll Finds," *Tampa Tribune* (27 October 1992), Metro–1.

32. Quoted in *Tampa Tribune* (17 July 1992), Nation/World–5.

33. From a Mason-Dixon poll reported by Gail Epstein, "Floridians Pick Perot in Survey," *Miami Herald* (4 June 1992), A1.

34. See also Suzanne L. Parker, "1992 Annual Policy Survey," *Governing Florida* (Fall/Winter 1992): 11–13. In this fall 1991 survey, Floridians ranked education, economic problems, government, crime, community development, social problems, and the environment, in that order, as the most important problem areas facing the state.

35. Bill Adair, "Washington High on Floridians' Hate List," *St. Petersburg Times* (28 October 1992), B1.

36. We used Florida's sixty-seven counties as the unit of analysis. The Florida supervisor of elections provided county-by-county election data, and other county-level variables were derived from census data.

37. The Democratic victories included in this analysis are Chiles's defeat of Martinez for governor in 1990, Graham's defeat of Hawkins for the U.S. Senate in 1986, and Graham's defeat of Bill Grant for the U.S. Senate in 1992.

38. Without knowing how Perot voters would have voted had Perot not been in the race, it is impossible to give a conclusive answer. We can only offer speculative conclusions based on Perot's share of the vote and the vote received by the two major parties in 1988 and 1992.

39. Pearson's $r = -.41$ for the Perot-Clinton vote, and Pearson's $r = -.17$ for the Perot-Bush vote. The Perot-Clinton correlation was statistically significant (.001 level), while the Perot-Bush correlation was not.

40. The term limit applies to, among others, Florida's U.S. House delegation, the Florida house and senate, and Florida's cabinet; Florida's U.S. Senators would be limited to two terms.

41. In a concerted effort to remove her from the court, anti-abortion groups and members of the Christian right were joined by anti–gun control groups (including the NRA) and a group of state prosecuting attorneys who accused her of being soft on crime. Three other state supreme court justices, all men with a record of judicial decisions similar to Barkett's, were also up for retention, but only Barkett attracted highly visible, well-financed opposition.

42. William E. Hulbary, Anne E. Kelley, and Lewis Bowman, "Florida: The Republican Surge Continues," in *The 1988 Presidential Election in the South: Continuity Amidst Change in Southern Party Politics*, ed. Laurence W. Moreland, Robert P. Steed, and Tod A. Baker (New York: Praeger, 1991), chapter 9.

43. Turnout figures are reported in Robert Pear, "55% Voting Rate Reverses 30 Year Decline," *New York Times* (5 November 1992), B4.

44. See Hulbary, Kelley, and Bowman, "Florida: The Republican Surge Continues."

45. Dade County (Miami) is unique. With the largest population in the state (more than 1.9 million in 1990), Dade County has by far the largest population of Hispanics (49 percent) and white Hispanics (43 percent) as well. Most of these are Cuban Americans, but a sizable percentage are from other Central and South American countries. In view of this uniqueness, we calculated the correlations in Table 9.1 for percentages of Hispanic and white Hispanic voters, first including and then excluding Dade County. The correlations were virtually identical either way, and we report them with Dade County included.

46. Kevin Phillips, "The Politics of Frustration," *New York Times Magazine* (12 April 1992), 38–42.

47. For an earlier analysis of this process in one part of Florida's party system, see Lewis Bowman, William E. Hulbary, and Anne E. Kelley, "Party Sorting at the Grassroots: Stable Partisans and Party-Changers Among Florida's Precinct Officials," in *The Disappearing South? Studies in Regional Change and Continuity*, ed. Robert P. Steed, Laurence W. Moreland, and Tod A. Baker (University: The University of Alabama Press, 1990), chapter 4.

10

North Carolina: Conflicting Forces in a Confusing Year

CHARLES PRYSBY

George Bush, Dan Quayle, Bill Clinton, and Al Gore spent a combined total of twenty days in North Carolina during the 1992 presidential campaign. Four years earlier, the presidential and vice-presidential candidates spent only half as many days in the state. The increased attention given to North Carolina by the candidates in 1992 indicated a more central role for the state in the presidential campaign. The identification of North Carolina as a battleground state accurately reflected its competitive status, as evidenced by the fact that North Carolina had the closest presidential race of any state in 1992. The final margin of victory was a scant 0.8 percent of the vote.

A brief examination of presidential elections in North Carolina during the 1980s does not immediately suggest that the state would be targeted as a battleground state in 1992. The 1980s were very good years for Republican presidential candidates. All three times the Republican candidate carried the state, and in the last two elections the state was three to four percentage points more Republican than the nation.

The 1980s also were successful years for North Carolina Republicans in congressional and state elections. John East defeated incumbent U.S. Senator Bob Morgan in 1980 to give North Carolina two Republican senators. The other senator, Jesse Helms, was reelected in 1984 in an expensive and notorious campaign over then Governor Jim Hunt. Additionally, Republican Congressman Jim Martin was successful in capturing the governorship that year, only the second time in this century that a Republican had been able to do so (the other time was in 1972, when James Holshouser was elected). In 1988, Jim Martin was easily reelected, and the Republican candidate for lieutenant governor, former Congressman Jim Gardner, also won, marking the first time in the century that Republicans had captured this office.

There were qualifications to this story of Republican success in the 1980s. Most of the key victories were recorded in presidential election years, when the party had the benefit of a strong candidate at the top of the ticket. Off-year elections were more favorable to the Democrats. The U.S. Senate seat won by East in 1980 was recaptured by Democrat Terry Sanford in 1986, for example. Elections for the U.S. House also displayed a surge-and-decline pattern. Republicans captured four of the eleven U.S. House seats in 1980 and five of the eleven in 1984, but in the following off-year elections, the Republicans lost two seats each time. Also, further down the ballot Democrat domination remained, although sometimes more tenuously. The state legislature, for example, maintained a Democratic majority in both houses throughout the 1980s.

Republican gains in North Carolina during the 1980s were built on a foundation that had been laid earlier. The breakthrough election was 1972, when Richard Nixon's strong showing in the presidential election helped Helms to first win election to the U.S. Senate and Holshouser to be elected governor. This marked the first time in modern state history that either the governor or a U.S. senator was not a Democrat. But the combined impact of the Watergate scandal and the 1976 presidential election halted Republican advances, and it was not until 1980, with Ronald Reagan at the top of the ticket, that the party was able to return to the competitive position it had earlier established.

Developments in North Carolina paralleled what was happening in the region. Southern politics during the 1970s and 1980s was characterized by Republican victories in presidential elections (1976 excepted), with the South becoming the most Republican region in the country. Republican success also was evident in key statewide races during the 1970s and 1980s; during this period, every state except Georgia and Mississippi elected a Republican governor, and every state except Arkansas and Louisiana elected a Republican U.S. senator. But Republican strength declined as one went down the ballot. In elections for the U.S. House and for the state legislature, for example, the South continued to be more Democratic than the rest of the country, albeit by a diminished margin.

A year prior to the 1992 election campaign, most observers felt that North Carolina would be solidly Republican in the presidential race, a judgment that was based on the recent history of presidential elections in the state and region and on President Bush's high approval rating in public opinion polls. But two factors conspired to make North Carolina a battleground state: (1) the precipitous drop in Bush's national approval rating, from 74 percent in August 1991 to 40 percent in August 1992;[1] and (2) the selection of two moderate southerners for the Democratic Party ticket, a strategy that presumably would make the party more appealing to southern voters. In a nationally competitive presidential election with a Clinton/Gore Democratic ticket, North Carolina was a logical battleground state. Its fourteen electoral college votes made it the third largest southern state, and the two larger ones, Texas and Florida, were considered especially Republican. By contrast, North Carolina had been slightly less Republican than the South in the three presidential elections held during the 1980s.

Given the circumstances that existed in 1992, North Carolina could not be considered safely Republican, but it was hardly a state where the Democrats had a significant advantage.

The selection of North Carolina as a battleground state also must be seen in light of the national strategies of both parties. For Republicans, holding the South was an essential ingredient for any winning formula. Arkansas and Tennessee would have to be conceded as home states to the Democrats, but if the rest of the South would go for Bush, that would provide him with 130 electoral college votes, almost one-half of what he would need for victory. Democrats sought to disrupt this strategy by making concerted appeals in a few southern states. If Clinton could win some southern states in addition to Arkansas and Tennessee, it not only would deprive the Republicans of needed electoral college votes, but also would force them to devote resources to defend what used to be considered their presidential strongholds, resources that thus would be unavailable for use elsewhere.

THE CAMPAIGN

The Presidential Race

The Democratic presidential strategy in North Carolina emphasized two key elements: (1) the poor economic performance of the Bush administration and (2) the fact that the Democratic ticket consisted of two moderate Democrats. This same strategy was used throughout the country, and it addressed what many observers felt were the primary reasons for Democratic presidential defeats in the 1980s: Voters judged the Republicans as better able to manage the economy and viewed the Democratic candidates as too liberal.

The Republican strategy focused on attacking Clinton's personal characteristics and on portraying the Democrats as liberals. Several questions about Clinton, including his marital fidelity and draft record, emerged during the primary season. These were amplified into more general concerns about Clinton's honesty and integrity. Highlighting the "slick Willie" image that had been discussed in the national media, Republicans attempted to paint Clinton as an individual who would not be forthright on the issues and could not be trusted to be president. Additionally, Clinton was attacked as a "tax and spend liberal Democrat" who would have to raise taxes on the middle class to pay for all his programs despite his claims that any tax increase would be limited to upper-income groups.

Democrats responded to charges about Clinton's personal character by arguing that the Republicans were trying to avoid the real issues in the campaign and by claiming that Bush broke his 1988 pledge never to raise taxes and therefore was himself lacking in integrity. Republican claims that Clinton and Gore were liberals in moderate clothing were dismissed by Democrats as typical campaign misrepresentation. But while Democrats felt that they had to respond to Republican charges, lest they repeat the Dukakis mistakes of 1988, they attempted as much as possible to focus attention on the economy. The Clinton strategy was to make the election a referendum on the performance of the Bush administration.

The Republican response to these charges about the failures of the Bush administration built on three themes: (1) The Bush administration had great accomplishments in the area of foreign affairs, including success in waging the war against Iraq and in overseeing the collapse of communism in Europe; (2) the economy was not that bad, and voters would see that this was the case if the media presented a more balanced account; and (3) many of the economic problems were a result of the Democrats in Congress stymieing Bush's economic proposals. While Republicans believed that it was necessary to defend the record of the Bush administration, they did not want to make the election a referendum on this record. Their goal was to make the election a question of which candidate could best be trusted to be president, a contest that Republicans were confident Bush would win.

Complicating these strategies was the fact that this election was not a simple two-candidate race. H. Ross Perot's original entry had made the presidential race very interesting; in June, all three candidates were extremely close together in the national public opinion polls, with no one having more than one-third of the vote preferences.[2] Perot's withdrawal from the race in July simplified the situation, but his reentry on October 1 reintroduced confusion into the campaign. Both major parties were unclear about whose supporters were more likely to defect to Perot, uncertain about how best to respond to Perot's campaign charges, and confused over the dynamics of a three-candidate race. Democrats feared that Perot would draw voters who had definitely rejected Bush, but who also felt uncomfortable about Clinton's personal characteristics. From the Republican standpoint, Perot would be another voice attacking the record of the Bush administration, lending more credence to Democratic campaign charges. Furthermore, Perot's presence might make it more difficult to focus attention on Clinton's personal character.

Although concerned, North Carolina Democrats were not greatly threatened by Perot. His appeal in the state was significantly lower than his appeal nationwide, and it seemed that the Perot vote would not come disproportionately at the expense of the Clinton vote. Blacks, who were about 20 percent of the electorate in the state, were unlikely to vote for Perot, and there were enough solidly Democratic white groups to make Democrats feel comfortable about a three-candidate race. In the eyes of some analysts, Perot would more likely draw off independents and weak Democrats, along with disaffected Republicans. Since independents and weak Democrats were important components of the Republican southern presidential coalition in the 1980s, simply keeping these voters out of the Bush camp might be enough to ensure a Clinton victory. But the danger in the Perot candidacy was that if he became a strong and creditable candidate, he could draw off many potential Clinton voters, especially if these voters began to seriously question whether Clinton really possessed presidential character.

The conflicting forces described above indicate that the outcome of the presidential race in the state was highly uncertain during the campaign, especially after Perot's reentry. Polling data reinforce that conclusion. Statewide polls in late August and early October showed that while Clinton had a modest lead over Bush both times, support for both candidates was soft. Neither candidate was viewed favorably by a majority of the voters in either poll.[3] The October poll showed that opinions of Perot were even more negative, but he nevertheless was a wild card who might siphon off some of the soft support for the other candidates.

Because North Carolina was defined as a battleground state, the Democratic and Republican candidates made numerous trips to the state.[4] Gore led the list with eight trips, covering nine days and seventeen different cities, some more than once. Gore's frequent appearances were not surprising, given his appeal as a southern Democrat and a candidate who won the state's presidential primary in the 1988 Super Tuesday contest. Clinton came to the state four times and visited thirteen different cities, many of them as part of a two-day bus trip with Gore. The Republican candidates visited the state less, but the frequent Democratic trips forced the Bush campaign to devote attention to the state. Bush appeared three times, visiting eight cities, while Quayle made two trips, appearing in eleven cities. Campaign surrogates, including spouses, also were heavily involved, most notably Marilyn Quayle, who made four trips on her own to the state. These candidate and surrogate appearances enhanced the visibility of the presidential campaign in the local media. Coverage in the local newspapers and exposure on local television stations accompanied each visit. The campaign messages delivered during these trips differed little from what the candidates said nationally. The visits basically served to reinforce the national campaign themes, stimulate voter interest in the campaigns, and generate local campaign enthusiasm.

The presidential campaigns were also extremely visible to North Carolina voters through televised political advertisements. The national strategies of the campaigns differed. The Clinton campaign spent most of its television money buying local time, feeling that it was more efficient to target funds to the competitive states and avoid spending in states that were safe for either candidate.[5] Since North Carolina was a battleground state, it received a heavy infusion of money. The Bush campaign spent heavily on national network time, and this is primarily how they reached North Carolina voters. Perot also spent heavily on national network time, buying both more conventional short spots and highly unusual thirty-minute "informercials," which featured Perot lecturing about the nation's economic problems and using numerous charts to make his points. These commercials, along with the exposure he received on national news programs, effectively constituted his campaign in the state, as Perot eschewed more traditional campaign techniques and established only a very limited grassroots effort in the state.

The content of the political advertisements matched the campaign themes outlined above. Several Republican ads focused on questions of Clinton's trustworthiness. Another Republican commercial claimed that the average family would see tax increases ranging from $1,000 to $2,000 per year under Clinton's proposals.[6] Democratic advertisements argued that the Bush administration had a dismal economic record and that Bush had broken his pledge on taxes. The Perot commercials also emphasized the economic woes of the country, singling out the budget deficit as the root cause of these problems.

The Democratic presidential campaign effort in North Carolina was much stronger in 1992 than it had been four years earlier. More resources were available, better coordination existed between the national and state campaigns, and more enthusiasm was displayed by those involved in the campaign effort. National campaign staff arrived in the state in mid-September, stayed through the election, and, unlike 1988, were able to effectively work with the state party.[7] A major effort was aimed at "persuadable" voters, defined as under sixty, white, registered voters in swing precincts.[8] These "persuadables" were hit with seven different pieces of campaign mail. Also, a very substantial get-out-the-vote drive was conducted. Aimed especially at black voters in urban areas, this effort involved phone calls, mailings, and door-to-door visits.[9]

The Republican campaign, by contrast, had fewer resources than in 1988. Less money was raised in the state and less was received from the national campaign, with the result that there was only one-half as much money to spend in 1992 as in 1988.[10] National help was lacking in other ways, too. For example, campaign paraphernalia, such as buttons or bumper stickers, were not provided by the national campaign, just the opposite of what had been done in 1988.[11] Fewer resources translated into less activity. Phoning was limited to 125,000 calls, most of which were made late in the campaign.[12] Mailings were down as well, although 4 million pieces still went out, targeted at Republicans, swing precincts, and areas around military bases.[13]

The Republican presidential campaign in North Carolina also was less well organized than in 1988. The national campaign provided less direction in terms of themes and targeted voter groups, so it was more difficult to provide a clear focus for the state campaign. Scheduling also was more disorganized, especially with respect to visits from candidates and campaign surrogates. Energy among campaign workers appeared down in 1992, but late in the campaign there was a noticeable surge in activity and enthusiasm among campaign workers and party activists.[14]

Congressional and State Elections

While the presidential contest was the most visible in the state, the gubernatorial and senatorial campaigns also attracted considerable attention. Former Democratic Governor Hunt faced Lieutenant Governor Gardner in a gubernatorial election marked by harsh attacks. As in several previous elections, such as the 1984 and 1990 reelection efforts of Helms, North Carolina voters were served a full course of negative televised commercials. Hunt criticized Gardner's business dealings, claiming that he had avoided paying business debts.[15] Gardner was equally forceful in attacking Hunt, as he compared Hunt to Hitler and charged near the end of the campaign that Hunt had broken the law by having a campaign worker electronically eavesdrop on phone calls made by Gardner.[16] The televised debates between the two candidates were equally vitriolic. Both campaigns spent heavily, especially for broadcast time, but Hunt had a decided advantage here. He spent $6.7 million in 1992, compared to $4.1 million for Gardner.[17]

The U.S. Senate election between incumbent Sanford and Republican challenger Lauch Faircloth was more polite and civilized. The early weeks of the campaign saw surprisingly little activity. Sanford did not appear to be devoting intense effort to his reelection, and Faircloth was almost invisible on the campaign trail. But in September Faircloth intensified his television and radio campaign, attacking Sanford on a number of issues. Faircloth's campaign was being run by the Congressional Club, the organization founded by Helms in the 1970s, which was following a strategy similar to what it had successfully employed in previous campaigns. The focus was on defining Sanford as ideologically out of touch with North Carolina values, while attempting to avoid debate over Faircloth's issue positions. Complicating Sanford's reelection bid was his hospitalization for two weeks in October for heart valve surgery, which not only removed him from the campaign trail, but also raised questions about his health and vigor, especially because he was seventy-five years old. To drive home this point, Faircloth aired an ad in October wishing Sanford a speedy recovery from his difficult surgery. Faircloth slightly outspent Sanford, $3.0 million to $2.6 million, but these expenditures were far less than what was spent in the gubernatorial race or in the 1990 senatorial contest between Helms and Gantt.[18]

Elections for the U.S. House received less attention than the senatorial and gubernatorial campaigns, but the congressional redistricting plan adopted earlier in the year made at least some of the races quite interesting. North Carolina was awarded an additional U.S. House seat for 1992, bringing the total to twelve for the state. It was understood that the new district plan would create at least one district that would have a black majority. The state legislature adopted such a plan in 1991, but it was rejected by the U.S. Justice Department, which argued that a second minority district should have been drawn.[19] Republicans felt that this was a victory for them, as concentrating blacks into two districts would drain off many reliable Democratic voters from the remaining districts. However, Democrats in the state legislature were able to produce a plan that not only contained two black–majority districts, but also placed the six incumbent Democratic congressmen seeking reelection into fairly safe districts.[20] The plan received considerable criticism, as the districts were in many cases oddly shaped, oftentimes not being very compact and sometimes just barely contiguous, but it did pass legal scrutiny. The plan left the Republicans solidly in control of three of the four congressional seats they held, but their hold on their fourth seat, the Eleventh District, was more tenuous. The Eleventh District had been highly competitive throughout the 1980s, and the redistricting did not substantially alter the district's partisan balance. Moreover, Republican prospects for capturing additional seats were uncertain. Only two of the six Democratic congressmen running for reelection appeared vulnerable, and neither extremely so, plus the two new black-majority districts were sure to be captured by Democrats.

RESULTS

Presidential Election

Despite the fact that Clinton led Bush by five percentage points nationally and the fact that the Republican campaign in North Carolina was beset by the problems described above, Bush still managed to carry the state. Bush received 43.4 percent of the vote, Clinton 42.7 percent, and Perot 13.7 percent.[21] North Carolina was the only state targeted by the Clinton campaign that was not carried by the Democrats, so Republicans in the state had reason to be positive about the outcome. However, Bush's winning margin was extremely slender—only 20,600 votes out of a total of over 2.6 million. The narrowness of the victory naturally had no effect on the electoral college votes, but it may have provided an insufficient boost for other Republicans on the ballot.

A Bush victory had not been predicted by the pre-election polls, although most had accurately called for a close election. The Carolina poll, conducted in late October by the University of North Carolina's School of Journalism, showed Clinton ahead by three points.[22] Similarly, a Mason-Dixon poll conducted a week before the election had Clinton ahead by one point.[23] However, movement in the Bush direction was evident—an early October Mason-Dixon poll showed Clinton ahead by six points, for example—so a narrow Bush victory was not entirely unexpected.[24]

Voting patterns in 1992 were in many ways similar to 1988 patterns. Table 10.1 presents the relationship between voting behavior and several social and demographic factors, based on the exit poll conducted by Voter Research and Surveys. Race stands out as the most critical characteristic. Clinton received over 90 percent of the black vote, but only about one-third of the white vote, a pattern very similar to what Dukakis received in 1988.[25] The data on racial voting patterns might lead one to erroneously believe that Bush would have won easily had it not been for the Perot vote, which came primarily from whites. Although the combination of the Bush and the Perot votes in 1992 is very similar to the Bush vote in 1988, both in the overall total and in the racial breakdown, the Perot voters indicated on the exit poll that they would have split their votes evenly between the other two candidates had Perot not been in the race. If the Perot vote were evenly divided between Bush and Clinton, the latter would have received over 40 percent of the vote of whites in North Carolina, a relatively good showing for a Democratic presidential candidate and very close to what would be needed for victory.

Other demographic factors also were significant, although none was as important as race. (See Table 10.1.) Bush did worse among the lower-income

Table 10.1
North Carolina Voting by Selected Social and Demographic Variables, 1992 (in percent)

Variable	President			U. S. Senate	Governor
	Bush	Clinton	Perot	Faircloth	Hunt
All voters	44	43	14	52	54
Race					
White (83)	50	34	15	60	47
Black (17)	5	91	3	7	93
Income					
Under $30,000 (42)	35	51	14	45	62
$30,000-$50,000 (28)	52	35	13	61	45
Over $50,000 (29)	49	36	15	56	48
Education					
High school only (34)	45	41	13	55	52
Some college (27)	44	42	14	52	50
College degree (25)	46	39	15	59	51
Postgraduate work (14)	33	54	12	37	71
Gender					
Male (50)	47	39	14	56	51
Female (50)	41	46	13	49	56
Age					
18-29 (22)	43	41	15	51	54
30-44 (33)	42	43	15	53	55
45-59 (25)	47	40	13	55	49
Over 59 (16)	43	49	9	49	57
Church attendance					
Attend weekly (51)	50	39	11	58	47
Attend less often (49)	38	47	17	46	61

Note: Percentages are to be read across each row (*e.g.*, 50 percent of whites voted for Bush, 34 percent for Clinton, and 15 percent for Perot); rows may not total exactly 100 percent because of rounding. For the Senatorial and Gubernatorial elections, only the percentages for the winning candidates (Republican Faircloth and Democrat Hunt, respectively) are shown; these were essentially two-candidate races, so in each case the remaining vote went almost entirely to the other major-party candidate in the race. The number in parentheses following each social or demographic category indicates the percent of exit poll respondents in the category (*e.g.*, 83 percent of the respondents were white). N = 1563.
Source: Voter Research and Surveys 1992 North Carolina exit poll; used by permission.

groups, as we would expect, but education is not similarly related to the vote. The only clear difference that emerges on education is that those with very high levels of education were more strongly for Clinton. The results for education may seem anomalous, but they match the 1988 pattern.[26] The expected gender gap is evident in both elections. Age is only weakly related to the vote in either year, except that those over sixty were more Democratic. The important religious distinction in North Carolina is not between Protestants and non-Protestants, as there are too few of the latter, but between those of different religious commitment. Those who attend church regularly were substantially more likely to vote for Bush, who also did very well among whites who said that they were "born again." On the whole, the demographic patterns found here reflect the usual and expected differences between the two parties, especially in the South.

The Perot vote is not clearly defined in demographic terms, other than the fact that most Perot voters were white. Perhaps surprisingly, Perot's appeal had little relationship to socioeconomic status, at least in terms of education and income. His vote also is unrelated to gender. We might have expected that, as an independent candidate, Perot would appeal very strongly to young voters, who have not yet formed deep partisan attachments, but the only connection to age is the limited support provided to him by those over sixty. For an independent candidate, Perot's support was remarkably diverse.

More important than demographic factors are attitudinal ones. Party identification is an important influence on voting, and one that has been used to explain Republican success in past elections in the South. Republican candidates have won by getting nearly all of the votes of self-identified Republicans, most of the votes of independents, and even a significant minority of votes from Democrats. This is exactly what Bush did in 1988, but in 1992 the independent vote split evenly between Bush and Clinton, with about one-fourth going to Perot. (See Table 10.2.) Clinton therefore would have won if he had done as well among Democratic voters as Bush did among Republican voters, as there were somewhat more Democrats than Republicans among those who voted. However, there were more defections in the Democratic ranks, allowing Bush to narrowly win the state.

The impact of party identification on the presidential vote is even clearer if we focus on white voters only. (See Table 10.3.) This analysis is useful because blacks are so overwhelmingly Democratic, both in identification and in voting behavior. The variation in voting that requires explanation exists primarily among whites. Clinton did well among white Democratic voters, but still lost about one vote in three. The southern and moderate character of the Democratic ticket was insufficient to prevent a sizable minority of white Democrats from defecting, although many went for Perot rather than Bush. And Clinton's appeal to white independents was limited, although again a significant share went to Perot.

Ideology is another basic orientation that has been cited as key to the failure of Democratic candidates in southern elections. The attempt by the Clinton campaign strategists to cast their ticket as new and more moderate Democrats appears to have had some impact. Clinton won about one-half of the votes of self-classified moderates, compared to only one-third for Bush. (See Table 10.2.) Conservatives still went decisively for Bush, although not nearly as strongly as in 1988. If we examine white voters only, we find that Clinton still matched Bush in appeal among moderates, who made up nearly one-half of all white voters. (See Table 10.3.) These ideological orientations should be related to specific policy issues, and the available data suggest that to be the case. For example, attitudes on abortion are fairly clearly linked to presidential vote.[27]

Table 10.2
North Carolina Voting by Selected Political Orientations, 1992 (in percent)

Variable	President			U. S. Senate	Governor
	Bush	Clinton	Perot	Faircloth	Hunt
All voters	4 4	4 3	1 4	5 2	5 4
Party identification					
Democrat (45)	1 5	7 3	1 3	2 2	8 2
Independent (18)	3 6	3 8	2 6	4 9	5 2
Republican (37)	8 4	7	9	9 1	1 8
Ideology					
Liberal (15)	1 3	7 2	1 5	1 7	8 3
Moderate (47)	3 5	4 9	1 6	4 6	6 2
Conservative (38)	6 9	2 0	1 0	7 6	3 0
National economy					
Good (28)	8 8	7	4	8 7	2 1
Fair (45)	3 6	4 8	1 5	4 6	5 8
Poor (26)	1 0	7 0	2 0	2 6	8 0
Economic situation					
Better (27)	7 4	1 9	9	8 0	2 9
Same (33)	5 1	3 7	1 3	5 6	5 1
Worse (38)	1 1	7 0	1 9	2 5	7 6
1988 presidential vote					
Bush (54)	6 9	1 8	1 2	7 8	3 1
Dukakis (25)	4	8 3	1 3	9	9 2
Did not vote (16)	3 2	4 9	2 0	4 3	6 0

Note: Percentages are to be read across each row (e.g., 15 percent of Democrats voted for Bush, 73 percent voted for Clinton, and 13 percent voted for Perot); rows may not total exactly 100 percent because of rounding. For the senatorial and gubernatorial elections, only the percentages for the winning candidates (Republican Faircloth and Democrat Hunt, respectively) are shown; these were essentially two-candidate races, so in each case the remaining vote went almost entirely to the other major-party candidate in the race. The number in parentheses following each orientation category indicates the percentage of exit poll respondents each category (e.g., 45 percent of the respondents were Democrats). The item on the national economy asked each respondent for his or her opinion of the condition of the nation's economy. The item on economic situation asked each respondent how his or her personal situation had changed over the last four years. N = 1563.
Source: Voter Research and Surveys 1992 North Carolina exit poll; used by permission.

Unfortunately, not enough information on specific policy issues exists to allow us to determine the relative impact of different issues, especially when controlling for party identification and ideology.

Party identification and ideology are fairly stable general orientations that influence the vote. Short-term forces also are important for explaining the vote. The most important short-term forces influencing presidential voting are retrospective evaluations of government performance, especially regarding the economy, and assessments of the personal characteristics of the candidates. As we have discussed above, both evaluations of government economic performance and the personal characteristics of the candidates received great attention in the

Table 10.3
North Carolina Voting by Selected Political Orientations for White Voters, 1992
(in percent)

Variable	President			U. S. Senate	Governor
	Bush	Clinton	Perot	Faircloth	Hunt
All white voters	50	34	17	60	47
Party identification					
Democrat (38)	19	64	17	29	77
Independent (19)	40	33	27	54	47
Republican (43)	84	7	9	91	18
Ideology					
Liberal (13)	17	65	18	19	81
Moderate (47)	40	41	18	53	56
Conservative (40)	74	15	11	82	24
National economy					
Good (32)	90	6	4	88	20
Fair (45)	42	41	18	53	53
Poor (22)	13	61	26	33	74
Economic situation					
Better (31)	77	14	10	83	27
Same (40)	56	30	14	62	46
Worse (28)	14	63	24	33	69
1988 presidential vote					
Bush (62)	71	17	12	79	30
Dukakis (20)	5	77	18	13	89
Did not vote (14)	36	40	25	53	53

Note: Percentages are to be read across each row (*e.g.*, 19 percent of white Democrats voted for Bush, 64 percent voted for Clinton, and 17 percent voted for Perot). For the senatorial and gubernatorial elections, only the percentages for the winning candidates (Republican Faircloth and Democrat Hunt, respectively) are shown; these were essentially two-candidate races, so in each case the remaining vote went almost entirely to the other major party candidate in the race. The number in parentheses following each orientation category indicates the percent of exit poll respondents each category (*e.g.*, 38 percent of the white respondents were Democrats). The item on the national economy asked each respondent for his or her opinion of the condition of the nation's economy. The item on economic situation asked each respondent how his or her personal situation had changed over the last four years. *N* = 1252.
Source: Voter Research and Surveys 1992 North Carolina exit poll; used by permission.

presidential campaign, so these attitudes should have played an important role in determining individual voting.

Exit poll data on retrospective economic evaluations are available. Voters were asked (1) whether their financial situation was better or worse off compared to 1988, and (2) what they felt about the condition of the nation's economy. As Tables 10.2 and 10.3 show, both assessments are very strongly related to the vote. An equally strong relationship existed in 1988. The difference is that in 1992 public opinion was more pessimistic. Only about one-fourth of the 1992 electorate felt that the national economy was good or that they were better off compared to four years earlier.

Regrettably, exit poll data on voter evaluations of the personal characteristics of the candidates are very limited. Given the general importance of these attitudes in presidential elections and the particular attention paid to Clinton's characteristics in 1992, there is good reason to believe that such evaluations were important in influencing the vote, but this suspicion cannot be fully supported with direct evidence. It is true that one-fourth of the exit poll respondents said that Clinton's draft record was an important factor in their vote decision, suggesting that voters were concerned about such matters. Indirect evidence also can be presented. The Mason-Dixon pre-election polls conducted in North Carolina asked respondents whether they had a favorable or an unfavorable opinion of each candidate. We do not directly know whether the opinions reflect assessments of personal characteristics, issue positions, or, in the case of Bush, performance in office because follow-up questions regarding why respondents had a favorable or an unfavorable opinion were not asked. But we can compare opinions of Clinton and Gore. While 43 percent of the respondents in the late October poll gave Clinton an unfavorable rating, only 27 percent did so for Gore.[28] Since Clinton and Gore were ideologically fairly similar, this difference is unlikely to reflect differences in how the voters assessed the issue positions of the candidates. The difference also cannot reflect a greater appeal of Gore based on regional ties, religion, or age, since Gore and Clinton did not differ on these factors. Thus, we infer that the difference reflects a more negative assessment of Clinton's personal characteristics, not surprising given the attention devoted to these factors in the presidential campaign. The unfavorable ratings for Bush and Quayle do not differ very much (42 percent and 45 percent, respectively), which suggests that their ratings are based more on performance evaluations and issue positions.

We conclude that voting in the 1992 presidential election in North Carolina was strongly influenced by party identification, ideological orientation, evaluations of government economic performance, and assessments of the personal characteristics of the candidates. Clinton was advantaged by the widespread negative opinions held by voters about the economic performance of the Bush administration. His image as a more moderate Democrat also made him somewhat more acceptable to moderate white voters than recent Democratic presidential candidates. But he was damaged by negative assessments of his personal characteristics. Similarly, Bush was helped by some forces and hurt by others. The election outcome cannot be explained in terms of a single factor. All of the above variables significantly affected the result, and the tightness of the race reflects the conflicting pull of these forces.

Congressional and State Elections

Below the presidential level, both parties had reason to cheer about the results. Republicans were most pleased with the U.S. Senate race, where Faircloth defeated the incumbent Democrat, Sanford. Faircloth's victory was a result of three factors discussed above: (1) an effective campaign by Faircloth to characterize Sanford as a liberal who was out of touch with North Carolina voters; (2) a weak campaign by Sanford, who failed both to respond to Faircloth's charges and to vigorously campaign for reelection; and (3) Sanford's health problems, including his hospitalization in October. Faircloth's victory indicates that the Congressional Club remains a force in North Carolina politics. Five of the last six Senate elections in North Carolina have been won by Republican candidates associated with the Congressional Club. The lone exception was Sanford's 1986 victory, which occurred when the Republican candidate was not tied to the Congressional Club.

The data in Tables 10.1 through 10.3 indicate how a Republican can win a statewide office. Faircloth attracted about 60 percent of the white vote, around the minimum necessary for a Republican to be successful. He did so by running very well among Republicans, splitting the independent vote, and capturing a reasonable minority of Democrats. Party affiliations have shifted sufficiently so that a Republican no longer has to win an overwhelming share of the independent vote or draw away large numbers of Democrats. The key is being able to win at least one-half of the white moderate voters, which Faircloth did. This share of the moderate white vote, combined with most of the conservative white vote, can add up to a majority.

The U.S. House races were more favorable to the Democrats, who carried the two black-majority districts (the First and Twelfth Districts) and reelected the six incumbent Democrats running for reelection. Republicans did retain the four congressional seats they held, but they had hoped for more. The Democrats, although pleased to have won what they did, were somewhat disappointed in their failure to win the Eleventh Congressional District, a traditionally competitive seat that they felt could be won in a year when the Republican presidential candidate was not particularly strong.

State elections represented a bigger success for the Democratic Party. Hunt defeated Gardner in the gubernatorial election, ending eight years of Republican control of the executive branch, and the party also recaptured the lieutenant governorship from the Republicans. The other statewide elected offices, including attorney general and secretary of state, were retained by the Democrats, although in some cases by narrow margins. And in the state legislature, the Democratic Party essentially maintained its strength, losing three seats in the house, but adding three in the senate.

The gubernatorial election data in Tables 10.1 through 10.3 outline how Democratic candidates can fashion a black-white coalition that is capable of winning top state offices. Hunt attracted nearly one-half of the white vote, more than a Democratic candidate normally needs. He did so by being competitive for independent and moderate white voters and even enticing a modest number of Republicans and conservatives to vote for him. In fact, 30 percent of Hunt's support came from independents and Republicans, and 20 percent of his vote came from conservatives.

CONCLUSION

The results of the 1992 elections send conflicting signals about the future of electoral politics in North Carolina. Focusing on the Senate race provides a favorable sign for Republican prospects. Examining the gubernatorial and congressional elections suggests otherwise. Some of the confusion can be cleared up by realizing that North Carolina has become a competitive state, but one in which competition varies by office, and thus we must analyze competition with this in mind.

Despite the southern ticket put forth by the Democrats, the Republican percentage of the two-party presidential vote in North Carolina was four points greater than the national figure. Since the Perot voters indicated that they would have divided evenly between Clinton and Bush in the absence of Perot, the same difference would have existed in a two-candidate race. An almost identical margin existed in 1988. Given the difference in the Democratic ticket between those two presidential elections, it is surprising that the Democrats did not do better in North Carolina in 1992, relative to the national vote. The obvious implication is that the moderate strategy followed by the Democrats was not a particularly southern strategy. Clinton may have benefited from the perception that he was less liberal than Dukakis, but that helped him in the North as much as in the South. If a Clinton/Gore ticket ran worse in North Carolina than nationally, the likelihood is that the state will retain its Republican advantage in subsequent presidential elections.

Which party wins North Carolina in the future presidential elections will depend on what happens nationally. If in 1996 Clinton runs and is reelected with 55 percent or more of the vote, he most likely will carry the state. If he wins reelection by a narrow margin, he probably will not win the state. And if he loses reelection, he almost certainly will lose North Carolina by a significant margin. Thus, Republicans should have a good chance of winning the state except when the Democratic presidential candidate begins to approach a national landslide.

Below the presidential level, future elections in the state are likely to be highly competitive at the top of the ticket. The U.S. Senate election demonstrates that Republicans are capable of defeating a reasonably popular incumbent even without the advantage of a highly popular presidential candidate at the head of the ballot. Democratic victories in the congressional and state elections suggest that they also do not require a strong presidential ticket to be successful. More support for the expectation of intense two-party competition, at least for important offices, comes from an examination of winning margins. The three most important statewide offices—U.S. senator, governor, and lieutenant governor—all were won with less than 56 percent of the vote. While no incumbent congressmen were defeated, four were reelected with less than 56 percent of the vote, signaling that these seats cannot be considered safe.

North Carolina voters are now sufficiently independent in behavior to create a fairly volatile electoral situation. Significant ticket splitting occurs. In the gubernatorial and presidential elections, for example, one-fourth of the Hunt voters did not vote for Clinton, and one-fifth of the Gardner voters did not vote for Bush.[29] Some of this results from the presence of Perot, but even comparing just the gubernatorial and senatorial elections, 13 percent of the voters split their tickets. Considerable volatility exists across time as well. The 1988 Dukakis voters might be expected to be hard-core Democrats, but 17 percent did not vote for Clinton, 9 percent did not vote for Sanford, and 8 percent did not vote for Hunt.[30]

The future of North Carolina politics should be one of two party competition, especially for key offices. Divided election outcomes are quite likely to occur. Congressional and state elections surely will be affected by national forces, especially because the major state elections are held in presidential years. But candidates and campaigns will count, too. Both parties are capable of winning when they have good candidates running strong campaigns. The biggest question for Republicans is whether they can parlay their successes at the top of the ticket into victories further down the ballot, such as for the state legislature. If that occurs, North Carolina will be a real two-party state.

NOTES

A number of individuals contributed to this study. Seth Effron, formerly of the *Greensboro News and Record*, shared his insights with me and provided polling data. Jennifer O'Lear, Institute of Government, University of North Carolina at Chapel Hill, provided me with the Carolina poll data. Lee Shapiro, Voter Research and Surveys, provided the exit poll data. Jack Hawke, North Carolina Republican Party chairman, supplied valuable information about the Republican campaign. Christopher Geis and Christopher Hains, North Carolina Democratic Party, did the same for the Democratic campaign. Thad Beyle, University of North Carolina at Chapel Hill, read the manuscript and made useful suggestions. I appreciate the assistance provided by all of the above individuals. Any errors of fact or interpretation that remain are my responsibility.

1. *The Gallup Poll Monthly* (September 1991), 19; (September 1992), 13.

2. Richard Morin, "It's Clinton's Turn to Have an Insignificant Lead," *Washington Post National Weekly Edition* (6–13 July 1992), 37.

3. *Mason-Dixon North Carolina Poll Survey Report, August 1992 and October 1992* (Columbia, Md.: Mason-Dixon Political/Media Research, Inc., 1992).

4. Seth Effron, in "Politics Stranger Than Fiction in North Carolina," *Greensboro News and Record* (1 November 1992), A1, details the visits made through October. There was one candidate visit, by Gore, in November.

5. Howard Kurtz, "The Candidates' Ad Campaigns Go Their Separate Ways," *Washington Post National Weekly Edition* (28 September–6 October 1992), 13.

6. *Charlotte Observer* (7 October 1992), A2.

7. Interview with Christopher Geis, director of media and research, North Carolina Democratic Party, 22 January 1993.

8. Interview with Christopher Hains, political director, North Carolina Democratic Party, 22 January 1993.

9. Interview with Christopher Geis.

10. Interview with Jack Hawke, chair, North Carolina Republican Party, 22 January 1993.

11. Interview with Jack Hawke.

12. Interview with Jack Hawke.

13. Interview with Jack Hawke.

14. Interview with Jack Hawke.

15. *Raleigh News and Observer* (8 October 1992), 2B.

16. Rob Christensen and Van Denton, "Race Ending As It Started—Negatively," *Raleigh News and Observer* (2 November 1992), 1A.

17. Figures supplied by the Campaign Reporting Office, North Carolina State Board of Elections.

18. Figures supplied by the Campaign Reporting Office, North Carolina State Board of Elections.

19. John Conway, "Assembly Passes Redrawn Districts," *Greensboro News and Record* (25 January 1992), A1.

20. Conway, "Assembly Passes Redrawn Districts," A1.

21. Calculated from figures supplied by the North Carolina State Board of Elections.

22. The Carolina poll was conducted by the School of Journalism, University of North Carolina at Chapel Hill (24–29 October 1992).

23. *Mason-Dixon North Carolina Poll Survey Report, November 1992* (Columbia, Md.: Mason-Dixon Political/Media Research, Inc., 1992).

24. *Mason-Dixon North Carolina Poll Survey Report, October 1992* (Columbia, Md.: Mason-Dixon Political/Media Research, Inc., 1992).

25. For exit poll data for the 1988 election, see Charles Prysby, "North Carolina: The Confluence of National, Regional, and State Forces," in *The 1988 Presidential Election in the South: Continuity Amidst Change in Southern Party Politics*, ed. by Laurence W. Moreland, Robert P. Steed, and Tod A. Baker (New York: Praeger, 1991), 185–200.

26. Prysby, "North Carolina."

27. The Carolina poll (24–29 October 1992).

28. *Mason-Dixon North Carolina Poll Survey Report, October 1992.*

29. Voter Research and Surveys North Carolina exit poll.

30. Voter Research and Surveys North Carolina exit poll.

11

Tennessee: Favorite Son Brings Home the Bacon

DAVID M. BRODSKY AND ROBERT H. SWANSBROUGH

The early line on the 1992 presidential election in Tennessee installed George Bush as the odds-on favorite to carry the Volunteer State. Several factors pointed to a Bush victory. First, the Republicans had carried Tennessee in all but two elections since Eisenhower's breakthrough in 1952. Second, George Bush's 1988 triumph, when he blanked the Democratic ticket in traditionally Republican east Tennessee and nearly scored a shutout in usually Democratic west Tennessee, eclipsed the near-perfect 1984 performance of superstar Ronald Reagan. Third, Bush's successful orchestration of Operation Desert Storm seemed to give him a substantial edge with Tennessee's generally conservative electorate. Finally, the absence of a proven slugger in the lineup of Democratic hopefuls pointed to a Bush win.

On election day, however, Bill Clinton and Tennessee favorite son Al Gore hit the ball out of the park. In this chapter, we examine the campaign, looking for the factors that caused the Bush/Quayle team to lose their early lead and that prevented them from finding a closer to shut down the Democrats in the late innings.

THE CAMPAIGN

Bush and Clinton Break on Top

In an early Tennessee poll, conducted by the University of Tennessee's Social Science Research Institute, George Bush emerged as the clear front-runner among Tennessee's Republican voters, receiving 78 percent of GOP primary ballots. Challengers Pat Buchanan and David Duke trailed with 17 percent and 3 percent, respectively.[1] Encouraged by the president's home run in the Gulf War and by his apparent support among Republican voters, most of Tennessee's GOP party leadership supported his reelection bid.

The strong public and party support for the president led his campaign team to look past the primary season to the general election. However, Pat Buchanan's surprisingly strong showing in New Hampshire, and the apparent effectiveness of his hard-hitting attacks on Bush for breaking his "no new taxes" pledge, redirected their attention. The threat of a Buchanan challenge forced the state's Bush supporters to create a campaign organization early in the election year.[2] The Bush team named Tennessee's popular retired U.S. senator, Howard Baker, as its state campaign chair and Tennessee's three Republican congressmen as co-chairs. The Tennessee Bush/Quayle campaign strategists then immediately began bringing the state's leading Republicans firmly into their camp.

On the Democratic side, Arkansas Governor Bill Clinton emerged as the clear front-runner. Clinton's candidacy for the Democratic nomination received endorsements from Governor Ned McWherter, all six Democratic members of the U.S. House of Representatives, and forty-seven state legislators. Tennessee's Democratic U.S. senators, Jim Sasser and Albert Gore, Jr., withheld their primary endorsements in deference to the presidential candidacies of their colleagues Tom Harkin and Bob Kerrey.

Buchanan Seeks to Move Up on the Right

The early poll results suggested Pat Buchanan had the potential to embarrass the president in Tennessee's primary. First, the conservative challenger enjoyed the support of one in five Republican primary voters, a base that might expand if Tennessee Republicans decided to vent their anger at the Bush administration's performance. As Tommy Hopper, Tennessee Republican chair, warned, "I think Buchanan's going to do pretty well here. . . . There are people who will vote for him to send a signal that they are dissatisfied with the direction of the president's campaign."[3] Second, Democrats angry at Bush's economic policies might take advantage of Tennessee's lax primary laws to cross over and vote for Buchanan. Certainly, the state's long history of crossover voting in primary elections made this a very real threat to the Bush/Quayle forces.

The collapse of Buchanan's support after New Hampshire limited his appearances in Tennessee. He made his only campaign visit to the Volunteer State on March 5, when he attacked Bush as "King George" during a Vanderbilt University address. Buchanan reasserted his "America First" theme after he arrived at the campus as a passenger in a Tennessee-made Saturn automobile.[4] His Tennessee campaign spokesperson, Jeannette Henderson, stated that Buchanan wanted "to stay with positive ads in Tennessee. We feel there's insufficient knowledge out there of who Pat Buchanan is and what he stands for. . . ."[5]

The Bush/Quayle team took the Buchanan threat seriously. They scheduled five pre-primary visits to Tennessee by either President Bush or Vice-President Dan Quayle, visits interpreted by State GOP Chair Hopper as indications that "there is significant concern about how close this will be." Moreover, the campaign relentlessly attacked Buchanan. For example, Bush's state director, Frank Barnett, hit Buchanan's "America First" message: "What he is saying is appealing, but it is not real world stuff."[6] And President Bush took his own oblique swipe at Buchanan when he observed during a Memphis visit that "Protectionism comes from fear."[7]

"I Gave at the Office"

Former Senator Paul Tsongas took his presidential campaign only to Nashville. Speaking at a black Baptist church, Tsongas acknowledged he was on Clinton's regional "turf." Tsongas admitted he sought simply a second-place "silver medal" in the South.[8]

Senator Bob Kerrey's campaign director in Tennessee, Jeff Clark, hit the state's Democratic leaders for flocking to the Clinton camp. "The easiest thing to do is to endorse Bill Clinton. He is the neighboring governor. Then when Bob Kerrey or someone else calls, they can say, 'I gave at the office.' "[9] But when Senator Kerrey withdrew from the presidential race on the eve of the Democratic primary, Clark himself publicly endorsed Clinton.

Both Bill and Hillary Clinton made last-minute campaign stops in the Volunteer State, while Governor Jerry Brown visited Memphis. Hillary Clinton visited both Nashville and Memphis as part of Clinton's final campaign push. Speaking to a crowd of 1,000, accompanied by Congressman Harold Ford and Tennessee House Speaker Jimmy Naifeh, Mrs. Clinton called for the reversal of "the insane programs of the Reagan-Bush administrations."[10]

Tennessee Secretary of State Bryant Millsaps noted, "This primary is driven largely by the performance of candidates in other primaries and the media attention they get."[11] The Tennessee poll, conducted February 22–26, appeared to support that observation. It revealed that Clinton held a clear lead with 51 percent of the Democratic primary voters, followed by Tsongas, a distant second with 16 percent support, and the rest of the Democratic contenders.[12]

Leading from Wire to Wire

The Tennessee primary results, including a turnout of one in five registered voters, surprised few people. President Bush received almost three-fourths of the Republican ballots, soundly defeating Buchanan (22 percent) and Duke (3 percent). Bush's Tennessee campaign coordinator, Don Rothwell, said of the election returns, "I think the President has heard the [Buchanan voters'] message and that's why a lot of people have come on board with him."[13] Another Bush staffer, Frank Barnett, offered a slightly different interpretation of the results: "Tennessee is a strong middle-of-the-road state that is not prone to extremism and simple answers."[14] He called for Buchanan to get out of the presidential race. Lester Firstenberger, Buchanan's Tennessee field director, tried to explain the loss: "I think the weather hurt us. One thing we could not compete with in the final analysis was the George Bush machine in Tennessee."[15]

Governor Clinton garnered two-thirds of the votes cast by Tennessee Democrats.[16] Nevertheless, he faced an uphill battle to win the Volunteer State's electoral votes in the fall. In a Tennessee poll trial heat, 46 percent of Tennessee voters preferred George Bush, 39 percent preferred Bill Clinton, and 15 percent reported no preference.[17] Despite the bad news in the trial heat, the poll also included an encouraging sign for Clinton—evidence of strong support among both black and white Democratic voters.

Enter the Favorite Son

Clinton's decision to select Senator Albert Gore, Jr., as his running mate clearly altered the dynamics of the general election campaign in Tennessee and in the South. Doug Hale, Clinton's southern coordinator, observed that the South "is going to be the battleground for the rest of the campaign."[18] At best, the Clinton team appeared to think a solid "southern" ticket would win some of the electoral votes that the region had come to give to the Republicans with monotonous regularity. At worst, the Democrats thought they could weaken the Bush/Quayle campaign by forcing the Republicans to expend substantial resources in order to hold their southern base. In either scenario, Gore brought such assets as experience in Washington, expertise in environmental and arms control issues, military service, and an attractive family to the ticket.

In Tennessee, the Clinton campaign hoped to benefit from Gore's popularity and from his statewide organization. A Mason-Dixon poll conducted after the GOP convention suggested the strategy worked as expected. The poll results revealed that the Clinton/Gore team held an eight-point lead over the Bush/Quayle ticket, 49 to 41 percent, with 10 percent of the state's registered voters undecided.[19] In contrast to 1984 and 1988, the Republican nominee enjoyed only a six-point margin (48 to 42 percent) among white voters.

Gore stood out as a key factor in the support for the Democratic ticket. When asked whom they would vote for if Gore were not Clinton's running mate, 45 percent picked Bush to only 42 percent for Clinton, with 13 percent undecided. Tennessee voters also held a very positive image of their junior senator. His 56 percent favorable rating surpassed Clinton (44 percent), Bush (41 percent), Quayle (33 percent), and Perot (18 percent). In contrast, his negative image ratings (22 percent) fell well below those assigned to Clinton (33 percent), Bush (43 percent), Quayle (54 percent), and Perot (58 percent).

Gore's presence also inspired strong support from the state's leading Democrat, Governor Ned McWherter. The governor not only spoke on behalf of the Democratic ticket, but also made his former state campaign coordinator, Jim Hall, available to head Clinton's Tennessee operation. McWherter had warned against overconfidence as early as the Democratic convention in New York: "Tennessee will be tight. . . . President Bush has a lot of support in Tennessee, and, if they get my friends Howard Baker and Lamar Alexander out there, it will be tight as a tick.''[20] Hall echoed that assessment: ''Anyone who thinks Tennessee is a lock for Clinton-Gore isn't looking at the 1984 and 1988 results. . . . [T]his is a competitive, two-party state in presidential elections, and it has been for 20 years.''[21]

Perotomania

H. Ross Perot complicated the Democratic and Republican campaign strategies when his supporters filed qualifying papers in Tennessee even though the deadline to appear on the ballot had passed. Perot trumpeted his volunteers' efforts: ''Tennessee is the first state to prove all the experts wrong. The experts said it was impossible for ordinary people to get together and organize.''[22] Perot's sudden withdrawal from the race in July angered many of his Tennessee supporters. Therefore, when Perot reentered the presidential contest, Steve Fridrich, his Tennessee chairman, had to adjust his plans in light of limited volunteer support. ''I do not think we will open offices across the state. . . . We're going to have to, just because we're so late getting kicked off here, depend on major media to get our message across.''[23]

Trouble in the East Tennessee Hills

The Bush/Quayle team members stepped up their efforts in Tennessee, sending the president on September 29 to visit the Tri-Cities, Knoxville, and Chattanooga in east Tennessee as well as Clarksville and Nashville in middle Tennessee. The September 29 visit represented Bush's third campaign appearance in Tennessee during a period of four and one-half weeks. Bush/Quayle staffer Frank Barnett viewed the five-city visit as a critical boost for the campaign: ''I would suspect with this Perot thing, if we roll him back into it and take the Bush visit combined, it ought to tighten up Tennessee very snug.''[24]

The decision to send the president to Tennessee, a state with only eleven electoral votes, for an all-day visit just five weeks before the election suggested the Bush/Quayle ticket saw a need to solidify support among their core constituents, especially in east Tennessee. Indeed, a comparison with how the Bush/Quayle schedulers used Bush's Tennessee campaign visits in 1988 supports such an assessment. Against Democratic nominee Michael Dukakis, Bush planners scheduled only two Volunteer State appearances, both in the Democratic strongholds of west and middle Tennessee; Quayle visited the traditional Republican heartland of east Tennessee, seeking votes for the ticket.[25] In contrast, Bush made three of his September 29 stops in solidly Republican east Tennessee. Instead of reaching out to Reagan-Bush Democrats elsewhere in the state, Republican unhappiness with the president forced the campaign to use its major asset to firm up his shaky political base. Howard Baker recognized the problem when he noted, "We have found more enthusiasm in Middle and West Tennessee than in East Tennessee. . . . We had better be careful."[26]

A Tightening Race

The reentry of Perot into the presidential race, and Bush's intensified activity in Tennessee, concerned the Clinton camp. Clinton's southern coordinator acknowledged to supporters, "This state is going to be a little tougher than we would have liked. Just consider yourselves the fire wall."[27]

As the race tightened, both campaigns sent their candidates and surrogates into the Volunteer State. Vice-President Quayle and First Lady Barbara Bush visited Tennessee. The campaign also used former Senator and White House Chief of Staff Howard Baker, former Tennessee Governor and then Secretary of Education Lamar Alexander, and former Senator Bill Brock to build support for the president. Secretary of Health and Human Services Dr. Louis Sullivan campaigned in Memphis on Bush's behalf.

On the Democratic side, Senator Sasser and Congressman Harold Ford visited black churches to build support for the Clinton/Gore ticket. Both Tipper Gore and Hillary Clinton stumped in Tennessee for votes. The Clintons and the Gores attended an August "One Woman, One Vote" rally in Memphis to celebrate the seventy-second anniversary of women getting the vote. Clinton also stopped briefly in Nashville for a rally and a hot dog on Music Row. He told 600 supporters, "I don't think Bush would have liked Elvis very much: that's another thing that's wrong with him."[28]

Nashville's country music stars lent their glitter to the candidates. President Bush enjoyed the support of Lee Greenwood and the Oak Ridge Boys, Wynonna Judd, Mark Chesnutt, Baillie and the Boys, Ricky Skaggs, the Gatlin Brothers, and Crystal Gayle. Democrat Clinton received the endorsements of Jimmy Buffet, Gary Morris, Mary-Chapin Carpenter, and Nanci Griffith. Perot won the support of Willie Nelson and Kris Kristofferson. Some of these country stars expressed their support with evident passion. For example, Ricky Skaggs, campaigning with President Bush, stated at one stop, "the dark side really wants him [Bush] out of there. God talked through a bush a long time ago, and . . . He can talk through a Bush again."[29]

The Mason-Dixon poll conducted between October 2–4 found Governor Clinton enjoying a 46 to 34 percent lead over President Bush, with Perot obtaining only 6 percent support after his reentry; 14 percent of the state's voters remained undecided.[30] Significantly, Bush led Clinton by only one point in Republican east Tennessee (40 to 39 percent). Clinton led the president with majorities of the voters in traditionally Democratic middle Tennessee (51 to 24 percent) and west Tennessee (50 to 37 percent). Only 36 percent of the state's voters viewed Bush favorably. Clinton enjoyed strong backing from blacks and had a slim lead among white Tennesseans (40 to 39 percent). A majority (53 percent) of Tennesseans viewed Perot unfavorably.[31]

The Tennessee poll, conducted 7–12 October, showed Clinton leading Bush by twelve points (47 to 35 percent) among all registered voters, with 5 percent selecting Perot and 9 percent undecided. This survey found Bush trailing Clinton by three points in east Tennessee. Clinton also earned a plurality (44 percent to Bush's 30 percent) among self-identified independents.

The final Mason-Dixon pre-election poll, conducted 25–26 October, found Tennessee's presidential race getting tighter, with Clinton holding a narrow 44 to 39 percent lead over Bush, his narrowest lead since July 1992.[32] Perot received 10 percent of the respondents' votes, with 7 percent undecided. Bush had regained his support in Republican east Tennessee (46 to 39 percent), while Clinton led in middle Tennessee (47 to 36 percent) and west Tennessee (47 to 35 percent).

Brad Coker, president of Mason-Dixon, stated, "Gore's place on the ticket is probably making the difference in the race here at the moment." In contrast, Republican State Chair Tommy Hopper downplayed the impact of Gore on the Democratic ticket: "I think the biggest effect Gore has had has been to energize the Democrats and help raise a lot more money." He recalled that in 1990, with the winners Governor McWherter and Senator Gore at the top of the Democratic ticket, the GOP gained seats in both houses of the Tennessee legislature. Hopper also emphasized that additional Republican resources were being sent to Tennessee because of Bush's improved poll standings. "We've been gaining about a point a day nationally for the past week."[33]

RESULTS AND ANALYSIS

What Happened to the Republican Presidential Lock?

The 1992 presidential election results in Tennessee represented the latest setback in a mounting string of defeats suffered by Republican candidates in statewide elections. Prior to 1976, Tennessee's Republicans appeared to have reached a position of virtual parity with the Volunteer State's traditionally dominant Democratic Party. However, Jimmy Carter's success in gaining Tennessee's electoral votes and Democrat Jim Sasser's upset victory over Senator Bill Brock marked the first steps in what became an extended recovery in the fortunes of Tennessee Democrats. Indeed, between 1976 and 1992 Tennessee Republicans won only three statewide races—Howard Baker's surprisingly narrow reelection in 1978 and Lamar Alexander's two victories in the gubernatorial contests of 1978 and 1982—in addition to the successive wins by Ronald Reagan in 1980 and 1984 and George Bush in 1988. With Bill Clinton's defeat of George Bush by a margin of 47 to 42 percent, the Democrats cleared the last barrier in their climb back to the pinnacle of Tennessee politics. Moreover, as shown in Table 11.1, the Democrats did it by carrying majorities of the popular vote in traditionally Democratic middle and west Tennessee and a substantial 41 percent of the vote in reliably Republican east Tennessee.

The county-by-county returns suggest the scope of the Clinton/Gore victory

Table 11.1
Popular Vote by Tennessee Region

Region	Total Number of Votes	Percent of Votes for			
		Bush	Clinton	Perot	Other
West	573,582	41.8	51.0	6.8	0.4
Middle	673,527	37.3	50.8	11.5	0.4
East	735,528	47.6	40.6	11.4	0.4
Totals	1,982,637	42.4	47.1	10.1	0.4

Source: Compiled by the authors from certified election returns provided by the Tennessee Secretary of State.

Table 11.2
Republican Counties by Tennessee Region

Region	1988		1992		Change	
	Number	Percent	Number	Percent	Number	Percent
West (21)	18	86	4	19	-14	-67
Middle (41)	23	56	2	5	-21	-51
East (33)	33	100	23	70	-10	-30
Totals (95)	74	77	29	31	-45	-46

Note: Number in parentheses following each region indicates the total number of counties in the region.
Source: Compiled by the authors from certified election returns provided by the Tennessee Secretary of State.

and the extent to which it represented a dramatic reversal of past Democratic fortunes (See Table 11.2). First, the Democratic ticket carried sixty-six of Tennessee's ninety-five counties, eight fewer than Carter and Mondale managed in 1976, the last time the Democrats carried the Volunteer State. Second, Clinton and Gore captured seventeen of twenty-one counties in west Tennessee, more than five times the number carried by Dukakis and Bentsen in 1988. Third, the Democrats swept thirty-nine of forty-one middle Tennessee counties, one more than Carter in 1976 and more than double the performance of the Democratic tickets in 1984 and 1988. Finally, Clinton and Gore managed to carry ten counties in Republican east Tennessee, a significant improvement over the shutouts suffered in 1984 and 1988.

The Democratic ticket's 1992 performance in the state's major metropolitan counties also represented a substantial improvement over 1988. Clinton and Gore won a majority of the votes in middle Tennessee's Davidson County (Nashville) and west Tennessee's Shelby County (Memphis). More important, the Democrats enjoyed substantial margins in each of these counties (14 percent in Davidson and 10 percent in Shelby). Although the Clinton/Gore team lost east Tennessee's Knox (Knoxville) and Hamilton (Chattanooga) counties, the Democrats held the Republicans to plurality victories.

Viewed from the Republicans' perspective, the Bush/Quayle 1992 performance represented a nightmarish mirror image of 1988 when they swamped the Democrats, winning 58 percent of the popular vote and carrying each of Tennessee's three grand divisions, winning 53 percent of the vote in west Tennessee, 55 percent in middle Tennessee, and 65 percent in east Tennessee. In 1992, however, their statewide percentage fell to 42 percent, a decline of 16 percent. They lost ground in each of the three grand divisions as their share of the vote fell by 11 percent in west Tennessee, 18 percent in middle Tennessee, and 17 percent in east Tennessee.

The county-by-county results present an even more dismal picture. The GOP ticket's twenty-nine counties carried in 1992 represented a loss of 46 percent from 1988. Within the grand divisions, the decline ranged from 30 percent in east Tennessee to 51 percent in middle Tennessee to 67 percent in west Tennessee.

The Perot Factor

It is hard to gauge the effect of the Perot candidacy on the results of the presidential contest. Perot carried one in ten Volunteer State voters. His share of the vote ranged from 7 percent in west Tennessee to 11 percent in east Tennessee to 12 percent in middle Tennessee. An examination of the vote total shows that if Bush and Quayle had received all of the Perot votes, a highly unlikely prospect, they would have carried Tennessee by a 52 to 48 percent margin. However, given the anti-incumbent nature of the Perot vote and George Bush's high negative ratings in the polls, it seems unlikely that he would have secured enough votes to carry the state.

The Impact of Reapportionment

Reapportionment had little apparent effect on congressional races in Tennessee. The voters returned each of the state's nine incumbent U.S. representatives, in most cases without much of a contest. However, in the Third Congressional District, long-time Representative Marilyn Lloyd barely managed to squeak past her Republican challenger, Zach Wamp, with 51 percent of the vote. The race turned increasingly ugly, especially as the Lloyd campaign tried to stave off a looming defeat with a barrage of negative commercials attacking Wamp.

Despite its limited effect on the congressional races, reapportionment profoundly influenced races for the Tennessee General Assembly. The Democrats, especially in the house, made every effort to redraw the districts to accomplish one of two goals—to create new districts where Democratic candidates would have a chance to win or to force incumbent Republicans to run against each other. In Hamilton County (Chattanooga), for example, the Democrats managed to accomplish both objectives. First, they created a new district that included portions of areas previously represented by Republican incumbents David Copeland and Ken Meyer, forcing them to run against each other. Second, they drew a new district that stretched from heavily Democratic areas in rural Hamilton County south into the City of Chattanooga. The Democratic candidate carried the district in November.

The redistricting plan had its desired effect in the house, where the Democrats increased their advantage from fifty-six/forty-three to sixty-three/thirty-six, their biggest majority since 1976. The election results show that much of the Democratic gain resulted from placing incumbent Republicans in the same district. Indeed, Tommy Hopper, Republican State Party chair, blamed redistricting for the Republican losses.

Despite the successes in the house, many observers felt the Democratic redistricting backfired in the Tennessee senate. Although the Democrats won one of two open seats in east Tennessee, they suffered surprise defeats in the losses of Senate Majority Leader Riley Darnell (by 142 votes) and Charles Beaty in a new "Democratic" district in middle Tennessee. Thus, the Democrats finished election day with a nineteen-to-fourteen margin, a net loss of one seat.[34]

A Battle for the Soul of the Republican Party

Historically, the intensity of the contests fought between Tennessee's Democrats and Republicans paled in comparison to the ferocity evidenced in many of the primary battles fought among the factions competing within the Democratic Party.[35] Although the Republicans have experienced some factional strife,[36] they usually have managed to avoid a unity-threatening controversy. However, the primary challenge by Pat Buchanan, conservative dissatisfaction with the policies of George Bush and his reelection campaign, and the "heat" of the internecine legislative battles that resulted from the Democratic reapportionment plan appear to have given birth to a battle for control of the Republican Party. In the words of (now former) Republican Party Chair Tommy Hopper, "There's going to be a battle for the heart and soul of the Republican Party nationally. . . . I think there's going to be a similar battle that's going to be fought in Tennessee."[37] Hopper's very conservative views and harsh partisan attacks on Governor McWherter particularly raised concerns. McWherter declared, "I think Tommy Hopper is a fine young man who overplays his partisanship with his mouth." Hopper replied by depicting McWherter as "an old-style, backroom, good ol' boy politician." State Representative Ronnie Davis, a moderate Republican, took out an ad in his local newspaper criticizing conservative Republicans and Tommy Hopper, declaring "I'm going to first represent the district and do partisan things secondary. . . . "[38] An angry ex-Representative David Copeland, defeated in a reapportioned district by fellow Republican Ken Meyer, whom he labeled a "Hopper protégé," also lashed out at Hopper. "The ship of the Republican Party appears to have run aground. It's very likely that responsibility will be affixed to the captain of that ship and accountability required."[39] Political infighting for control of the heart and soul of Tennessee's Republican Party had already begun.

CONCLUSIONS

The election of 1992 suggests a number of lessons. The first lesson applies to the Democrats: Resist the temptation to interpret the success of the Clinton/Gore ticket as indicating a return to Democratic dominance of presidential politics in the Volunteer State. As Senator Jim Sasser observed, "I think Gore's being on the ticket clinched Tennessee for Clinton. Without Gore, it would have been doubtful."[40] The remaining lessons apply to both Democrats and Republicans. First, success at the polls depends on the extent to which candidates address (or appear to address) the issues concerning the voters, not the issues concerning only party activists. In 1992, Clinton and Gore did the better job at this. Their emphasis on economic issues dovetailed nicely with the concerns reflected in several statewide polls. For example, three of five respondents in a Mason-Dixon poll pointed to the economy as the most important problem influencing their vote. Taxes and spending (9 percent) and family values (5 percent), key Republican themes, trailed far behind.[41] Second, if candidates fail to enter a general election contest with a secure base, their campaigns will suffer as they divert scarce resources to shore up their core constituencies. The Bush/Quayle team's shortfall in middle and west Tennessee may have resulted, at least in part, from the perceived need to concentrate the president's appearances in Republican east Tennessee. Third, although the presidential election results appear to reaffirm the historic partisan affinities of voters in the state's three grand divisions, the evidence from several state legislative races suggests the continuing erosion of party loyalties based on regional factors. Fourth, do not ever take anything for granted. Surely the Democrats failed to foresee Senate Majority Leader Darnell's loss in heavily Democratic middle Tennessee, while the Republicans could not have expected Bill Clinton to transform Tennessee and the South into battle-ground states by naming Al Gore as his running mate. Finally, the political future in Tennessee offers the prospect of continuing volatility, especially if voters continue to respond to more temporal factors in the calculus that drives their political decision making.

NOTES

1. *Memphis Commercial Appeal* (9 March 1992), A–1.
2. *Nashville Tennessean* (11 March 1992), A–10.

3. *Chattanooga Times* (2 March 1992), A–1.

4. *Memphis Commercial Appeal* (9 March 1992), A–8.

5. *Memphis Commercial Appeal* (9 March 1992), A–8.

6. *Nashville Tennessean* (2 March 1992), A–7.

7. *Nashville Tennessean* (6 March 1992), A–8.

8. *Nashville Tennessean* (8 March 1992), A–1.

9. *Nashville Tennessean* (2 March 1992), A–7.

10. *Memphis Commercial Appeal* (7 March 1992), A–8.

11. *Memphis Commercial Appeal* (9 March 1992), A–1.

12. *Memphis Commercial Appeal* (9 March 1992), A–1.

13. *Memphis Commercial Appeal* (11 March 1992), A–10.

14. *Nashville Tennessean* (11 March 1992), A–10.

15. *Nashville Tennessean* (11 March 1992), A–1.

16. *Memphis Commercial Appeal* (11 March 1992), A–1.

17. *Chattanooga Times* (2 March 1992), A–3.

18. *Nashville Tennessean* (4 October 1992), A–2.

19. *Chattanooga Times* (2 September 1992), A–1.

20. *Chattanooga Times* (2 September 1992), A–1.

21. *Chattanooga Times* (2 September 1992), A–1.

22. *Nashville Tennessean* (6 March 1992), A–1.

23. *Nashville Tennessean* (2 October 1992), A–4.

24. *Nashville Tennessean* (4 October 1992), D–1.

25. David H. Brodsky and Robert H. Swansbrough, "Tennessee: A House Divided," in *The 1988 Presidential Election in the South: Continuity Amidst Change in Southern Party Politics*, ed. Laurence W. Moreland, Robert P. Steed, and Tod A. Baker (New York: Praeger, 1991), 201–219.

26. *Knoxville News Sentinel* (24 October 1992), A–7.

27. *Nashville Tennessean* (4 October 1992), A–2.

28. *Nashville Tennessean* (7 October 1992), A–1.

29. *Nashville Tennessean* (4 October 1992), A–21.

30. *Chattanooga Times* (7 October 1992), A–1.

31. *Nashville Tennessean* (9 October 1992), A–4.

32. *Chattanooga Times* (30 October 1992), A–1.

33. *Memphis Commercial Appeal* (18 October 1992), B–7.

34. *Memphis Commercial Appeal* (4 November 1992), A–21.

35. Robert H. Swansbrough, *Political Change in Tennessee* (Knoxville: University of Tennessee Bureau of Public Administration, 1985), 1–18.

36. Norman L. Parks, "Tennessee Politics Since Kefauver and Reece: A Generalist View," *Journal of Politics* 28 (February 1966): 144–168.

37. *Chattanooga Times* (9 November 1992), B–3.

38. *Chattanooga Times* (9 November 1992), B–3.

39. *Chattanooga Times* (9 November 1992), B–3.

40. *Nashville Tennessean* (4 November 1992), A–1.

41. *Chattanooga Times* (2 September 1992), A–1.

12

Texas: Friends, Neighbors, and Native Sons

FRANK B. FEIGERT AND JOHN R. TODD

BACKGROUND

The Importance of Texas in Presidential Politics

Both parties must give serious consideration to Texas in planning presidential campaign strategy. As the third most populous state, Texas has thirty-two electoral votes, three more than it enjoyed under the 1980 census. This is enough to make any presidential candidate take notice. Both parties have considered Texas a strategic state since the 1950s, when Republican presidential candidates first began to do well in the state. In the ten presidential elections from 1952 to 1988, Republicans carried Texas six times. Democrats put much stock in the fact that no Democrat had been elected president without carrying Texas. As a result, Texas has assumed a significant place in the strategy of both parties.

Texas also established its centrality in the campaign by being a source of substantial campaign gifts. By early March of 1992, Texans had given $2 million to presidential candidates—more than had any other state. Most of that money (almost $1.8 million) had been contributed to George Bush.[1] Texans were also to be generous to Clinton. In May, Clinton was able to raise about $400,000 at a single fund-raiser held in Austin. This was reported to have put his contributions from Texas over the $1 million mark.[2] And, of course, Texas is the home of the most self-financed candidate in our history, H. Ross Perot.

Party Strength in Texas

To understand contemporary party competition in Texas, it is important to understand the changes in party identification that have taken place in the last thirty years. In 1964, 65 percent of Texans identified with the Democratic Party. Ten years later, 59 percent of Texas adults still identified with the Democratic Party. After another ten years, identification with the Democratic Party was down to a third of the electorate. By 1989, the Texas poll found Texas party identifiers to be about equally divided between the Democratic and the Republican parties.[3] In 1991, polls found Democrats and Republicans to be tied, with about 30 percent of the electorate identifying with each.[4] In thirty years, the distribution of party loyalties has undergone a sea of change, from overwhelming identification with the Democratic Party to neck-and-neck competition between the parties.

In addition to party identification, the shift to the Republican party has been evident in Texas in other ways. In 1978, a Republican won the governorship for the first time since Reconstruction. Since then, each gubernatorial race has been competitive. No longer can the Democrats coast to victory in the governorship. Republicans have also won other statewide offices, such as the state treasurer's office and several supreme court justiceships. The Republicans have also increased their representation in the state legislature and in the state's congressional delegation. The party had hoped to win enough seats in the legislature to control the reapportionment process in 1991. Failing that, the party did successfully overturn in court the senate districting plan drawn by the Democrats. What the party could not do at the polls and in the legislature, it tried to do with the assistance of a Republican federal district judge. This was expected to give them a substantial opportunity to increase the party's presence in the state senate from nine to sixteen seats, a majority of the thirty-one-member chamber.

The Democratic Party has remained competitive at the state level. Ann Richards' victory for the governorship in 1990 provided encouragement to the party. The party continues to hold a majority in both houses of the state legislature and continues to dominate local offices in most counties—except the most metropolitan areas.

Issues

The 1992 election found Texas suffering from the recession like the rest of the country. The state had been through its own recession since the mid–1980s when the Organization of Petroleum Exporting Countries (OPEC) collapsed and the world price of oil plummeted. The Texas oil and gas businesses were dealt a blow from which they may never recover. Thus, being dragged down by a national recession in the 1990s was particularly troublesome for Texas. The economy and jobs were certainly on the minds of Texans.

Taxes were also a matter of concern. Because of expanding demands and falling revenues, Texans have been subjected to a barrage of tax increases in recent years. The Texas legislature raised taxes in 1984, 1985, 1986, 1987, and 1990.[5] Thus, while Texas is not a high-tax state, it is weary of tax increases.

The president's breaking of his "read my lips" 1988 campaign pledge rubbed a raw nerve in Texas.

THE PRIMARIES

The Texas primaries were held on March 10, as a part of the Super Tuesday sweep. By joining the Super Tuesday states, Texas had hoped to increase its role in the nominating process. However, in 1992, by the time Super Tuesday rolled around, each party's field of contenders had been trimmed. On the Democratic side, the field had narrowed to Bill Clinton, Paul Tsongas, and Jerry Brown. Clinton had already established himself as the Democratic Party front-runner. Being the governor of a neighboring state pushed Clinton even further ahead in Texas. The Republican field included President Bush, Pat Buchanan, and David Duke. It was apparent by Super Tuesday that Buchanan was not going to be able to wrest the nomination away from the president, and Duke was widely regarded as an unacceptable extremist.

The outcomes of the primaries were lopsided. Bush got 74 percent of the vote in the Republican primary, and Clinton almost 69 percent of the vote in the Democratic primary. The front-runners polled comfortable majorities in every region of the state.

An exit poll of primary voters indicated that the three issues that mattered most to Clinton voters were the economy/jobs (51 percent), health care (27 percent), and education (20 percent). The three issues that mattered most to Bush voters were the economy/jobs (36 percent), education (27 percent), and taxes (26 percent).

Clinton's primary support came almost equally from males (47 percent) and females (53 percent). The racial/ethnic breakdown indicated that 66 percent of Clinton's vote came from whites, 21 percent from African Americans, and 13 percent from Hispanics. Bush also drew equally from males (48 percent) and females (52 percent). The racial/ethnic breakdown of his vote included 92 percent whites, 2 percent African Americans, and 5 percent Hispanics.[6]

THE CAMPAIGN

Geography, Demography, and Political Strategy

To understand the campaign strategies of the two parties in Texas, it is necessary to know something about the geographical and social bases of each party's supporters. The Republican Party in Texas is overwhelmingly urban-based. It draws its greatest strength from such metropolitan centers as Dallas, Fort Worth, and Houston. In fact, the Republican Party has supplanted the Democrats in these metropolitan centers. The Democratic Party does much better in the non-metropolitan centers, with the most solid base being the east Texas yellow-dog Democrats.

In socioeconomic terms, the Republican Party has built its base in Texas among affluent city dwellers who would be called Yuppies in other states. Democrats have drawn their strength from the urban poor and minorities and from the rural, working-class Bubbas. In this election, attention came to be focused on an in-between group that newspaper writers called the Yubba vote. Yubbas are suburban dwellers who make less money than Yuppies, but are Yuppie ''wanna-bes.''

As the race developed, the movable part of the electorate increasingly came to be identified as the Reagan Democrats and the Yubbas. Both groups were likely to have been adversely affected by the recession and were therefore considered persuadable.[7]

Each party's campaign strategy was shaped by these geographic and demographic realities. The Republican state party chair believed that the party needed to concentrate on winning the major metropolitan centers. Gary Mauro, state land commissioner and state campaign manager for Clinton, indicated that the Democratic Party's strategy was to split the urban areas and carry the rural counties. Mauro also indicated that white males (Bubbas and Yubbas) would be a pivotal group. Mauro said that this group had been the pivotal group in Texas elections in the past ten years. Without them the Democratic party loses; with them it wins.[8]

Some have argued that the Democrats never really tried or expected to win Texas. It was widely believed that the true Democratic strategy was simply to give the president enough competition in Texas to force him to commit more time and resources to the state than the Republicans would originally have thought necessary. There is some merit to this belief, since we learned after the election that Texas was not one of the targeted states that James Carville had designated as essential for Clinton's victory. Thus, Clinton's campaign advertising was slowly withdrawn in the final weeks of the campaign, while that for Bush appeared to be much more intensive. Hence, both the president and a good deal of his resources were pinned down defending his adoptive home state, while Clinton could seek votes elsewhere. Only in the literal final day, when it appeared that Clinton might pull off an upset, did he make two whirlwind appearances at airport rallies.

The Perot Factor

Campaign strategy for each of the parties was complicated by the on-again, off-again involvement of native son Ross Perot in the campaign. Perot entered the campaign in the spring after floating the idea of his candidacy on the ''Larry King Live'' show on CNN. He quickly put together an organization, he hired veteran campaign consultants Ed Rollins and Hamilton Jordan, and his candidacy appeared to build support. In July, Perot left the race as abruptly as he had entered it, indicating that the parties, especially the Democrats, were addressing the issues in which he was interested and that he feared his candidacy would throw the race into the House of Representatives and cause national chaos. *Newsweek* carried Perot's picture on its cover with the caption "The Quitter." Shortly after Perot dropped out of the race in July, a *Dallas Morning News* poll indicated that Clinton would be the prime beneficiary of his withdrawal. The poll indicated that 40 percent of former Perot supporters would back Clinton and only 28 percent were ready to support the president.[9] In October, Perot rejoined the race, and the party strategists had to worry once more about whose votes he would take.

Both parties made it clear that they were concerned about the effect of the Perot candidacy on their ability to win Texas. When Perot announced that he was considering rejoining the race in late September, the Bush and Clinton campaigns sent delegations to Dallas to meet with and court Ross Perot by presenting their own economic plans. The Republican team included Senator Phil Gramm, and the Democratic team included Senator Lloyd Bentsen. Running his campaign from his Dallas headquarters, Perot thus gave the country the spectacle of the two major parties willingly humbling themselves before him.

Texas in the Party Conventions

Texas played a prominent role in the conventions of each party. When the Democrats met in New York, Texans were in full view. Governor Ann Richards served as the permanent chair of the convention, giving her television coverage each night of the convention. Richards had become a Democratic Party star after her keynote address at the 1988 party convention in which she thoroughly ridiculed George Bush, accusing him of having a "silver foot in his mouth." African-American Barbara Jordan, a former member of the U.S. House of Representatives, was a featured speaker. Of special interest, as we shall see, was the speech by State Railroad Commissioner Lena Guerrero, whose own electoral fortunes were to complicate Clinton's later in the race.

The Republican convention was held in Houston—the president's adopted home town. Governor Richards had quipped that "in Texas we don't call a man who has a hotel room in Houston a Texan—we call him a tourist." The convention seemed shaped by Perot's presence in the race. With Perot in, the party had to play to its conservative base. The convention's theme seemed designed to do just that. There was little effort to expand the tent and let more people in. It took on the tone of a revival meeting for the faithful. In a state perceived to have some of the staunchest foes of "secular humanism," a constant state party theme, these conservative appeals may have helped Bush with his voter base, although he never identified himself with either the platform or the remarks of, for instance, Pat Buchanan.

Texans were among the featured speakers at the Republican convention. Senator Phil Gramm, considered a likely presidential candidate in 1996, was the principal keynote speaker. There is little to suggest that his appearance and speech helped his cause for the 1996 nomination, much less election. Kay Bailey Hutchison, state treasurer, was also featured.

The Campaign in Texas

Because both parties perceived Texas to be a critical part of a strategy to win nationally, both parties' candidates made frequent visits to the state. Clinton and Gore made one of their bus trips through central Texas. Even before the Republicans met in Houston, Clinton flew to Houston to receive the endorsement of a police association in that city. Gore made visits to the Hispanic centers of El Paso and the Rio Grande Valley. Texas was one of the eight states visited by Governor Clinton on election eve.

The Bush team also made a number of visits. Bush made six visits to the state between mid-May and mid-September—far more than might have initially been thought necessary.[10] Barbara Bush also made several tours of the state, including a visit to a Dallas area phone bank where she made calls for a while. Included in the president's visits was a trip to the General Dynamics plant in Fort Worth to announce the authorization of F–16 fighter plane sales to Taiwan. This decision was expected to save thousands of jobs at the General Dynamics plant in a state that had already been hit hard by the recession and announced military base closings. It was also expected to save thousands of votes. This was followed by Vice-President Quayle's visit in which he announced authorization to modify the F–16, guaranteeing even more job security for Texans.

The Horse Race in the Polls

While Bush was expected to have an edge in Texas because of his status as a favorite son, in August the Texas poll reported Clinton to be leading Bush in Texas: 49 percent for Clinton, 35 percent for Bush.[11] By Labor Day, a *Dallas Morning News* poll revealed that Bush and Clinton were running neck and neck (Clinton, 42 percent; Bush, 40 percent).[12] At this point, neither candidate had really won the hearts of Texans. Sixty-one percent of those who planned to vote for the president indicated that they did not like his views, and 55 percent of those planning to support Clinton indicated that they did not like his views.[13]

On October 11, the day of the first presidential debate, newspapers reported that the Texas poll still found the race too close to call. By this time, 35 percent supported Bush, 35 percent supported Clinton, and 17 percent supported Perot.[14] On October 25, with just over a week to go in the campaign, the polls still reported the race to be a dead heat. A *Dallas Morning News* poll reported 38 percent supporting Bush, 36 percent supporting Clinton, and 20 percent supporting Perot.[15] These results are included with other statewide polls, shown in Figure 12.1. While it might appear that Perot's belated reentry into the race on September 30 cut away at the president's support, it should also be pointed out that the campaign had already demonstrated a high degree of volatility, but

Figure 12.1
The Candidates in Selected Texas Polls, 1992

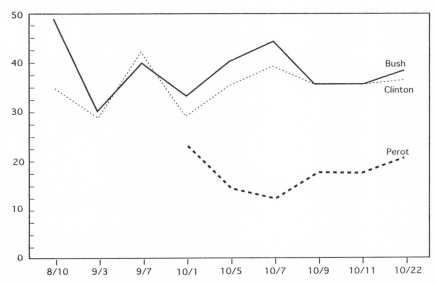

Source: See text and "The American Enterprise" in The Public Perspective
4 (November/December, 1992), 104.

within a narrow range. That is to say, speculation as to who was hurt and who
was helped by Perot's entrance can be just that—speculation. The only point
from which we might draw conclusions is at the very end, when a narrow race
between Clinton and Bush widened somewhat, as both Perot and Bush edged
up marginally.

RESULTS AND ANALYSIS

In the final analysis, the Clinton strategy in Texas worked quite well. The
president was forced to defend his base, spending time and money there, while
carrying the state by less than four percentage points (40.6 percent Bush, 37.1
percent Clinton, 22.0 percent Perot). This was down sharply from the 12.7
percent margin he had enjoyed in 1988. In Table 12.1 we present results for the
6 most populous and the 6 smallest of the 254 counties. Geographically, the
president's victory was an amalgam, basically carrying the state in a broad
diagonal swath from the panhandle to the central coast, with some success in
those east Texas counties immediately to the east of Dallas and Tarrant Counties.
Clinton's greatest successes came in a swath from El Paso south and east along
the Rio Grande Valley counties, historically both Hispanic and Democratic.
Clinton also captured most of his party's historic base in east Texas. Perot won

Table 12.1
1992 Presidential Election Results in the Largest and Smallest Texas Counties (in percent)

County	Bush	Clinton	Perot	(Total Votes)
Largest counties				
Bexar (San Antonio)	40.7	41.5	17.4	415,276
Dallas	38.7	35.0	25.8	661,252
El Paso	34.9	50.1	14.6	135,163
Harris (Houston)	43.1	38.2	18.3	942,947
Tarrant (Fort Worth)	38.9	33.1	27.6	471,396
Travis (Austin)	31.9	47.3	20.3	276,235
Smallest counties				
Borden	48.7	28.0	23.0	378
Glasscock	66.0	17.4	16.2	574
Kenedy	39.7	50.0	10.3	174
King	41.8	28.6	29.6	189
Loving	32.3	20.8	46.9	96
McMullen	61.9	17.6	20.1	443

Note: Totals may not equal 100 percent because of scattered votes for other candidates.
Source: General Election Returns/County by County Totals Report, Texas Secretary of State (Austin, TX: 28 November 1992).

only six widely scattered small counties. However, note that, in a classic example of "friends and neighbors" politics, his best performance in the largest counties came in Dallas and Tarrant. Similarly, Bush's best showing in these counties came in his adopted Harris County. Returns for the smallest counties show a considerably greater variance than do those for the largest counties.

There is some reason to believe that Clinton might have won Texas, although it was not one of his targeted states. Recall that early polls had shown him in a dead heat with Bush. However, he might very well have been the victim of "reverse coattails," owing to a scandal involving Lena Guerrero, the railroad commissioner who had been showcased as a speaker at the Democratic convention. A former state legislator, as a female Hispanic she appeared to many to be the embodiment of a new Democratic Party. Consequently, she had been appointed to head the State Railroad Commission by Governor Ann Richards. Late in the campaign her opponent revealed in a series of devastating campaign ads (using her own voice, taped at another commencement) that, her protestations to the contrary, Guerrero had never graduated from the University of Texas as she had claimed. Later confessing that she "thought" she had completed her degree requirements and had graduated, she received only 39.5 percent, as compared to her GOP opponent's 53.5 percent, possibly hurting Clinton's chances at carrying the state.[16]

Elsewhere in down-ticket races, each party was able to claim victory of sorts, since each increased its delegation to the U.S. House, a consequence of Texas

Table 12.2
Selected Texas Election Results, 1964–1992

Year	National Elections				State Elections				
	Dem PV %	Dem Senators	U.S.House Dem	Repub	Dem GV %	State Senate Dem	Repub	State House Dem	Repub
1964	**63.3**	1	23	0	**73.8**	31	0	149	1
1966		1	21	2	**72.8**	30	1	147	3
1968	**41.1**	1	20	3	**57.0**	29	2	142	8
1970		1	20	3	**53.6**	29	2	140	10
1972	33.3	1	20	4	47.9	28	3	132	17
1974		1	21	3	**61.4**	28	3	134	16
1976	**51.1**	1	22	2		27	4	131	19
1978		1	20	4	49.2	26	5	127	23
1980	41.4	1	19	5		24	7	114	35
1982		1	22	5	**53.2**	25	6	114	36
1984	36.1	1	17	10		26	5	98	52
1986		1	17	10	46.0	25	6	94	56
1988	43.3	1	19	8		23	8	93	57
1990		1	19	8	**49.5**	23	8	94	56
1992	37.1	1	21	9		18	13	92	58

Note: Dem PV % = Democratic presidential vote percentage; Dem GV % = Democratic gubernatorial vote percentage. Boldface percentages indicate the winners, including those with no majority.
Sources: For national elections, Congressional Quarterly, *Guide to U. S. Elections* (Washington: Congressional Quarterly, Inc., 2d ed., 1985); and *Congressional Quarterly Weekly Report* (7 November 1992). For state elections, U. S. Bureau of the Census, *Statistical Abstract of the United States* and *Book of the States* (Lexington, KY: Council of State Governments).

being allocated an additional three seats following the 1990 census. However, none of the three new seats went to a Republican. Rather, the single replacement of an incumbent came with the defeat of Albert Bustamante, a Democrat who had been implicated in the House banking scandal, with 30 "*cheques calientes*," as his Hispanic opponent characterized the bad checks.[17] Bustamante was also the target of a federal investigation involving the award of a bingo contract on an Indian reservation. Two other Texas Democrats with bad checks (Ron Coleman—673; Charles Wilson—81) were able to weather criticism of their involvement.

These results are cast in a longer perspective, using 1964 as a base, in Table 12.2. From this date, Texas has been fairly solid as a national Republican state, winning five of the last six presidential elections. However, its state office fortunes have been more erratic, slowly building toward a position of strength. In the state senate, the judge-drawn reapportionment was supposed to yield a GOP majority of sixteen seats, but the GOP fell short of this goal. Despite this, the ability to block Democratic legislation and the governor's agenda was achieved in both chambers.[18]

CONCLUSIONS

At the outset, it was widely assumed that Texas was an essential state for each party to carry, given its status as the third largest state, with 32 votes in the electoral college. Recognizing this, both parties showcased any number of Texas speakers at its national conventions. And Texas supplied yet another candidate, Ross Perot.

Faced with the oddity of two native sons—one a true native, one adoptive—and a candidate from a neighboring state, Texas continued, more or less, in its recent pattern as a national Republican state. It backed a Republican for president for the fourth straight time, and for the fifth time in six elections. As elsewhere, the Perot factor was doubtless a complicating one for Texas voters. However, what evidence is available suggests that his influence was primarily in the area of turnout, up 3.9 percent from 1988 in Texas.[19] Despite this, the turnout in Texas, at 49.1 percent, was still substantially less than that for the rest of the country.

What influence did this race have on Texas voters? The contest for railroad commissioner might very well have cost Clinton the opportunity to carry Texas. However, in the final analysis, the immediate importance of the state to the Democratic Party was diminished by its successes in so many other states. Thus, despite having the third largest vote in the electoral college, Texas proved valueless to the Democrats, other than forcing Bush to defend his turf. For Bush, there can be scant consolation in knowing that Texas was the largest state he carried in a losing effort.

In other contests, Texans retained their strongly Democratic delegation to the U.S. House of Representatives, but showed a willingness to elect more Republicans to the state legislature. GOP gains were more noticeable in the state senate, where the party approached majority-party status for the first time since Reconstruction. Nonetheless, it remains difficult to describe Texas as a truly competitive two-party state at this time. Indeed, there is substantial evidence of distinct subregional differences in the state, as revealed by the presidential and subpresidential votes. Each party has its own strongholds and competes for other offices to varying degrees.

In the final analysis, it can be observed that Texas was essentially irrelevant to a campaign that successfully targeted so many other states. Yet, when the campaign was finally over, the state produced two cabinet members—Senator Lloyd Bentsen was tapped to serve as secretary of the treasury and former San Antonio Mayor Henry Cisneros was designated as secretary of housing and urban development. The vacancy created by Bentsen's resignation from the Senate produced a lengthy search by Governor Ann Richards for an interim replacement. In the end, she selected Railroad Commissioner Bob Krueger, a former representative who had lost the primary for the U.S. Senate in 1984. Under Texas law, the vacancy was filled in a special election in May 1993. Easily won by

Republican Kay Bailey Hutchison, this election provides further evidence that Texas continues its slow march toward a competitive two-party system.

NOTES

1. "Texas Leads in Campaign Contributions," *Dallas Morning News* (9 March 1992), 6A.

2. "Clinton Passes Milestone," *Dallas Morning News* (20 May 1992), 6A.

3. *The Texas Poll Report* 6 (Fall 1989): 1.

4. "Fewer Texans Polled Identify with GOP, Democrats," *Dallas Morning News* (31 May 1992), 30A.

5. Texas Comptroller of Public Accounts, *Breaking the Mold: New Ways to Govern Texas, A Report from the Texas Performance Review*, vol. 1 (Austin: Texas Comptroller of Public Accounts, 1991), 27.

6. "What Texas Voters Said," *Dallas Morning News* (11 March 1992), 21A. Primary returns are from Secretary of State, *Official Primary Returns*.

7. "Yubba Bloc May Hold Key to Lone Star Presidential Vote," *Dallas Morning News* (7 September 1992), 16A.

8. "Yubba Bloc," *Dallas Morning News*.

9. "Perot Supporters: Bush vs. Clinton," *Dallas Morning News* (19 July 1992), 1A.

10. David Jackson, "Campaigns Differ on Bush Visits," *Dallas Morning News* (14 September 1992), 1A.

11. "Clinton Leads Bush in Texas, Poll Indicates,' *Dallas Morning News* (10 August 1992), 1A.

12. "Clinton, Bush in Dead Heat in Texas, Poll Says," *Dallas Morning News* (6 September 1992), 1A.

13. "Clinton, Bush in Dead Heat," *Dallas Morning News*.

14. Sam Attlesey, "Texas Poll Finds Bush, Clinton Even," *Dallas Morning News* (11 October 1992), 1A.

15. Sam Attlesey, "Bush, Clinton Neck-and-neck in Texas Poll," *Dallas Morning News* (25 October 1992), 1A.

16. Christy Hoppe and George Kuempel, "GOP Says Elections Hurt Richards; Democrats Scoff," *Dallas Morning News* (5 November 1992), 21A.

17. Phil Kuntz, "Overdrafts Were a Potent Charge," *Congressional Quarterly Weekly Report* (7 November 1992), 3575.

18. The state senate normally operates by suspending the rules in order to consider and vote on legislation. The state house does not operate in this fashion, but a two-thirds vote is required in order to recommend constitutional amendments to the voters.

19. Texas Secretary of State, *General Election Returns/County by County Totals Report* (Austin, Texas: 28 November 1992) and *Statistical Abstract of the United States: 1992*.

13

Virginia: A Different Story with the Same Ending

JOHN J. McGLENNON

THE REPUBLICAN LOCK ON THE OLD DOMINION

From the opening shot of the 1992 presidential campaign, Virginia was seen as one of the safe havens for George Bush and the Republican presidential ticket. If some southern states might be put in play by the nomination of two moderate Democrats from the region for president and vice-president, Virginia was not expected to be one of them. Even the presidential candidacy of the state's chief executive, L. Douglas Wilder, the first popularly elected African-American governor in the nation's history, did not appear to threaten GOP presidential hegemony in Virginia.

Unlike the other ten southern states, Virginia alone had rejected regional appeals to support Jimmy Carter for president in 1976 and had produced the South's only electoral votes for Republican Gerald Ford. Since 1952, the Democratic presidential nominee had carried Virginia only once, in Lyndon Johnson's 1964 landslide. Even then, Virginia's Republican vote was well above the national GOP performance.

In 1988, when Republican vice-presidential nominee J. Danforth Quayle was regarded as a liability to the Bush campaign, the Republicans sent him to Virginia for the last weekend before the election. The trip was widely interpreted as an indication of how safe Virginia was for the GOP.[1] Virginia voters were spared much of the barrage of television ads throughout the 1980s as neither party committed substantial resources to winning the Old Dominion.

Although the end result in 1992 continued Virginia's unbroken string of GOP victories in presidential contests, the outcome was by no means certain, and the race was the closest in sixteen years. Suddenly, Virginians were being actively courted by both major parties, but especially by the Republicans, who spent much more money and far longer than normal to win a clear, but uncomfortably narrow, plurality victory.

In the end, Virginians showed up at the polls in record numbers to join with most southern states in supporting the reelection of George Bush. But that end came only after H. Ross Perot collapsed as a serious challenger for the presidency, and after Republicans held off a surge of support for Clinton following his second debate performance. That debate, not coincidentally, took place in Richmond.

Unlike in 1976, Virginia was neither unique among the southern states, nor even unusual, as it had been in 1928 and the 1950s. The Old Dominion was one of seven southern states to support George Bush's losing campaign, giving him neither his highest nor his lowest margin in the region.

THE CAMPAIGN: A LITTLE SUSPENSE FOR A CHANGE

The Nominations

Virginia is not used to being in the presidential spotlight. The participation of the state in the Super Tuesday southern regional primary in 1988 turned out to be a one-time fling with high-visibility presidential nominating contests. Voters demonstrated little interest in the primary, with fewer than one registered voter in four bothering to cast a ballot.[2]

The Old Dominion abandoned its experiment with the primary in 1992 and reverted to selecting its national convention delegates through a caucus/state convention system. By the time Virginians had selected their convention delegates, both George Bush and Bill Clinton had become the presumptive favorites for their party nominations.

On the Republican side, more attention was devoted to the election of a new state party chair and the growing influence of the Christian right in the party organization than to the presidential preferences of the state convention delegates, who overwhelmingly favored the president.[3]

Governor Wilder had already abandoned his presidential campaign before the first ballots were cast in Iowa or New Hampshire, as Virginians registered their disapproval of his national ambitions.[4] When the Democratic caucuses took place in April, Wilder had been joined on the sidelines by three presidential also-rans, Senators Bob Kerrey and Tom Harkin and former Senator Paul Tsongas. Only former Governor Jerry Brown remained as an active candidate challenging Clinton, though a group of party activists close to Wilder organized an effort to elect uncommitted delegates.[5]

For the Democrats, the determination of the Virginia delegation to the Democratic National Convention is a three-stage process. Open caucuses are held in each city and county of the state to elect a number of state/district convention delegates proportional to the area's population and Democratic vote performance. The delegates are awarded in accordance with the proportion of voters at the caucus supporting each candidate or declaring themselves "uncommitted."

At congressional district–level conventions, a set number of national convention delegates (again based on the district's population and voting behavior) are awarded to the candidates based on the percentage of state/district convention delegates in attendance who support each candidate. Finally, at the state convention, an additional set of national convention delegates is selected, again based on the proportion of delegates attending the state convention in support of each candidate. Delegates elected in support of a candidate may not switch their support to another candidate unless their first choice has less than a 15 percent threshold level of support. Delegates who are elected as uncommitted may switch to a candidate at any level of the process, but the switch is final.

Clinton took a majority (52 percent) of the state convention delegates, with the uncommitted category finishing second (36 percent) and Brown earning 12 percent, less than the 15 percent of the delegates required to win a share of the state's at-large delegates. Brown appeared to win a share of the national delegates elected at congressional district conventions, primarily due to his support among college students in Richmond and Norfolk, but the failure of the Brown delegates to attend district conventions suppressed his already low vote.

Clinton took the lion's share of the state's pledged delegates at the state convention, as many of the uncommitted delegates declared their preference for the Arkansas governor. As at the Republican convention, more attention was focused on the state chairmanship when the Democrats met in Roanoke. An abortive attempt to oust or weaken Wilder's handpicked state chairman, Paul Goldman, occupied most of the news coverage that the convention received.

Wilder himself became the focus of intense speculation due to persistent rumors that he was willing to be considered as vice-presidential running mate for independent candidate Perot. The main question surrounding his convention speech was whether or not he would declare his support for the all-but-nominated Clinton. He did not.[6]

Wilder kept the speculation alive up until the Democratic National Convention, as news-starved television reporters posed the possibility of a Wilder bolt to Perot as one of the few potential dramas in a well-scripted, tightly organized nomination spectacle for Bill Clinton. Wilder disappeared from all proximity to center stage when Perot announced the first "end" of his presidential bid on the third day of the convention, citing the revitalized Democratic Party as a major factor in his decision to quit.[7]

The Buchanan revolt in the Republican Party never took hold in Virginia, where delegates were elected without having to declare their candidate preference. President Bush won all of the state's convention votes, as most attention centered on the battle for the state chairmanship. That contest was eventually won by Patrick McSweeney, a strong conservative aligned with the Christian right, sending yet another signal of the growing influence of Pat Robertson and other evangelical conservatives in the state GOP.[8]

The third major candidate for the presidency, Ross Perot, had not yet been certified for the Virginia ballot when he seemingly withdrew from the race on

July 15, but his supporters had gathered far more than the signatures necessary
to earn him such designation. In fact, Perot was scheduled to make one of his
infrequent campaign stops in Virginia the Saturday after his withdrawal. However, in what was perhaps a sign that he was going to return to the race at a
later date, Perot informed state officials that he did not want his name removed
from the Virginia ballot despite his withdrawal.

The Fall Campaign

The post–Democratic convention "bounce" in public opinion polls enjoyed
by Clinton gave the impression that no state was any longer safe for the Bush
campaign. Even so, analysts generally concluded that as the campaign wore on,
Virginia would be among the first states to be secured by the president's reelection
effort. But the seriousness with which the GOP viewed the prospect of losing
the Old Dominion became evident in the travel schedule of the president and
the vice-president.

Bush made a Labor Day visit to the headquarters of Pat Robertson's new
Christian Coalition in Virginia Beach[9] and followed that a few days later with
a major address on small-business initiatives at a hardware store in Fredericks-
burg.[10] Quayle made visits to Richmond and Norfolk in hopes of solidifying
support among conservative business people and the military. Barbara Bush
made a late campaign appearance in Newport News. Bush/Quayle television ads
flooded the airwaves, primarily attacking the character and the record of Clinton.

Although Virginia Democrats were optimistic about the prospects of the Clin-
ton/Gore ticket, they had a hard time convincing the national campaign that it
ought to focus the ticket's time on a state where the prospects of winning were
still questionable. Clinton did make a highly profitable visit to the Middleburg
estate of Democratic patron Pamela Harriman for a fund-raising dinner, which
produced in excess of $3 million. He and Gore both made brief forays into the
northern Virginia suburbs of Washington, D.C., but otherwise Virginia was
originally not on the itinerary of the Democratic candidates.

The resurrection of a series of presidential debates suddenly made Virginia
much more central to the Clinton/Gore campaign. The original proposal of the
bipartisan Presidential Debate Commission had included the University of Richmond as one of the three sites for meetings between the presidential candidates.
When the Bush campaign rejected the commission's schedule and format, it put
the Richmond event very much in doubt. Ultimately, the Republicans agreed to
a series of debates or joint appearances, and Richmond again was selected as a
site.

This second presidential debate proved to be a major triumph for Clinton, and
it had a strong, if short-lived, effect on the Virginia electorate. As he would for
each debate, Clinton set aside several days for preparation and for resting his
voice. For more than two days, he and his campaign set up shop in Williamsburg,
the original capital of Virginia and the site of the famous restored eighteenth-

century city. Clinton jogged the streets of the city, shook hands with hundreds of local residents and tourists, and gained invaluable attention from local television stations and newspapers.

The "debate" itself was the most unconventional format of the three presidential appearances. A moderator, ABC News Correspondent Carole Simpson, directed questions to the candidates from a pre-selected group of about 200 undecided voters assembled at the University of Richmond's basketball arena. Public opinion polls and analysts overwhelmingly concluded that Clinton had shone in this format, with an easy, direct, conversational style that allowed him to display both an impressive command of the details of policy questions and an ability to relate to the concerns of these "average voters."

Ross Perot, who would be more effective in both the first and the third debates, seemed to have little to say in this venue, usually ending his comments after his familiar snappy one-liners. But the most peculiar performance came from President Bush, who was spotted conspicuously looking at his watch during other candidates' answers and, most damaging of all, seemed unable to understand a question about how the national economic downturn had affected him personally. Fairly or not, the president's inability to "get it" became a metaphor for his seeming lack of understanding and concern over the public's anxiety about the economy.

Virginia viewers watched post-debate coverage of Clinton staying behind for nearly an hour after the debate, talking individually with many in the debate audience, while Bush and Perot both immediately left the arena. Bush's appearance at a post-debate rally in downtown Richmond was a curious affair, with not a single leading Virginia Republican in evidence to television viewers. The president was introduced by the singer/bandleader who had kept the audience, primarily high school and college students, entertained throughout the evening.

Clinton's eventual arrival at a downtown hotel rally of 2,000 was also broadcast, and he capped his visit by staying overnight in the Governor's Mansion with former rival Wilder and then appearing at a morning rally in Capitol Square. This rally brought together the Democrats' top officials, including Wilder and his intraparty nemesis, U.S. Senator Charles Robb. Newspaper reports described the rally as the largest political event other than a gubernatorial inauguration ever held on the Capitol grounds.[11]

Despite the strong surge of momentum that Democrats experienced in the commonwealth after this debate, the considerable Republican advantage in the electorate was reinforced by several public opinion polls. While late spring polls had shown Perot taking a lead over Bush, with Clinton running at about 20 percent, few state observers believed that those figures would hold up. When Clinton took a seven-point lead in a Mason-Dixon poll conducted after the Democratic convention and Perot's withdrawal, again the expectations were that the GOP would eventually return to dominance.[12]

Throughout the fall campaign, the surprise was that the president could not seem to move beyond a lead of less than the statistical margin of error in statewide surveys and that he wound up in a tie with Clinton (with Perot far behind) in two polls conducted immediately after the Richmond debate. Even this, of course, still put Virginia among the top prospects for Republicans, as the number of states where Bush led Clinton could be counted on the fingers of one hand. Finally, a series of late polls indicated that the GOP was likely to win the state, with margins ranging from four to eleven percentage points.[13]

Complicating the predictions for election day 1992 was the substantial upsurge in interest among Virginia's electorate. Like the rest of the nation, Virginians were excited by this contest, as more than 400,000 new voters were registered. The combination of a close race, a strong independent candidate, several hotly contested U.S. House races, economic anxiety, and anger at the political system energized the voters. Registrars across the state noted dramatically increased absentee voting and prepared for a record turnout.

These predictions proved to be accurate as 84.5 percent of an expanded pool of voters showed up on election day, keeping polling places busy in sunny, pleasant weather. The 7 percent jump in turnout among registered voters translated into a 55 percent voting rate among the voting age population, easily exceeding any previous election turnout in the state and marking the first time that Virginia's turnout in a presidential election approximated the national average.

RESULTS AND ANALYSIS: AS EXPECTED, BUT BARELY

The Presidential Election

Virginians once again resisted a Democratic presidential victory, as George Bush won 45.0 percent of the total vote, a plurality that gave him the commonwealth's thirteen electors. Bill Clinton's 40.6 percent earned him the closest second place for any Democrat since Jimmy Carter's showing in 1976. Ross Perot fell considerably below his national showing, with 13.6 percent of Virginians casting ballots for him, and the other three independents on the ballot combined to draw less than 1 percent.[14]

In its simplest terms, the 1992 presidential election in Virginia was entirely predictable. The Republican candidate won the state for the seventh straight time, and for the tenth time out of the last eleven contests. No other southern state has such a lengthy and unbroken streak of presidential wins for one party. Virginia and Indiana are the two largest states to continue the string, and the only two east of the Mississippi River.

George Bush won in Virginia's suburbs, the base of GOP victories in the state. Bush carried all of the major suburban counties in the state except the reliably Democratic (and mostly urban) Arlington. Albemarle County, surrounding Charlottesville, split almost evenly between Bush and Clinton. In fact, the fourteen largest suburban jurisdictions, which cast 46 percent of the statewide vote in 1992, provided Bush with a margin of 112,224, almost precisely his statewide margin over Clinton (111, 867).

As impressive as that margin sounds, it represented only a plurality of the suburban vote for Bush (47 percent), with Clinton drawing 38 percent and Perot winning 15 percent in these localities. That marked a substantial decline from Bush's nearly two-to-one win over Michael Dukakis in the same areas (65 to 35 percent) as he received less than half of his 281,338 suburban edge in 1988. In addition, the advantage that Bush took out of the state's smaller suburbs and rural areas was completely offset by Clinton's edge in the state's urban areas. Dukakis had lost the nonsuburban remainder of the state by a margin larger than Bush's total advantage in 1992.

The Republican presidential vote total was the lowest since 1980, when 700,000 fewer votes were cast in the state. Bush also received the lowest GOP presidential percentage in the Old Dominion since Richard Nixon's plurality win in 1968 against Hubert Humphrey and George Wallace. Bush won in eight of the state's eleven congressional districts, though he won a majority (54.4 percent) in only the Seventh District. While the state underwent major reapportionment in 1991, adding a new district and creating a predominantly African-American district, the erosion of Bush's support is evident in that he had carried all ten districts in 1988. That year his margins in nine of the ten districts exceeded his largest district margin in 1992.

Despite the weakness of the incumbent president, Democrats were still denied a victory in Virginia. Once again, even a candidate with strong regional appeal, a centrist who seemed to represent the kind of Democrat Virginians have comfortably elected to state offices, fell short of victory. As the prospects of a national Clinton win improved, Virginia Democratic organizations increased their efforts. They hoped to avoid being left out of the ranks of states contributing to the first Democratic presidential victory in sixteen years.

The efforts fell a bit short, but Clinton did achieve several notable results. Drawing the largest Democratic percentage since Jimmy Carter in 1976, Clinton easily set a record for the most votes ever received by a Democratic presidential candidate in Virginia. He topped Dukakis's showing by nearly 180,000 votes, despite the three-way contest. Clinton kept the race competitive everywhere in Virginia. He carried 42 of the 136 localities (compared to 25 for Dukakis) and nearly tied Bush in several others. Clinton did especially well in cities or counties with large black populations, but he also reduced the Bush advantage in the suburbs, most notably in vote-rich, suburban northern Virginia. In Fairfax County, the state's largest jurisdiction comprising roughly 12 percent of Virginia's population, Clinton exceeded even Carter's 1976 performance.

The Democratic presidential percentage increased over 1988 in only fourteen states as a result of the three-way contest. In this case, Virginia joined every one of the other states of the South except Texas (due to Perot's strong showing in his home state), along with three border states (Maryland, Delaware, and Kentucky) and the District of Columbia. As in a number of these states, Clinton could take the Democratic percentage higher because of his Southern heritage and because Ross Perot took a smaller portion of the overall vote.

The three congressional districts that the Democrats carried represented the three corners of Virginia's triangular geography. He won a plurality in southwestern Virginia's "Fighting Ninth" District, an area of historically strong party competition, bordering Albert Gore's Tennessee, Kentucky, and West Virginia. Organized labor is a powerful presence in the coal-mining counties of the district, and this had been Dukakis's best district in 1988.

In addition, Clinton won a majority in northern Virginia's Eighth Congressional District. This district had been reconstituted by the General Assembly to include reliably Democratic Arlington County and the city of Alexandria in order to protect freshman Representative James Moran (D–Alexandria). Clinton just missed carrying the new Eleventh District, added as a result of the rapid population growth in northern Virginia.

The biggest Democratic win, however, came in the Third Congressional District, a predominantly African-American constituency, which stretches from Norfolk, on the Atlantic Ocean, across the port of Hampton Roads along both sides of the James River to Richmond, some eighty miles inland, and then north through several rural counties. The district, the product of a sophisticated computer analysis of Virginia's racial demography, was designed to meet the demands of the federal Voting Rights Act that states take appropriate steps to create "majority minority" districts wherever possible. The district produced 65 percent for Clinton.

Ultimately, the defeat resulted from the continuing rejection by suburban Virginians of Democratic presidential nominees. The same voters who helped elect three Democratic governors in the 1980s were still unwilling to endorse the party's choice for the White House. Especially in the Richmond suburbs, Clinton lost by margins of landslide proportions, even as he improved on the showings of Dukakis, Mondale, and Carter. The fact that these areas constitute a growing segment of the state's electorate poses a continuing obstacle for the Democrats. In addition, the anxiety among defense workers and those dependent on military spending over Clinton's larger proposed defense cuts blunted his appeal in the Tidewater region of the state. Finally, although Ross Perot did not do particularly well in Virginia, his presence on the ballot may have siphoned off pro-choice Republicans who had voted for Governor Wilder in 1989 and were disaffected by President Bush's abortion stance, but hesitant to cross over to Clinton.

The Perot Factor

Despite early expectations that Virginia would be fertile ground for the Perot candidacy, the Texas billionaire fell more than 5 percent off his national pace in the Old Dominion. The willingness of Virginians to support independent candidacies (Harry Byrd, Jr., had been elected to the U.S. Senate twice without major-party endorsement) and their reputation for fiscal conservatism suggested that Perot ought to have an appeal. Perot also had a ready-made organization in the many POW–MIA activists, especially in the military-influenced Tidewater area.

When the votes were counted, however, Perot had failed to persuade Virginia voters. Except for Florida and Texas, Perot did poorly in the South, and the fact that Virginia was among his weaker states is somewhat surprising. Perot had little appeal among black voters, but Virginia's African-American voting population is not among the highest in the region. The more suburban nature of the Virginia electorate should have favored the Texan, and Virginia's relatively high income level suggests that it should have been more like Texas and Florida, both of which gave Perot above-average percentages.

The Second Congressional District, dominated by Navy interests and the suburban city of Virginia Beach, gave Perot his largest percentage, but even here he fell two points behind his national average. Northern Virginia and Richmond area suburbs were not particularly hospitable to the "Perotista" attacks on government, perhaps because of the high levels of national and state government employment. But Perot's appeal fell flat across the commonwealth. He carried no district, county, or city and did not even place second anywhere. In his best district, his vote was less than half of either of the two major-party candidates.

The explanation for Perot's relative weakness in the Old Dominion is probably found in a number of factors: his general weakness in the South, the large number of government employees and government-related businesses and industries, the substantial minority population, and even the unprecedented nature of the Perot candidacy. A state described as "fixated by its traditions"[15] is a poor prospect for the kind of radical upheaval preached by the Texan.

Though he did not run as well in Virginia as in other states, Perot's candidacy certainly helped to keep the outcome in doubt for much of the election. Few believed that Clinton had any realistic chance of winning Virginia in a two-way contest. The fact that Perot was likely to draw his vote most heavily from the areas of GOP strength was seen as benefiting the Democrats. At the same time, Perot's support in Republican-leaning areas reflected a basic dissatisfaction with George Bush, and many of these voters had been comfortable voting for Democrats in state elections.

In the end, Perot's vote would have been likely to split among Clinton, Bush, and abstention. It was not large enough to change the outcome unless the vote moved decisively in one direction or the other, and national surveys gave little indication that such a movement was likely.

Virginia's Elections for the House of Representatives

The same factors that promised to bring wholesale change to the U.S. House of Representatives in 1992 produced a lively year for Virginia's House delegation. Nationally, a combination of scandals, retirements, anti-incumbency, and reapportionment led to predictions that a record number of freshman representatives would be elected in 1992. In Virginia, everything but scandal produced a relatively modest change of three new members in a delegation expanded by one.

Virginia was a winner in the decennial reallocation of seats in the House. With a population growth rate of 16 percent, 4 percent above the national average, the state saw its number of House districts increased from 10 to 11. Reapportionment in Virginia would begin with the happy necessity of creating a new district. Complicating matters considerably was the pressure to create a predominantly African-American district in order to ensure that the state's 22 percent black population would be able to elect a member of the House for the first time since Reconstruction.

The creation of a "majority minority" district had not been seen as inevitable even by black politicians ambitious to serve in the Congress. Virginia's black population is dispersed widely across the state, with no single region containing enough African Americans to guarantee a voting majority. A number of black leaders, including Governor Wilder, suggested that it might suffice to create a couple of "minority influence" districts, where 35 to 45 percent of the population was black and where a black candidate with appeal to white voters might prevail.

The operating principle for the Justice Department in reviewing state reapportionment plans was that if it could be demonstrated that it was *possible* to create a predominantly black district, the burden was on the legislature to explain why such a district should not be drawn. When the *Norfolk Virginian-Pilot* newspaper commissioned a computer analysis of the state to find whether such a plan was possible, the computer drew a district that essentially hugged the shores of the James River as it flowed into the harbor at Hampton Roads, carving out the black neighborhoods of Norfolk, Portsmouth, Newport News, and Hampton. It then moved westward, darting back and forth across the James to pick up pockets of black voters in rural and suburban counties on the way into the predominantly black sections of Richmond before heading north through several rural counties with substantial minority populations.

Once this proposal was advanced, it became almost certain that the state would adopt a version of it, in the process dramatically altering surrounding districts. Three Tidewater-based districts and one Richmond area constituency had to be altered, making them generally whiter and more Republican.

Within the constraints of having to carve out a new district in northern Virginia and a minority district in the eastern and central parts of the state, the legislature made some other significant alterations. In the past, Virginia's General Assembly had made only the necessary modifications in district lines, usually not demonstrating a particularly partisan approach to the process despite commanding Democratic majorities in both houses.

Perhaps because of the increasing competition between the parties at every level, the General Assembly was more willing to consider the partisan ramifications of its reapportionment decisions in the 1990s. In northern Virginia, the two evenly balanced suburban districts were replaced by three districts, one each securely in the hands of a major party, with the third being divided as closely as possible between the parties.

Even with the growth of the state delegation, the northern Virginia and minority districts were destined to squeeze one Republican incumbent out of his district. After some intense jockeying, the loser was Republican George Allen, Jr., son of the former Washington Redskins coach, who had only been elected to Congress in November 1991 to fill a vacancy. After several unsuccessful attempts to find a district in which to run, Allen announced his retirement from the House in order to plan a 1993 run for governor. The remaining districts were modified only slightly, generally in an attempt to give them a modestly more Democratic cast.

The legislature's handiwork was modified by Governor Wilder, who made several amendments to the plan, primarily by shifting more black voters into the new minority-dominated Third District at the expense of Second District Representative Owen Pickett and Fourth District Representative Norman Sisisky, both Democrats who were already seeking reelection in substantially more Republican districts.

One final piece to pre-election maneuvering found Representative James Olin announcing his retirement from the House after ten years and creating an open seat based in the Roanoke area. Three open-seat contests were sure to produce new House members from Virginia, and when the dust cleared in November, all eight incumbents seeking reelection had been returned to office. None won less than 55 percent of the vote, although Pickett saw the impact of his new district in a substantially reduced margin. On the other hand, Representative Herbert Bateman won comfortably after a near upset in 1990, as thousands of Democratic (African-American) votes were excised from his First Congressional District.

The three newcomers included a Republican white male, a Democratic black male, and a Democratic white woman. The Republican, Robert Goodlatte, easily won the open Sixth District seat, which had been in Republican hands for thirty years prior to Olin's tenure. The Third District gave a landslide to state senator Robert Scott, a classmate of Vice-President Albert Gore at Harvard and a fifteen-year veteran of the General Assembly, making him the first African American elected to Congress from Virginia in this century. The new Eleventh District had the closest race in the state, with victory going to state delegate Leslie Byrne, the first woman ever elected to Congress from the Old Dominion.[16]

The House delegation continued its tilt toward the Democrats, having come from the 1980 election of a nine-to-one GOP contingent to the 1992 result of seven Democrats and four Republicans. But the first election conducted under the district lines for the 1990s suggested that a number of districts will be highly competitive if popular Democratic incumbents step down.

In all four GOP-held districts, Bush won at least 49 percent of the vote and led Clinton by margins of 12 to 24 percent, suggesting a significant Republican edge in the electorate. In all four, the successful House candidates won by even larger margins. Of the seven Democratic winners, all outpolled Clinton by margins ranging from 5 to 29 percent. The Second District will be hardest for the Democrats to retain, and, given Bush's twelve-point edge there, Pickett's similar reelection margin was impressive.

CONCLUSION: THE REPUBLICAN LOCK HOLDS, BUT FOR HOW LONG?

In the end, the winners and losers of Virginia's 1992 general elections might have looked inevitable. George Bush won Virginia's thirteen electors for the GOP for the seventh straight time by decisively carrying the state's growing suburbs. All eight House incumbents were returned to office and were joined by three newcomers elected to open seats.

But the surface predictability masked some historically important developments in Virginia politics. The state that once trailed the nation in voter participation set a new record both for number of registered voters and for turnout in a presidential election. For the first time in its modern history, Virginia's turnout approximately equaled the national rate, an even more remarkable feat as the national number surged upward.

Although the Democrats failed to deliver the state, Bill Clinton exceeded the vote totals for any previous party nominee and even in a three-way race won the highest percentage of the vote of any Democratic candidate for president in twelve years—and the second highest percentage since Lyndon Johnson carried the state in 1964.

Ross Perot ran a surprisingly weak third in the Old Dominion despite the abundance of affluent suburban voters who nationally were so attracted to the independent. Virginia behaved much more like the typical southern state than the Rim South states of Texas and Florida, both of which produced above-average percentages for Perot.

As one of eighteen states (and seven in the South) that supported the reelection of George Bush, Virginia would seem to be beyond the reach of Democrats in future contests. But the closeness of the Virginia vote, like that in the other southern states, suggests an opportunity for the Democrats. Can a President Clinton break down the image held by southern white voters of Democratic presidential nominees who are outside of the mainstream?

Bill Clinton's roots in the Democratic Leadership Council (DLC), the party's moderate, heavily southern faction, suggest that he is the kind of Democrat who ought to have appeal to the decisive suburban bloc of Virginia voters. Like his fellow-DLC-leader Charles Robb, and even sometimes-DLC-critic Doug Wilder, Clinton may have the potential to compete effectively for the decisive bloc of suburban, independent voters who hold the key to Virginia elections. If he can, the experience of Virginia Democrats in statewide elections suggests that the Old Dominion may see effective two-party competition once again.

NOTES

1. *Richmond Times-Dispatch* (7 November 1988), A1.

2. State Board of Elections, *Official Results: Democratic Presidential Primary Election, March 8, 1988* and *Official Results: Republican Presidential Primary Election, March 8, 1988* (Richmond: March 28, 1988).

3. Congressional Quarterly, *Guide to the 1992 Republican National Convention, Congressional Quarterly Weekly Report* 50, supplement to no. 33 (August 8, 1992): 59.

4. *Washington Post* (12 January 1992), A4.

5. Congressional Quarterly, *Guide to the 1992 Democratic National Convention, Congressional Quarterly Weekly Report* 50, supplement to no. 27 (July 4, 1992): 56.

6. *Richmond Times-Dispatch* (7 June 1992), A15.

7. *New York Times* (14 July 1992), A14.

8. *Washington Post* (31 May 1992), B3.

9. *Washington Post* (12 September 1992), A10.

10. *Richmond Times-Dispatch* (17 September 1992), B1.

11. *Richmond Times-Dispatch* (17 October 1992), A1.

12. *Newport News Daily Press* (29 July 1992), A1.

13. *Richmond Times-Dispatch* (1 November 1992), A1.

14. State Board of Elections, *Official Election Results 1992* (Richmond: Commonwealth of Virginia, November 23, 1992).

15. Michael Barone and Grant Ujifusa, *The Almanac of American Politics 1992* (Washington, D.C.: National Journal, 1991), 1262.

16. *Richmond Times-Dispatch* (24 November 1992), B3.

PART IV

CONCLUSION

The South and the 1992 Presidential Election

HAROLD W. STANLEY

In the 1992 presidential vote, the South was not a vital region. Bill Clinton's victory would have been safe without a single one of the thirty-nine electoral college votes he secured from the southern states. In 1992, winning the White House for the Democratic Party meant nominating two southerners whose relative appeal outside the South, not a strong southern base, made victory prospects viable. Ironically, an all-southern Democratic ticket proved electable, but had not required southern electoral votes. Indeed, the South favored George Bush, forming the most favorable Republican region. In one sense, the South proved less hospitable, and the other regions more hospitable, than Clinton had hoped: The only state Clinton forces targeted to win, but lost, was in the South (North Carolina); the only states Clinton won without such targeting were outside the South (New Hampshire and Nevada).

Hindsight and electoral college arithmetic suggest that the South was not vital to the outcome of the 1992 presidential election. Such a conclusion does not mean that writing off the South occurred or would have been smart politics for either party. To the contrary, southern states figured prominently in the general election campaign plans of both Clinton and Bush. Clinton forces sought to put the southern states "in play," making Republicans compete there, forcing Republicans to shore up their recently acquired presidential base. This strategy succeeded, preventing Republicans from taking southern states for granted in order to focus campaign resources on battleground states outside the South. Republicans ended up campaigning strenuously to hold southern states—a solid indication of Bush's political plight in 1992: "Although the Democrats' southern strategy did not pay off handsomely in electoral votes, it did tie down GOP resources—money plus the time of Bush and Dan Quayle, who had to barnstorm the South right up until the end to secure most of their GOP base."[1] Moreover, southern states not only were "in play" for the general election, but also played a critical role in the successful nomination quest of Clinton as the "Comeback Kid"—a critical role the architects of the southern Super Tuesday had anticipated for 1988.

This chapter reviews from a regionwide perspective topics discussed in the earlier state chapters: the dynamics of the nomination process; the campaign strategies, particularly for Clinton; what the results reveal about the success of that presidential strategy; and the state of the parties in presidential and in subpresidential politics.[2]

SUPER TUESDAY 1992: DID IT WORK THIS TIME?

Did the existence of a southern Super Tuesday advantage Clinton? Southern Democrats, smarting from losing the presidency in 1984, had combined to create a regional primary for 1988. The express goal was to benefit mainstream Democratic presidential candidates and to help stop the trend among whites in the region toward presidential Republicanism.[3] Given that in 1992 a more moderate or "new" kind of Democrat secured the nomination and won the presidency, one would do well to wonder, as Charles S. Bullock III does when discussing the nomination process, the extent to which Super Tuesday's creators contributed to Clinton's nomination and general election victories.

For 1992, the southern contingent of Super Tuesday was reduced in size. Four states (Alabama, Arkansas, North Carolina, and Virginia), disappointed with the 1988 experience, moved the delegate election process to later dates, abandoning the quest to mount a regional presence at the front of the process and thus to exert greater leverage over the nominee. A fifth southern state, Georgia, also jumped ship by moving up earlier in the calendar, snagging greater media and candidate attention as the curtain raiser for the six southern states remaining in Super Tuesday. (South Carolina Republicans had shown the advantage of such timing in 1988.)

The dynamics of the 1992 nominations differed from those of 1988. The absence of nationally known figures such as Jesse Jackson left the field open to lesser-known candidates who had to establish themselves. The absence of other southern and border state candidates benefited Clinton. In 1988, U.S. Senator Al Gore had sought to jump-start his campaign in the South on Super Tuesday (having tested the waters in Iowa and New Hampshire, but having found them unfriendly). The results of Super Tuesday 1988 produced a three-way win, with Dukakis, Jackson, and Gore each claiming victory. Unfortunately for Gore, having jump-started his campaign in the South, he could not mount an effective campaign in subsequent states. He did not have momentum going into Super Tuesday, and going out of Super Tuesday, he failed to find a receptive non-southern state, dropping out of the campaign after the New York primary.

In 1992, Clinton did not pursue a South-first strategy. The Iowa Democratic caucus was written off by all because of the home-state advantage of Senator

Tom Harkin. New Hampshire was the first real test, and Clinton had a trial by fire: The Gennifer Flowers story raised allegations of marital infidelities, and doubts over Clinton's draft status began to surface. Clinton met these charges head-on and waged a nonstop campaign to recover. In New Hampshire, Clinton placed second to ex-Senator Paul Tsongas of neighboring Massachusetts. Proclaiming himself the "Comeback Kid," Clinton headed South to roll up wins in primaries in Georgia and South Carolina (held in advance of Super Tuesday 1992) as well as in five other southern states balloting on Super Tuesday (March 10). Clinton's successes did not stop there. Unlike Gore, he continued his winning ways after Super Tuesday, racking up wins in eight of the nine primaries held between Illinois (March 17) and Pennsylvania (April 8).

Overall, southern presidential primary turnout lagged behind the 1988 levels. Excluding South Carolina and Virginia Democrats (because primaries were not held in both years), the number of southerners voting in presidential primaries dipped between 1988 and 1992 from 10.7 to 9.9 million. Republicans made notable gains in certain states: The number of Georgians choosing to participate in the Republican primary matched the Democratic primary turnout (453,987 to 454,631—in 1988, Republican turnout had been less than two-thirds the Democratic level). In South Carolina in 1992, Republican turnout surpassed the Democratic turnout (148,840 to 116,414). Of the southern states holding primaries on Super Tuesday or before in 1992, Republican primary turnout was a larger share of Democratic primary turnout than it had been in 1988 for each state except Texas.[4] What Brad Lockerbie and John A. Clark noted for Georgia may be true more broadly: Pat Buchanan's presence on the Republican ballot may have enticed more white conservatives into the Republican primaries just as Jesse Jackson's absence on the Democratic ballot meant lower black mobilization in the 1992 Democratic primaries.

THE DEMOCRATIC GENERAL ELECTION STRATEGY

Democratic prospects for retaking the White House in 1992 were dim. Recent electoral history suggested the Republicans held an electoral college lock on the presidential quest. The Democratic base had shriveled as Republicans swept five of the last six presidential elections. The South, once solid for the Democrats, had voted solidly Republican in those five Republican wins.[5] Any Democratic presidential candidate would have to work hard to overcome "the stigma of the Democratic party as the home of losers and liberals."[6] From the vantage point of early 1991, when prospective Democratic presidential contenders were considering suiting up for the quest, President Bush's record-setting approval ratings in the wake of the Gulf War gave several Democrats pause.

Bush had difficulties in mounting an effective reelection campaign. The anemic economy was the principal sore point. His strengths reminded some voters of his weaknesses: Foreign policy achievements such as the Gulf War fueled public misgivings that the president had spent too much time on foreign policy, too little on domestic problems. Falling back on a campaign strategy reminiscent of what had worked so well against Dukakis, Bush sought to raise doubts about Clinton's personal fitness to be president. The ungrammatical slogan for 1992—"Who do you trust?"—may have struck home in better times, but for too many voters such personal attacks seemed to be a desperate attempt to divert attention and to sidestep accountability for poor on-the-job performance.

The electoral map since 1968 was forbidding, but bad economic times in 1992 made a Democratic electoral college majority thinkable. H. Ross Perot's independent candidacy added uncertainty to any attempt to predict the 1992 outcome on the basis of previous elections. Moreover, Perot had the ability to saturate the airwaves with heavy buys of media beyond the general election constraints imposed on the publicly financed major-party campaigns. This made targeting to establish and hold bases of support both more necessary and more difficult.

Clinton mounted an effective campaign.[7] From the depths of May and early June, when the Democratic nomination was being secured in primaries and caucuses while national polls showed Clinton running a poor third behind Bush and Perot, Clinton made a very impressive comeback. The Clinton campaign was broke and in debt, but, taking Perot's lead, effectively resorted to nontraditional media venues ("The Arsenio Hall Show," MTV, television talk shows, the network morning shows, etc.) to reach the public. The Bush and Perot campaigns cooperated by attacking one another, giving Clinton's candidacy an "above-the-fray" aspect. Clinton presented an economic plan that initially lost out in the media focus on the Bush-Perot charges and countercharges. As the economic news worsened, the previous release of an economic plan made Clinton appear all the more presidential and prepared.

The selection of another southerner, Gore, as running mate presented a ticket of "two southern progressives without the baggage of liberal excess"[8] and was not a ticket-balancing move. In a year marked by a public yearning for something other than politics-as-usual, the move resonated well, signaling and reinforcing the notion that Clinton was an unconventional Democrat.[9] Gore had a galvanizing effect, bringing to the ticket additional political weight that proved more helpful than the Clinton forces had anticipated.[10]

When Perot withdrew (on the day of Clinton's Democratic convention acceptance speech) from a presidential race he had yet to enter, Clinton's status as the candidate of change, the only alternative to Bush, was intensified. After the Democratic convention, Clinton, Gore, and their wives embarked on a mid-America bus tour that powerfully symbolized, among other things, that these candidates were in touch with the public.

From June to August, the national polls showed Clinton going from a distant third to a comfortable first. Clinton forces did not bask in the hope that such a leading margin in August was enough and would stick, but had carefully cut the nation's states into categories echoing the triage employed in battlefield medical care. Clinton forces divided the states into three categories—"top end," "play hard," and "big challenge."[11] (See Table 14.1.) The strategy proved either

Table 14.1
Clinton Campaign's State Targeting for the 1992 General Election

"Top End"	"Play Hard"	"Big Challenge"
Heavily Democratic	Colorado	**Watch for developments**
Arkansas	Delaware	**Alabama**
District of Columbia	**Georgia**	Arizona
Hawaii	Iowa	**Florida**
Massachusetts	Kentucky	Kansas
Minnesota	**Louisiana**	New Hampshire
Rhode Island	Maine	Nevada
West Virginia	Maryland	**South Carolina**
	Michigan	South Dakota
Competitive, economically	Missouri	**Texas**
troubled	Montana	
California	New Mexico	**Minimal campaign effort**
Connecticut	New Jersey	Alaska
Illinois	**North Carolina**	Idaho
New York	Ohio	Indiana
Oregon	Pennsylvania	**Mississippi**
Vermont	**Tennessee**	Nebraska
Washington	Wisconsin	North Dakota
		Oklahoma
		Utah
		Virginia
		Wyoming

Note: Southern states are in boldface type.
Source: Adapted from "Bulls-Eye: Targeting Helped Clinton Use Resources Wisely," *Milwaukee Journal* (6 November 1992), 10, as reported in William J. Crotty, "Introduction: A Most Unusual Election" in *America's Choice: The Election of 1992*, ed. William J. Crotty (Guilford, Conn.: Dushkin Publishing Group, 1993), 10-11.

prescient or self-fulfilling: Only one targeted state (North Carolina) was lost (by 0.7 percent), and only two nontargeted states were won (New Hampshire and Nevada).

The thirteen "top end" states and the District of Columbia were counted as safe, the nineteen "big challenge" states were seen as beyond hope, and the eighteen "play hard" states received the brunt of Clinton's campaign resources. The strategy was a national one, but the focus in this chapter is regional. Of the southern states, only Arkansas, Clinton's home state, ranked among the safely Democratic "top end" states. The "top end" and the "big challenge" categories were ignored; most of the Clinton campaign attention went to the middle category: "play hard." Four southern states with forty-seven electoral votes—Georgia, Louisiana, North Carolina, and Tennessee—were among the eighteen battleground states. Preceding chapter discussions of the different states confirm this targeting and its importance in the campaign. These states were crisscrossed by the Democratic and Republican campaigns. Most of the remaining southern states received a visit or two from the different camps or several from campaign surrogates, but basically, as Patrick R. Cotter makes clear for Alabama, the campaign activity consisted of Bush or Quayle seeking to shore up the Republican base.

Six southern states with 94 electoral votes—Alabama, Florida, Mississippi, South Carolina, Texas, and Virginia—were essentially written off by the Democrats. Virginia had last voted Democratic in 1964, the rest in 1976. Resources were not "wasted" on these states, since Bush was deemed likely to hold them. Feints proved useful, however, particularly in Florida and Texas, with a combined 57 electoral votes. Rather than concede such electoral prizes, Clinton forces scheduled bus tours in these two states to make Bush defend his own base. The attention paid off: "The week after the Democrats visited Texas, for example, . . . the Bush campaign responded with a heavy run of television ad time in seven large Texas media markets, a significant expenditure for the last week of September in the president's home state."[12]

The Democrats targeted states to pick up; the Republicans targeted states to hold. In 1988, Bush had won 426 electoral votes; he could shed over one-third of those and still win. But, in 1992, the Bush base proved hard to hold. As John J. McGlennon discusses, Bush's political troubles in 1992 made even previously reliably Republican Virginia worthy of attention and resources, hardly a symptom of a robust Republican candidacy. As one analyst noted, "The South is supposed to be Bush's backbone, but it's not there for him. He's having to fight for it." Prior to the voting, journalists reported most southern states as competitive, winnable by either Bush or Clinton, with the only concessions being Arkansas and Tennessee by the Republicans.[13]

Although the presidential Democratic team wrote off six southern states, state and local Democrats, even in those six states, did not distance themselves from the national Democratic ticket. For white southern Democrats, the more mainstream Democratic nominees of 1992 were a far cry from 1984 and 1988.[14]

THE PRESIDENTIAL RESULTS

The South's position in the 1992 election was an unusual one: All the principal presidential candidates, Perot included, could claim southern ties. Obviously, simple home-court advantage could not figure prominently in campaign plans or the results. Bush did relatively better in winning the votes (if not the hearts and minds) of the region: Bush secured 42.6 percent of the vote, Clinton 41.2 percent, and Perot 15.8 percent. In fact, as Table 14.2 shows, the eleven southern states were, as in 1988, Bush's best region in terms of vote share, bettering his next best showing in the Rocky Mountain states by 4.5 percentage points. Almost two-thirds of Bush's electoral vote came from the South, a region with just over one-fourth of the nation's voters.

Clinton, despite a three-way race, notched up regional support slightly surpassing the level attained by Dukakis against Bush in 1988 (41.2 to 40.9 percent). Clinton's support exceeded Dukakis's in each southern state except Texas, the state both Bush and Perot called home. The three-way contest makes comparisons

Table 14.2
Presidential General Election Returns for Regions and the Southern States, 1988 and 1992

Region	1992						1988				
	Electoral Vote		Popular Vote				Electoral Vote		Popular Vote		
	Dem	Rep	Total Vote	Clinton %	Bush %	Perot %	Dem	Rep	Total Vote	Dukakis %	Bush %
South	39	108	27,552,565	41.2	42.6	15.8	0	138	23,250,412	40.9	58.3
Alabama	0	9	1,688,060	40.9	47.6	10.8	0	9	1,378,476	39.9	59.2
Arkansas	6	0	950,653	53.2	35.5	10.4	0	6	827,738	42.2	56.4
Florida	0	25	5,311,219	39.0	40.9	19.8	0	21	4,299,149	38.5	60.9
Georgia	13	0	2,321,125	43.5	42.9	13.3	0	12	1,809,672	39.5	59.7
Louisiana	9	0	1,790,017	45.6	41.0	11.8	0	10	1,628,202	44.1	54.3
Mississippi	0	7	981,793	40.8	49.7	8.7	0	7	931,527	39.1	59.9
North Carolina	0	14	2,611,850	42.7	43.4	13.7	0	13	2,134,370	41.7	58.0
South Carolina	0	8	1,202,527	39.9	48.0	11.5	0	8	986,009	37.6	61.5
Tennessee	11	0	1,982,638	47.1	42.4	10.1	0	11	1,636,250	41.5	57.9
Texas	0	32	6,154,018	37.1	40.6	22.0	0	29	5,427,410	43.3	56.0
Virginia	0	13	2,558,665	40.6	45.0	13.6	0	12	2,191,609	39.2	59.7
Border	37	8	8,233,114	44.2	37.3	18.1	8	38	7,147,304	47.5	51.9
Rocky Mtn.	20	20	5,969,828	36.3	38.1	24.1	0	40	5,013,851	40.8	57.6
Pacific Coast	76	3	15,513,943	45.1	32.7	21.4	21	50	15,507,490	48.2	48.2
New England	35	0	6,350,504	44.4	31.7	23.3	17	19	5,729,652	49.3	49.5
Mid. Atlantic	74	0	15,457,536	47.3	35.7	16.3	36	44	14,365,964	48.5	50.6
Midwest	72	12	19,101,674	42.9	37.2	19.4	11	79	16,982,097	46.0	53.2
Plains	17	17	6,241,723	39.1	37.2	23.2	18	18	5,588,050	49.0	50.0
TOTALS	370	168	104,420,887	43.0	37.4	18.9	111	426	91,584,820	45.6	53.4

Note: For composition of regions, see Harold W. Stanley and Richard G. Niemi, eds., *Vital Statistics on American Politics* (Washington, D.C.: Congressional Quarterly, 3d ed., 1992), 434.
Source: Adapted from *Congressional Quarterly Weekly Report* (1989), 139, and (1993), 233.

between 1988 and 1992 difficult, but Democrats, if they did indeed get a boost down South from the double-southern ticket of Clinton and Gore, might need minor miracles to turn around the southern states they initially wrote off: Florida was lost by only a couple of percentage points and Texas by 3.5, but Alabama (6.7 percent), Mississippi (8.9 percent), South Carolina (8.1 percent),and Virginia (4.4 percent) loomed farther from Democratic reach. Stephen D. Shaffer put it well: If Democrats ''are unable to carry the state with two 'moderate' southerners on the ticket at a time when an incumbent Republican is plagued by a stagnant economy, when will they be able to carry Mississippi in a national election?'' Viewed differently, Clinton and Gore carried their home states along with Georgia and Louisiana—hardly a resounding Democratic comeback in the region, not that such a comeback was required for winning the presidency.

Surprisingly, Perot fared poorly in the South, his home region, a region marked by past support for populist causes and protest politics. Indeed, the South was Perot's worst region, although he did better his national percentage of support (18.9 percent) in the two largest southern states, Florida (19.8 percent) and Texas (22.0 percent). The increase in voter turnout, which elsewhere seems to have been fueled by enthusiasm for Perot, also typified the South in the 1992 elections.[15] Presumably something more than fascination for the populist billionaire motivated the higher turnout in the South.

THE RESULTS BELOW THE PRESIDENCY

Republicans lost the White House, but below the presidency southern Republicans could find satisfaction—even, as Diane D. Blair makes clear for Arkansas, in Clinton's home state. Southern Republicans lost the governorship in North Carolina, but gained two U.S. Senate seats, nine House seats, and 44 seats in state legislatures (thirty-one in the state houses, thirteen in the state senates).

The 1992 results give no grounds for complacency for Democratic partisans. The southern Democratic base has taken further hits, and the election of Clinton of Arkansas may only mask them. Reflecting on the 1992 results, Clinton's campaign manager, James Carville, acknowledged the unfinished work remaining for Democrats in the South.[16] Unmistakable signs of Democratic rejuvenation in the South are rare and outnumbered by indications of Republican strength. As noted, the South was Bush's strongest region. Republicans gained nine U.S. House seats in the South, a figure matching the national net Republican increase. Redistricting following the 1990 census accounted for some of the Republican surge. Two southern Democratic senators fell to Republican challengers (Fowler in Georgia and Sanford in North Carolina) and a third narrowly escaped defeat: Fritz Hollings of South Carolina edged out his Republican challenger by only 51 to 49 percent.

Voting patterns below the presidential level also suggest growing Republican strength. White Protestants make up the lion's share of the region's voters. Such

Table 14.3
The South in Congress, Partisan Divisions by State, Pre– and Post–1992 Election

State	House Old Dem	House Old Rep	House New Dem	House New Rep	Senate Old Dem	Senate Old Rep	Senate New Dem	Senate New Rep
Alabama	5	2	4	3	2	0	2	0
Arkansas	3	1	2	2	2	0	2	0
Florida	9	1 0	1 0	1 3	1	1	1	1
Georgia	9	1	7	4	2	0	1	1
Louisiana	4	4	4	3	2	0	2	0
Mississippi	5	0	5	0	0	2	0	2
North Carolina	7	4	8	4	1	1	0	2
South Carolina	4	2	3	3	1	1	1	1
Tennessee	6	3	6	3	2	0	2	0
Texas	1 9	8	2 1	9	1	1	1	1
Virginia	6	4	7	4	1	1	1	1
South	7 7	3 9	7 7	4 8	1 5	7	1 3	9

Source: Adapted from Hastings Wyman, Jr., "GOP Gains in Legislatures," *Southern Political Report* (24 November 1992), 3.

voters have trended Republican in the region, voting more solidly Republican at the congressional level and increasingly identifying with the Republican Party, particularly so among the young. In 1988 and in the 1990 midterm elections, 54 percent of southern white Protestant voters supported Republican House candidates in the region. In 1992, that number rose to 58 percent. Southern white Protestants voting in 1992 identified as Republicans rather than Democrats by 52 to 26 percent among those less than thirty years old and by 54 to 22 percent among those thirty to forty-four years old.[17]

Voters were in an anti-incumbent mood in 1992, but in the South as in the nation, when the votes were counted, fewer incumbents were turned out of office than some expected. For the House, 91 percent of southern incumbents seeking reelection won, contrasted with 94 percent outside the south. More House members stepped down than were voted down: sixteen retirements, but only four primary and five general election defeats. Retirements, defeats, and redistricting produced thirty-five new faces among the South's 125 House members (28 percent, contrasted with 24 percent outside the South).[18]

The 1992 election results produced a more diverse body of elected officials, with blacks, Hispanics, and women gaining. The number of women in Congress from the South increased from three to eleven, with nine Democrats and two Republicans.[19] The percentage of women in southern state legislatures increased from 10 to 12.3 percent. State legislatures range from 6 percent female in Alabama to just over 18 percent in North Carolina; however, the proportion of

Table 14.4
Southern State Legislatures, Partisan Divisions by State, Pre– and Post–1992 Election

State	House Old Dem	House Old Rep	House Old Ind	House New Dem	House New Rep	House New Ind	Senate Old Dem	Senate Old Rep	Senate New Dem	Senate New Rep
Alabama	82	23		82	23		28	7	28	7
Arkansas	91	9		90	10		31	4	30	5
Florida	74	46		71	49		22	18	20	20
Georgia	145	35		127	53		45	11	42	14
Louisiana	89	16		89	16		33	6	33	6
Mississippi	98	23	1	93	27	2	41	11	39	13
North Carolina	81	39		78	42		36	14	39	11
South Carolina	80	43	1	73	50	1	33	13	30	16
Tennessee	57	42		63	36		20	13	20	13
Texas	94	56		93	57		23	8	18	13
Virginia	59	41		59	41		22	18	22	18
South	950	373	2	918	404	3	334	123	321	136

Note: In Alabama, Louisiana, and Virginia, there were no state legislative elections in 1992.
Source: Adapted from Hastings Wyman, Jr., "GOP Gains in Legislatures," Southern Political Report (24 November 1992), 3.

female legislators in the South still lags behind the national figure, which is 23 percent.[20]

The number of blacks from the South in Congress rose from five to twelve. Redistricting after the 1990 census had created twelve new black-majority districts in the South.[21] At the state legislative level, there was a net gain of thirty-eight blacks to state legislatures: twenty-nine in the lower houses and twelve in the upper. (See Table 14.4.) States such as North Carolina, at Justice Department insistence, created the maximum number of majority congressional districts populated by blacks, a protected class under the Voting Rights Act. In most southern states, congressional or state legislative redistricting was litigated, with federal court panels handing down new district lines in such states as Alabama and South Carolina.

CONCLUSION

Paradoxically, the South was both at the center and bypassed in the presidential election of 1992. The Democrats had an all-southern ticket, and both Bush and Perot claimed southern ties as well. These southern roots did not make the South the decisive battleground: "In nominating Clinton and Gore, it appeared that the Democrats had decided to fight for the South. The party's all-southern ticket, however, only skirmished in Dixie, and instead marched north to victory."[22]

Table 14.5
Southern State Legislatures, Black Elected Officials by State, Pre– and Post–1992 Election

State	House		Senate	
	Old	New	Old	New
Alabama	19	19	5	5
Arkansas	9	10	3	3
Florida	12	14	2	5
Georgia	27	31	9	9
Louisiana	24	24	8	8
Mississippi	21	32	3	10
North Carolina	14	18	5	7
South Carolina	16	18	6	7
Tennessee	10	12	3	3
Texas	13	14	2	2
Virginia	7	9	5	4
South	172	201	51	63

Note: In Alabama, Louisiana, and Virginia, there were no state legislative elections in 1992.
Source: Adapted from Hastings Wyman, Jr., "Black Gains Spell New Era in Southern Politics," *Southern Political Report* (24 November 1992), 1.

The Republicans could have unified and carried the South, but still would have lost the White House.

Clinton's presidential victory provides an opportunity for Democratic revitalization in the South: National Democrats need not be the "losers and liberals" many southerners had grown to expect. Whether that revitalization occurs will depend substantially on the economy and Clinton's performance in office. In some senses, Clinton's defeat of Bush resembles Reagan's defeat of Carter in 1980: The incumbent president, despite notable foreign policy accomplishments, was turned out of office by an electorate whose disenchantment was fueled by dissatisfaction over the domestic economy. Opinions of Reagan's presidential performance were molded by highly publicized congressional votes on the budget and tax cuts, but lingering economic weakness took its toll on Reagan's public standing in his first two years. For the 1982 election, Republican candidates shied away from appearances with the president. Two years later that changed as economic recovery in 1983 and 1984 figured prominently in Reagan's reelection.[23]

The early months of the Clinton administration have lacked Reagan's high-visibility congressional successes. The economy shows few signs of bouncing back. But the voters' perspectives from 1996 will encompass events and trends yet to unfold. Democratic revitalization, particularly in the South, is a possibility, but far from certain. The stagnant economy that made the incumbent George Bush easier to run against imperils incumbent Clinton. The Republican southern inroads below the presidential level, even in the 1992 election, have built a base from which further expansion is practical. Clinton as president makes Democrats a target for the unpopular tax hikes and spending cuts associated with budget deficits. Other decisions may be good policy, but bad politics. For instance, the South prided itself on military installations secured through congressional clout. The end of the Cold War and military cutbacks will mean a particularly hard hit in some southern locales.[24] A Democrat in the Oval Office can give these cutbacks partisan repercussions in those locales.

What southern Democrats found attractive about Clinton in the 1992 presidential election makes the success of the Clinton presidency more crucial for future evolution of the Democratic Party in the South. Clinton was a moderate, mainstream Democrat, politically close to the typical state and local southern Democrat. If Clinton's performance in the Oval Office comes up short, southern Democratic candidates will be hard pressed to distinguish Clinton's politics from their own. Clinton's success in the Oval Office could be uplifting for Democratic prospects in the South, but less than success could be disastrous.

NOTES

1. Hastings Wyman, Jr., *Southern Political Report* (10 November 1992), 1. See also Charles D. Hadley, "Southern Politics After the Election of President Bill Clinton: Continued Transformation into the Republican Party," *American Review of Politics* 14 (Summer 1993): 197–212.

2. For excellent reviews of the South in recent presidential politics, see Earl Black and Merle Black, *The Vital South: How Presidents Are Elected* (Cambridge, Mass.: Harvard University Press, 1992); Robert P. Steed, Laurence W. Moreland, and Tod A. Baker, eds., *The 1984 Presidential Election in the South: Patterns of Southern Party Politics* (New York: Praeger, 1986); and Laurence W. Moreland, Robert P. Steed, and Tod A. Baker, eds., *The 1988 Presidential Election in the South: Continuity Amidst Change in Southern Party Politics* (New York: Praeger, 1991).

3. Harold W. Stanley and Charles D. Hadley, "The Southern Presidential Primary: Regional Intentions with National Implications," *Publius: The Journal of Federalism* 17 (Summer 1987): 83–100; Charles D. Hadley and Harold W. Stanley, "Super Tuesday 1988: Regional Results, National Implications," *Publius: The Journal of Federalism* 19 (Summer 1989): 19–37; Charles S. Bullock III, "The Nomination Process and Super Tuesday," in *The 1988 Presidential Election in the South: Continuity Amidst Change in Southern Party Politics*, ed. Laurence W. Moreland, Robert P. Steed, and Tod A. Baker (New York: Praeger, 1991), 3–19; Barbara Norrander, *Super Tuesday: Regional Politics and Presidential Primaries* (Lexington: University of Kentucky Press, 1992).

4. In absolute numbers, Democratic primary turnout in 1992 bettered that for 1988 only in the three states that had moved the primary to a date later than Super Tuesday (Alabama, Arkansas, and North Carolina). Republican gains occurred only in Georgia and North Carolina. For every other southern state presidential primary, turnout in 1992 lagged behind that of 1988—Congressional Quarterly, *Guide to the 1992 Democratic National Convention* (Washington, D.C.: Congressional Quarterly, 1992), 69, 71; *Guide*

to the 1992 Republican National Convention (Washington, D.C.: Congressional Quarterly, 1992), 63; *Congressional Quarterly Weekly Report* (1988), 1894, 1950, 2254.

5. In the six presidential elections between 1968 and 1988, Virginia (with thirteen electoral votes after the 1990 census) voted Republican in all six; Florida (25), North Carolina (14), South Carolina (8), and Tennessee (11) in five; Alabama (9), Arkansas (6), Louisiana (9), Mississippi (7), and Texas (32) in four; and Georgia (13) in three. Nationally, the electoral lock was indicated by the Republican candidate's having carried thirty-four states with 336 electoral votes (66 more than required to win) at least five times between 1968 and 1988—Harold W. Stanley and Richard G. Niemi, eds., *Vital Statistics on American Politics*, 3d ed. (Washington, D.C.: Congressional Quarterly, 1992), 137.

6. Gwen Ifill, "President-elect—Road to Victory," *New York Times* (5 November 1992), A1.

7. For journalistic assessments of the Clinton campaign on which the following paragraphs are based, see Chris Black, "In 6 Weeks, a Race Reshaped," *Boston Globe* (5 November 1992), 27; David Lauter, "Clinton's Strategy of Triage," *Los Angeles Times* (5 November 1992), 1; Gwen Ifill, *New York Times* (5 November 1992), A1; Edward Walsh, "The Winners: Clinton Victory Founded on Discipline, Energy, GOP Miscues," *Washington Post* (5 November 1992), A31.

8. Cynthia Tucker, "Breaking Free of the Old South," *Atlanta Journal and Constitution* (1 November 1992), 1.

9. Al Fromm, director of the Democratic Leadership Council, as quoted in Ifill, *New York Times* (5 November 1992), A1.

10. The politically correct contemporary term for "redneck" seems to be "Bubba," and Clinton and Gore were, for the sake of journalistic spice, frequently referred to as "Bubbas." Charles Wilson of the Center for Southern Studies at the University of Mississippi came closer to the truth: "yuppie southerners" [in Jeanne Cummings, " '92 The People Decide," *Atlanta Journal and Constitution* (4 November 1992), A3]. John Hall said it well: "One of the great myths of this campaign is that of the 'double-Bubba' ticket. Whoever invented that phrase should be sentenced to the infield of the Darlington 500 in an 'I Love New York' shirt. Bill Clinton of Oxford and Al Gore of Harvard? Bubbas?" "Presidential Geography: Southern Ticket, Western Victory," *Atlanta Journal and Constitution* (9 November 1992), A11.

11. As the Clinton team decided which states to target for the general election, "southerness"—receptivity to a Democratic ticket headed by two southerners as evidenced by previous voting support for tickets headed by southerners—was a factor.

12. F. Christopher Arterton, "Campaign '92: Strategies and Tactics of the Candidates," in *The Election of 1992: Reports and Interpretations*, ed. Gerald M. Pomper (Chatham, N.J.: Chatham House, 1993), 87.

13. Hastings Wyman, Jr., quoted in Sam Attlesey, "Decisions in Dixie: Democrats Chip Away at GOP Hold on South," *Dallas Morning News* (5 October 1992), 1. See also Tom Raum, "Democrats Take Advantage of All-Southern Ticket" (Associated Press wire) 17 October 1992.

14. For 1984, see Harold W. Stanley, "The 1984 Presidential Election in the South: Race and Realignment," in *The 1984 Presidential Election in the South: Patterns of Southern Party Politics*, ed. Robert P. Steed, Laurence W. Moreland, and Tod A. Baker (New York: Praeger, 1986), 309–310.

15. Hastings Wyman, Jr., *Southern Political Report* (24 November 1992), 4.

16. James Carville, National Press Club luncheon, (19 January 1993).

17. Voter Research and Surveys exit poll data for 1992 as reported in James A. Barnes, "A Sinkhole for Democrats in Dixie," *National Journal* (13 February 1993), 429.

18. Walter Jones of North Carolina died in office after announcing his decision to retire. Jones is counted as a retirement in the count in the text. *Congressional Quarterly Weekly Report* (1992), 3577–3579.

19. *Southern Political Report* (24 November 1992), 3.

20. Data from Center for the American Woman and Politics, Rutgers University, as reported in *Southern Political Report* (8 December 1992).

21. *Southern Political Report* (24 November 1992), 1, 2.

22. Jerome M. Mileur, "The General Election Campaign: Strategy and Support," in *America's Choice: The Election of 1992*, ed. William J. Crotty (Guilford, Conn.: Dushkin, 1993), 52.

23. Clinton's 1992 win lacked at least two elements of Reagan's 1980 victory: a wider-than-expected election day victory and an unexpected Republican majority in the Senate. On southern politics and the Reagan years, see Harold W. Stanley, "The Reagan Legacy and Party Politics in the South," in *The 1988 Presidential Election in the South: Continuity Amidst Change in Southern Party Politics*, ed. Laurence W. Moreland, Robert P. Steed, and Tod A. Baker (New York: Praeger, 1991), 21–33.

24. Elizabeth A. Palmer, "Fighting on the Home Front: Charleston Defends Itself," *Congressional Quarterly Weekly Report* (8 May 1993), 1172–1175.

Selected Bibliography

Abramowitz, Alan, John McGlennon, and Ronald Rappaport. "The Party Isn't Over: Incentives for Activism in the 1980 Presidential Nominating Campaign." *Journal of Politics* 45 (November 1983): 1006–1015.

Abramowitz, Alan, and Walter J. Stone. *Nomination Politics: Party Activists and Presidential Choice*. New York: Praeger, 1984.

Baker, Tod A., Charles D. Hadley, Robert P. Steed, and Laurence W. Moreland, eds. *Political Parties in the Southern States: Party Activists in Partisan Coalitions*. New York: Praeger, 1990.

Baker, Tod A., and Robert P. Steed. "Southern Political Elites and Social Change: An Exploratory Study." In *Politics '74: Trends in Southern Politics*, edited by Tinsley E. Yarborough. Greenville, N.C.: East Carolina University Press, 1974.

Baker, Tod A., Robert P. Steed, and Laurence W. Moreland, eds. *Religion and Politics in the South*. New York: Praeger, 1983.

Bartley, Numan V., and Hugh D. Graham. *Southern Politics and the Second Reconstruction*. Baltimore: Johns Hopkins University Press, 1975.

Bass, Jack, and Walter DeVries. *The Transformation of Southern Politics*. New York: Basic Books, 1976.

Beck, Paul A. "Environment and Party: The Impact of Political and Demographic County Characteristics on Party Behavior." *American Political Science Review* 68 (September 1974): 1229–1244.

Bibby, John F., Robert J. Gibson, Cornelius P. Cotter, and Robert J. Huckshorn. "Trends in Party Organization Strength, 1960–1980: Institutionalization in an Era of Electoral Dealignment." *International Political Science Review* 4, no. 1 (1983): 21–27.

Black, Earl. "A Theory of Southern Factionalism." *Journal of Politics* 45, no. 3 (August 1983): 594–614.

Black, Earl, and Merle Black. *Politics and Society in the South*. Cambridge, Mass.: Harvard University Press, 1987.

―――. "Successful Durable Democratic Factions in Southern Politics." In *Contemporary Southern Political Attitudes and Behavior*, edited by Laurence W. Moreland, Tod A. Baker, and Robert P. Steed, 99–120. New York: Praeger, 1982.

―――. *The Vital South: How Presidents Are Elected*. Cambridge, Mass.: Harvard University Press, 1992.

Black, Merle, and Earl Black. "The Growth of Contested Republican Primaries in the American South, 1960–1980." In *Contemporary Southern Political Attitudes and Behavior*, edited by Laurence W. Moreland, Tod A. Baker, and Robert P. Steed, 121–143. New York: Praeger, 1982.

―――. "Republican Party Development in the South." *Social Science Quarterly* 57 (December 1976): 566–579.

Canon, Bradley C. "Factionalism in the South: A Test of Theories and a Revisitation of V. O. Key." *American Journal of Political Science* 22 (November 1978): 833–848.

Carter, Luther F., and David S. Mann, eds. *Government in the Palmetto State: Toward the 21st Century*. Columbia: Institute of Public Affairs, University of South Carolina, 1992.

Chambers, William N., and Walter Dean Burnham, eds. *The American Party Systems: Stages of Political Development*, 2nd ed. New York: Oxford University Press, 1975.

Colburn, David R., and Richard Scher. *Florida's Gubernatorial Politics in the 20th Century*, 11–32. Tallahassee: University Presses of Florida, 1980.

Cosman, Bernard. *Five States for Goldwater*. University: University of Alabama Press, 1966.

Cotter, Cornelius P., and John F. Bibby. "Institutional Development of Parties and the Thesis of Party Decline." *Political Science Quarterly* 95 (Spring 1980): 1–27.

Cotter, Cornelius P., and Bernard C. Hennessey. *Politics Without Power: The National Party Committees*. New York: Atherton Press, 1964.

Cotter, Patrick R. "Alabama: The Unsettled Electorate." In *Party Realignment in the American States*, edited by Maureen Moakley. Columbus: Ohio State University Press, 1992.

Crotty, William J. *America's Choice: The Election of 1992*. Guilford, Conn.: Dushkin, 1993.

―――. *Decision for the Democrats*. Baltimore: Johns Hopkins University Press, 1978.

―――. *Party Reform*. New York: Longman, 1983.

―――. *The Party Symbol: Readings on Political Parties*. San Francisco: W. H. Freeman and Co., 1980.

Crotty, William J., and John S. Jackson III. *Presidential Primaries and Nominations*. Washington, D.C.: Congressional Quarterly Press, 1985.

Crotty, William J., and Gary C. Jacobson. *American Parties in Decline*. Boston: Little, Brown, 1980.

Dauer, Manning J., ed. *Florida's Politics and Government*. Gainesville: University Presses of Florida, 1980.

Edsall, Thomas B., and Mary D. Edsall. *Chain Reaction: The Impact of Race, Rights, and Taxes on American Politics*. New York: W. W. Norton, 1991.

Eldersveld, Samuel J. *Political Parties: A Behavioral Analysis*. Chicago: Rand McNally, 1964.

―――. *Political Parties in American Society*. New York: Basic Books, 1982.

Fishel, Jeff, ed. *Parties and Elections in an Anti-party Age: American Parties and the Crisis of Confidence.* Bloomington: Indiana University Press, 1978.

Gibson, James, Cornelius P. Cotter, John F. Bibby, and Robert J. Huckshorn. "Assessing Party Organizational Strength," *American Journal of Political Science* 27, no. 1 (May 1983): 193–222.

Grantham, Dewey W. *The Democratic South.* New York: Norton, 1963.

Harmel, Robert, and Kenneth Janda. *Parties and Their Environments: Limits to Reform?* New York: Longman, 1982.

Harvard, William C. *The Changing Politics of the South.* Baton Rouge: Louisiana State University Press, 1972.

Huckshorn, Robert J. *Party Leadership in the States.* Amherst: University of Massachusetts Press, 1976.

James, Judson L. *American Political Parties in Transition.* New York: Harper and Row, 1974.

Jewell, Malcolm E., and David M. Olson. *American State Political Parties and Elections.* Homewood, Ill.: Dorsey Press, 1982.

Kayden, Xandra. "The Nationalizing of the Party System." In *Parties, Interest Groups, and Campaign Finance Laws,* edited by Michael J. Malbin. Washington, D.C.: American Enterprise Institute, 1980.

Kelley, Anne E. *Modern Florida Government,* rev. ed. Washington, D.C.: University Press of America, 1983.

Key, V. O., Jr. *Southern Politics in State and Nation.* New York: Alfred A. Knopf, 1949.

Kirkpatrick, Jeane Jordan. *Dismantling the Parties.* Washington, D.C.: American Enterprise Institute, 1978.

Kousser, J. Morgan. *The Shaping of Southern Politics: Suffrage Restriction and the Establishment of the One-Party South, 1880–1910.* New Haven, Conn.: Yale University Press, 1974.

Ladd, Everett C., Jr. *Where Have All the Voters Gone? The Fracturing of America's Political Parties,* 2d ed. New York: W. W. Norton, 1982.

Ladd, Everett C., and Charles D. Hadley. *Transformations of the American Party System.* New York: W. W. Norton, 1978.

Lamis, Alexander P. *The Two-Party South.* New York: Oxford University Press, 1984.

Lea, James F., ed. *Contemporary Southern Politics.* Baton Rouge: Louisiana State University Press, 1988.

Matthews, Donald A., and James W. Prothro. *Negroes and the New Southern Politics.* New York: Harcourt, Brace & World, 1956.

Miller, Warren E., and Teresa Levitin. *Leadership and Change.* Cambridge, Mass.: Winthrop, 1976.

Moreland, Laurence W., Tod A. Baker, and Robert P. Steed, eds. *Contemporary Southern Political Attitudes and Behavior.* New York: Praeger, 1982.

Moreland, Laurence W., Robert P. Steed, and Tod A. Baker, eds. *Blacks in Southern Politics.* New York: Praeger, 1987.

———, eds. *The 1988 Presidential Election in the South: Continuity Amidst Change in Southern Party Politics.* New York: Praeger, 1991.

Nie, Norman H., Sidney Verba, and John R. Petrocik. *The Changing American Voter.* Cambridge, Mass.: Harvard University Press, 1976.

Petrocik, John R. *Party Coalition: Realignments and the Decline of the New Deal Party System*. Chicago: University of Chicago Press, 1981.

Pierce, John C., and John L. Sullivan, eds. *The Electorate Reconsidered*. Beverly Hills, Calif.: Sage, 1980.

Polsby, Nelson W. *The Consequences of Party Reform*. Oxford: Oxford University Press, 1983.

Pomper, Gerald M. *The Election of 1992: Reports and Interpretations*. Chatham, N.J.: Chatham House, 1993.

———, ed. *Party Renewal in America: Theory and Practice*. New York: Praeger, 1980.

———. "Toward a More Responsible Two-party System? What, Again?" *Journal of Politics* 33 (November 1971): 916–940.

Price, David E. *Bringing Back the Parties*. Washington, D.C.: Congressional Quarterly Press, 1984.

Ranney, Austin. *Curing the Mischiefs of Factions: Party Reform in America*. Berkeley: University of California Press, 1975.

———. "The Political Parties: Reform and Decline." In *The New American Political System*, edited by Anthony King. Washington, D.C.: American Enterprise Institute, 1978.

Reed, John Shelton. *The Enduring South: Subcultural Persistence in Mass Society*. Lexington, Mass.: Lexington Books, 1971.

———. *One South: An Ethnic Approach to Regional Culture*. Baton Rouge: Louisiana State University Press, 1982.

Roland, Charles P. *The Improbable Era: The South Since World War II*. Lexington: University Press of Kentucky, 1975.

Rose, Douglas, ed. *The Emergence of David Duke and the Politics of Race*. Chapel Hill: University of North Carolina Press, 1992.

Schlesinger, Joseph. *Ambition and Politics*. Chicago: Rand McNally, 1966.

Seagull, Louis N. *Southern Republicanism*. New York: John Wiley and Sons, 1975.

Stanley, Harold W. *Voter Mobilization and the Politics of Race: The South and Universal Suffrage, 1952–1984*. New York: Praeger, 1987.

Steed, Robert P., Laurence W. Moreland, and Tod A. Baker, eds. *The Disappearing South? Studies in Regional Change and Continuity*. University: University of Alabama Press, 1990.

———, eds. *The 1984 Presidential Election in the South: Patterns of Southern Party Politics*. New York: Praeger, 1986.

———, eds. *Party Politics in the South*. New York: Praeger, 1980.

Strong, Donald S. "Further Reflections on Southern Politics." *Journal of Politics* 33 (1971): 239–256.

———. *Issue Voting and Party Realignment*. University: University of Alabama Press, 1977.

———. *Urban Republicanism in the South*. University: University of Alabama Bureau of Public Administration, 1960.

Sundquist, James L. *Dynamics of the Party System*. Washington, D.C.: Brookings Institution, 1973.

Swansbrough, Robert H. *Political Change in Tennessee*. Knoxville: University of Tennessee Bureau of Public Administration, 1985.

Swansbrough, Robert H., and David M. Brodsky, eds. *The South's New Politics: Realignment and Dealignment*. Columbia: University of South Carolina Press, 1988.

Tindall, George Brown. *The Disruption of the Solid South*. Athens: University of Georgia Press, 1972.

Toppin, John C. *Southern Republicanism and the New South*. Cambridge, Mass.: Harvard University Press, 1966.

Wilson, James Q. *Political Organization*. New York: Basic Books, 1973.

Wolfinger, Raymond, and Robert B. Arseneau. "Partisan Change in the South, 1952–1976." In *Political Parties: Development and Decay*, edited by Louis Maisel and Joseph Cooper, 174–210. Beverly Hills, Calif.: Sage, 1978.

Wright, Gavin. *Old South, New South*. New York: Basic Books, 1984.

Wright, Gerald C. "Community Structure and Voting in the South." *Public Opinion Quarterly* 40 (Summer 1976): 201–215.

Index

About the Editors and Contributors

ROBERT P. STEED is professor of political science at The Citadel.

LAURENCE W. MORELAND is professor of political science at The Citadel.

TOD A. BAKER is professor of political science at The Citadel.

DIANE D. BLAIR is associate professor of political science at the University of Arkansas.

LEWIS BOWMAN, retired, was professor of political science at the University of South Florida.

DAVID M. BRODSKY is The University of Chattanooga Foundation Professor of Political Science at the University of Tennessee at Chattanooga.

CHARLES S. BULLOCK III is Richard B. Russell Professor of Political Science at the University of Georgia.

JOHN A. CLARK is assistant professor of political science at the University of Georgia.

PATRICK R. COTTER is professor of political science at the University of Alabama.

FRANK B. FEIGERT is Regents Professor of Political Science at the University of North Texas.

CHARLES D. HADLEY is professor of political science at the University of New Orleans.

WILLIAM E. HULBARY is associate professor of political science at the University of South Florida.

ANNE E. KELLEY is associate professor of political science at the University of South Florida.

BRAD LOCKERBIE is assistant professor of political science at the University of Georgia.

JOHN J. McGLENNON is professor of political science at the College of William and Mary.

CHARLES PRYSBY is professor of political science at the University of North Carolina at Greensboro.

STEPHEN D. SHAFFER is professor of political science at Mississippi State University.

HAROLD W. STANLEY is associate professor of political science at the University of Rochester.

ROBERT H. SWANSBROUGH is professor of political science at the University of Tennessee at Chattanooga.

JOHN R. TODD is professor of political science at the University of North Texas.